Diana Wilde
I don't wear step-ins anymore.

A memoir
through letters
1968-1970

Copyright © Diana Wilde 2020
The moral rights of the author have been asserted.

All rights reserved. Except as permitted under the Australian Copyright Act 1968 (for example, a fair dealing for the purposes of study, research, criticism or review), no part of this book may be reproduced, stored in a retrieval system, communicated or transmitted in any form or by any means without prior written permission. All inquiries should be made to the author.

 A catalogue record for this book is available from the National Library of Australia

I don't wear step-ins anymore:
A memoir through letters 1968 to 1970
Wilde, Diana (Author)
ISBN 978-1-922452-98-6

Cover and book design by Green Hill Publishing

Typeset Adobe Minion Pro 11/16

To my dear cousins, Val and Mike.

*Thank you for telling me the truth.
If you hadn't, I may never have opened the box of nearly
300 letters written while I was overseas.*

Foreword

I had been lugging a box of letters around with me ever since I returned home from two years overseas, between 1968 and 1970. A line in one letter stood out: 'I don't wear step-ins anymore'. This piece of under-clothing went from the waist to the knees, and was similar to a girdle or corset. You stepped into them, as they were made of stretchy material. Then you gyrated all over the room, slowly pulling them up the legs, over the hips and around the waist. Some step-ins joined on to a brassiere to contain more flab and excess fat. They were very constricting, and I was fitted for one when my mother took me to Mark Foy's Department Store, Sydney, just before I commenced my first job with W.D. & H.O. Wills in Kensington. But I didn't want to be constricted. I wanted to be a free spirit and live my life my way.

A few months before my 21st birthday, after five years of saving and intense planning, I sailed to London on the Sitmar liner the *Fairstar*. In August 1968, it took five weeks to get from Sydney to London via the Pacific. The Suez Canal was closed due to the constant wars in this area. On my return home in September 1970, my mother handed me my letters and encouraged me to write about the two years I had been away. These letters joined the many hundreds of other letters and aerogrammes I had received while I was away. I placed them in a sealed cardboard box, and they moved with me to new flats, rentals, and a few purchased homes across Sydney.

Then in January 2012, my cousin Val, a close relative who lived nearby in the Blue Mountains village of Wentworth Falls, told me I had been adopted at birth. Her husband, Mike, had wanted to tell me that I was adopted for a very long time. Both my parents had died, my Dad in 1984 and my Mum in 2009. Now was the right time to open the box of letters that was sitting in my garage, collecting dust. I now wanted to get to really know the family which was not my blood, but had nurtured and cared for me all these years.

Part 1
Sea Voyage

The *Maori Farewell* song played in my head as I read the very first letter I had sent to my family after leaving home on the *Fairstar*[1]. Most ships sailing from Sydney during the 1960s were farewelled by this song, and it had blared out from speakers along the Pyrmont wharf from which my ship sailed. Coloured streamers were thrown from the wharf and the sides of the ship, and family members clung tightly to them until they snapped apart as the gap between the ship and wharf widened. I wrote the first letter to my family on the same day I sailed out of Pyrmont. My cousin Val had introduced me to her workmate, Jan, who was sharing a cabin with me.

5th August 1968

> Dear Mum, Dad & Denise,
> I still don't believe I am on a ship. Everything seems very strange, probably because after the last few hectic weeks, it is so different. I found your note Mum, and the newspaper clipping with the Gospels of John and Luke. I will keep it always and pray someday I have as much faith as you have in God.

---

1   This song was sometimes called 'Now is the Hour', as it began: 'Now is the hour when we must say goodbye, soon we will be sailing far across the seas...'.

Jan and I have a table to ourselves in the dining room, with a group of four right next to us. Our waiter is tremendous. He is one of those happy little energetic Italians who walk around and sing and laugh while serving our food. My stomach still feels as though it is not yet part of me, but by tomorrow, or the next day, I will be putting away the 6 courses quite easily.

We finally met our cabin mate Kris about 9pm last night. She is on her own, but so far has managed to dig up a chap who, as she says, asked her to come up and see the captain and get married. Last night she told him she would do his washing for him. Big chance she has, because Jan and I are going to have a few subtle words to say to her, if this starts happening. All the same, she isn't too bad, and I am sure when Jan and I get to know her better, everything will iron itself out.

6.8.68-As the 3 of us talked till 3.30am this morning, we didn't wake till 12 noon today, and consequently haven't seen breakfast for the past 2 days. I made a promise to myself to get to breakfast at least once before we reach England. I finally got my appetite back at lunch today, mainly because our waiter Gerardo, is so amiable and helpful to us. Last night he told me I was German.[2] He wouldn't believe I came from Australia, and I don't know whether to take this as a compliment or not. Everything is so cheap on the boat, and since we left, I've spent about $1.00 Australian. When I reach Tahiti, I am going to use the extra money for sightseeing.

We are having a Gala evening tonight, and I am going to wear my black cocktail dress. Jan is really going to kill them all and wear her low-cut cocktail dress. I know she won't experience much competition from me with my flat chest. However, I have my nice thick hair and height. I also have my bubbling personality to make up for all my physical handicaps, as you would say.

---

[2] In 2012 I found out I was adopted from birth, and after much research, I now knew that my great-grandmother, Willamena Berg, was born in Dresden, Prussia (now Germany).

I don't wear step-ins anymore.

7.8.68 to 12.8.68-The crew never seem to run out of entertainment for all the people on board. As the weather has been very overcast, the only thing to do is sleep in, and then go to the Zodiac lounge. This is where they run talent contests, bingo, and last night, a fancy-dress ball. The 3 of us decided to watch the ball and had a terrific time. I've made a lot of friends, but Jan is finding it very hard. She won't be patient, and continually moans about it to Kris and me. The young people attend a discotheque at 12 midnight every night through to 2am in the morning.

Tomorrow we arrive at Tahiti, and I am so looking forward to it. The boat has arranged tours, but a pile of us are hiring motor scooters for the day and seeing what we want to see. You would be proud of me. I've not touched any travellers' cheques yet, and don't think I will need to for a while. I also wash my undies out every night, and don't need to iron or wash any big stuff.

I miss you all so much, especially all the little things you used to do for me. After meeting so many people from so many walks of life, I realize now how much I love you all, and will come home a much wiser and tolerant human being. I display your photos in the cabin, and Kris remarked on how nice you all looked (I agree).

I will write again soon, so please keep well, and never forget I love you and Dad with all my heart and miss you very much. Lots of love, Dianne.

My great-grandmother on my birth mother's side had lived in Foxground, in the hinterland above Kiama on the South Coast of New South Wales. I knew her grave was in Berry Cemetery, and I intended to visit it in the not-too-distant future. I now had a collection of photos of my birth family and a two-inch-thick A4-sized book detailing what I had found out about my family history, but I knew nothing about my birth father. My Birth Certificate showed 'Unknown' where my father's name was to appear. I felt a chill pass through my body when I read the word. Half of me was 'unknown', a non-entity, only half made.

I had felt empty most of my life. Some nights I would crawl out of the hopper window in my bedroom. My room was situated at the back of the house, and my parents and sister slept at the front.[3] Especially when the moon was full, I'd grab my fox terrier, Trudy, and go into the backyard. I would perch myself in a position from which I could see the moon shine above Kingsford-Smith Airport. I wondered where I had come from, and why I had landed in this house with these parents. These feelings haunted me for most of my life, until I was told about my adoption. Then everything made sense.

The next letter I brought out of a tattered folder marked '1968', was the first letter my mother had sent to me on board the *Fairstar*, an aerogramme. Aerogrammes were the most popular and cheapest form of letter writing in the 1960s. They measured the size of an A4 sheet of paper, and the writer had the whole of one side and about a third of the other side to write on. Your writing had to be small to fit in what you wanted to say. Two-thirds of one page was kept for the address of the person you were writing to, and the final third was for the sender's name and address. There was an art in folding the paper and applying a small amount of spit to the sticky parts. If you didn't open the aerogramme correctly, much of the writing at the edges could be lost. My mother had a small and concise writing hand, and it was astounding how much she was able to fit on one aerogramme.

5th August 1968
Miss Dianne Lindsay Cabin
241 'B' Deck C/- 'Fairstar' Papeéte

To Our Darling Big Girl,

By the time you receive this letter, you will be established on the ship. We hope you are enjoying yourself, and food is everything you desire. Today (Bank Holiday) Dad took Denise and I down to

---

[3] Hopper windows were the type of window that swung out from the bottom, and made it very easy for a small child to crawl out of the house.

I don't wear step-ins anymore.

Wollongong. We had lunch at Coles Cafeteria. On the way home we went to the Cemetery, and then called in at Beverley's in Como. Aunt had been down to the school with Beverley, Kristin, Valmai and Lisa for Education Week. We had afternoon tea and came home about quarter to four. All the time Valmai had been away on Sunday, Lisa slept. When they arrived back at Beverley's, Valmai and Michael had to wake Lisa at half past eight for her bottle. Today I received a letter from Valda. She said David and she were looking forward to seeing you and Jan. The weather hasn't been too good, very overcast, and Valda said she was looking forward to winter, as she said it is cozier.

Tuesday, I went to Bowls today and the weather was very good. Mr. Rogers' dog has been barking since I came home from bowls and is getting a little tiresome. Denise has gone to a Drive-in to see those English Doctor Series. Yesterday and today we took guesses at where you most probably would be. Dad has brought the paint home to do your bedroom. I picked a pink for the walls, and white for the ceiling. I hope to start on it this weekend. Beverley has asked Aunty Betty, Beryl, and if Aunty Ruby can make it, to go down to Sutherland R.S.L. Club on Wednesday 28th August for 'Ladies Day'. They are going to eat at a smorgasbord. I rang Aunty Ruby last night to thank her for the tickets she got, so we could go to South Sydney club on Sunday night. She is trying to get some for another night to see 'Kathryn Grayson Show'.

I only wish, Dianne, you could have come to Church with Dad and I last Sunday morning, as I was looking forward to it.

Hope you had a good night's sleep on your first night at sea. I was very pleased you had a shower and toilet in your cabin. We hope you have met nice company and put your kangaroo coat in a safe place. Be careful with your money, don't trust anybody and look after your clothes. We hope the black frock Denise gave you fits. If it is a little short at the beginning, wear it without the belt, and after a while the dress will drop a little. I wore mine on Sunday without the belt. Well darling, I will close now hoping to hear from you as soon as you can post a card from Papeéte. Love and best wishes from Mummie, Dad and Denise xxx

Even though I was having a fantastic time on the ship, I seriously missed my family, especially my younger sister Denise. She was only two years and nine months younger than me, but got on with Mum much better than I did. I could not talk to my mother about anything, but I was able to tell Dad anything about boys I fancied, or even ask him to buy me *Modess* sanitary napkins from the chemist. He ran a family electroplating business in Marrickville, the next village towards Sydney from where we lived, and at one stage wanted me to help run it. His two brothers and one sister had sons, but this didn't seem to bother him. He knew I was very capable of running a business.

I wasn't a girlie girl like my sister, who was built like *Gidget*, a diminutive girl character in the surfie movies popular at the time. I was a tomboy. Big boned and with broad feet, I refused to wear proper shoes, preferring to escape to our local park with Ross from next door. We would play along the railway line between Bexley North and Turrella. I loved bodysurfing and playing cricket with the local boys in our wide, spacious Minnamorra Avenue.

I had been planning my escape to England and Europe for well over four years, during which time I saved as much money as I could. My father encouraged my dream by promising to double the money I eventually saved. I had a great job working as a secretary in the Manufacturing Department of W.D. and H.O. Wills in Kensington, and later in Macquarie Street, Sydney, where the company moved to a brand-new building in 1966.

On my way to work in Sydney, it was easy to walk the short distance to the Commonwealth Bank Travel Agency in Martin Place. I would stare longingly at the coloured travel brochures lining the tiled walls. As a teenager I had subscribed to *Life* and *National Geographic* magazines, and among my possessions were small books delivered every month, inside which were tear-out sticky-back pictures of places and sights from the country each issue talked about, such as Greece, France, India and Japan. At high school I began to communicate with a Japanese pen pal called Fusae. I still own a book she posted to me, called *Kokoro* by Soseki Natsume.

I was also an avid reader. Each morning on my way to Earlwood Primary School, I walked past the Public Library. I borrowed books from an early age, and continued doing so until I left on my overseas trip in August 1968, when I only had a few months to go till I turned 21. I devoured classics by Tolstoy, Dostoyevsky, Balzac, Hemingway, Flaubert and Shakespeare. I would continue devouring literature while I was overseas, and all through my life, culminating with a Bachelor's degree in English Literature from Macquarie University, which I completed in my 50s.

As I read these letters from the late 1960s, I became aware of how different I was to the family who had adopted me. No one else in my family read like I did, except for my maternal grandfather Ernest, who died before I was adopted. When my mother died in 2009, I found only romance novels by Barbara Cartland amongst religious texts from Billy Graham and Robert Schuller under her bed.

My second letter from the ship was written after my first stop in Tahiti, a place I had dreamed of visiting. It had taken ten days and two Thursdays to get there, so I kissed the soft earth when I finally walked down the gangplank.

13th August 1968

Dear Mum, Dad and Denise,
    Now to tell my story - I awoke 3.30am in the morning, a few hours before we were due to berth at Tahiti (Papeéte). Jan and I were trying to get dressed when Kris yelled to us, she could see lights out of the porthole. We didn't believe her at first because she is always pulling our leg. We nearly fainted when we saw the lights ourselves. We sat on deck for a while just looking at them. It was so exciting after not seeing land for so long.
    The humidity was unbelievable. Until I became accustomed to it, I found it hard to breathe. Papeéte was covered in very thick pink

clouds, and it looked like a postcard. We were told it rained every night, and you could see how muddy and moist the streets were. A lot of Tahitians were on the wharf all dressed in those flower print shirts and sarongs. All the girls have beautiful hair right down to their waists and their teeth shine.

We had a good breakfast and set off sightseeing at about 7am in the morning. After looking around some of the shops, which were all closed as it was a Sunday, we managed to change our money at one of the many bars along the main street. There were no men serving at the bars - only women - and all of them were chain-smoking. Kris, Jan and I decided to try the local beer. By the way, there are approx. 100 francs to an Australian dollar. 3 beers, very small bottles (Coke size) cost us 135 francs. This roughly equals 50c a bottle Australian currency, which is robbery. The girls at the bar made up for it by giving each of us a flower from the basket of flowers delivered to every store first thing in the morning.

We couldn't afford to hire a vehicle, but our prayers were answered, when we met 2 French Officers from a nuclear destroyer berthed next to the 'Fairstar'. Their names were Henri and Ives, and by means of sign language and a few French words, they asked us if we would like to go skin diving with them. They both seemed very nice, so off we went to a beautiful place about 20 miles from Papeéte called Tahiti Village. I did not believe there could be a place like it. I have only seen a resemblance to it in movies, maybe. I took plenty of photos to prove just how fantastic it really was. It was a hotel for tourists set on the sea, and there were about 20 huts (thatched roof and all), with a very large grass hut with a bar and tables and chairs (the chairs were weaved and glazed over for strength). So as not to spoil the landscape, the main hut had holes in the roof so coconut trees could grow out through them, which made it more effective. When we walked through to the terrace, the sea lay before us, and I just stood there in a daze. The sea was so beautiful, and the sun shining on it made it change to about 4 different shades from aqua to deep blue.

I don't wear step-ins anymore.

It was still very early, however the heat was really oppressive, so we changed into our swimmers and went down to the water. Henri lent me his face mask and showed me how to use the snorkel. I went under the water. Another world suddenly stared me in the face. About 10 yards from the shore was reef after reef of living coral, the colours so brilliant and varied. Swimming right under my nose were hundreds of tiny coloured fish. At first, I was scared - it was so eerie and something I had never seen before, except in books or at the movies. We were very sad when they told us they had to be back at the ship by 12.30pm.

We said goodbye and thanked them for the marvellous time we had. After lunch on board we decided to go touring again. This time we met a Frenchman called Christian Bonnier. We had been sitting outside the 'Mission for Lost Children' when he came along to ask us if we were from the 'Fairstar'. He told us he had been living in Papeéte with his parents for over a year, and his business involved a string of hotels situated throughout the Pacific. His English wasn't too bad, and he said he would like to show us around. He had a 10-year-old 'Citroen' motor car with a canvas top rolled back. By this time, we were all very sunburnt, and we were going to be even more burnt by the end of the day. We drove for miles looking at the scenery and stopping to take photos. The people of Papeéte seem very friendly and extremely happy with life generally. We found out 4 ships a week visit Papeéte. This is probably one of the reasons why the Tahitians do not stare at you, but simply walk past unconcerned. Their homes are very simple and some very untidy. Dogs and cats roam around the house, and hens and roosters live where they like. The children are beautiful, they laugh and sing all the time. There is no begging on the streets, and all look as healthy as we do. You would fall in love with the flowers. I have taken a lot of photos to show you. They are very conscious of their island's natural beauty and preserve it by making gardens of flowers right up to the roadside. It was really lovely driving along and seeing acres of flowers on one side, and different blues of the ocean on the other.

We arrived at the 'Paul Gauguin' Museum on the other side of the island but didn't have time to see through it. On the way back, we were driving behind a truckload of Tahitians, and me being a mad photographer, stood up and poked my head through the roof. I took photos of all the Tahitians, including a little baby all wrapped up in ever-present flower painted material. They were so taken by it all I had to take about 4 photos to keep them happy. Even then, they kept pulling faces and posing to attract my attention. Christian took us to his home to meet his family and gave us each a shell necklace. He also serenaded us with his guitar.

We had tea at night, and after such a busy day, I dropped on my bunk at 9.30pm and didn't wake (fully dressed) until 6.30am. I was very disheartened looking out of our porthole while Tahiti slipped away. It was such a beautiful place; I could have spent a week there and still not been satisfied. We do not reach Balboa for another 11 days, and the thought of shipboard life for so long just sickens me.

Our cabin mate Kris is very nice, and when I asked her the other day if she would flat with us in London, she was very happy. We all get on like a house on fire, especially Kris and me. She is 22 in November (15th I think), and we are planning a big double birthday party. All the time we were in Tahiti, Jan kept complaining about the heat. What would you expect when she wore stockings with wedge type sandals? She slipped on some rocks and complained of having a sore backside for the rest of the day. Her bed is a complete mess, and she throws her soiled underclothing under the bed. Your training has worked wonders. I hardly believe it myself. I scored the divan under the porthole, with plenty of room for my clothes etc. You wouldn't believe how tidy I am - Even Jan tells me I am too methodical! Kris is tidy too, so when we get a flat in London, we are going to give Jan a corner, screen it off from all view and let her go for her life!

You will be pleased to hear I have read a few passages out of the bible already and find it very helpful when I am feeling homesick. The one thing I miss the most is I don't have anyone close to me I can talk

I don't wear step-ins anymore.

to. Writing your troubles in a letter is not the same, it is not fast enough. I am very impatient. I am getting so depressed by looking at the sea every day. At first it was restful, now it is downright boring. If we had more ports, without these long stretches in between, it would be better. The young men on board spend most of their waking hours drinking at the bar, yet I have not seen one drunk person since we left Sydney. The 3 of us usually sit and talk to the waiters, Adriano and Giorgio. They told us a few days ago people are drinking so much, they have only one case of Bacardi Rum left on the ship! They say this is disgusting.

I've met a nice chap called Tony who usually joins me wherever I go. He is originally from England; however, he joined the Australian Army and was a Sargeant and served in Vietnam for 18 months. His trade is Interior Decorating. He is going home for a visit only and intends working his way around the world and settling back again in Australia.

We had our Equatorial Dinner last night and I haven't enjoyed a meal like it. There was lobster, turkey and Spanish wine on the house. Afterwards we all had champagne in the Zodiac Lounge. My waiter, Gerardo gave me 4 slices of turkey and 2 helpings of cranberry sauce. Much to Jan's dismay, I am still his favourite, and get a little embarrassed when he tells everyone I am his girlfriend (I hope he is joking). Jan is arranging for us to meet some of her relatives in Balboa from the Consulate, so we will probably enjoy our time there.

I am looking forward to this Treasure Hunt revue, because it may give me experience in making a fool of myself in front of hundreds of people. Thank goodness I won't be wearing my glasses. I won't be able to see all those laughing faces.

Give all my love to Denise and tell her I hope she is behaving herself and staying home a bit more than she usually does. Also, tell her she doesn't know what she is missing, and would be in her element on this ship. Make sure you all write to me (long letters filled with all the trivia of your daily life). It is very exciting to read your letters. Thinking of you all every day, Lots of love, Dianne.

I now had only a few stops before landing in England. My cousin Valda and her husband David wanted me to stay with them in Barnet, Hertfordshire, when I arrived. They had been in the UK for over a year and had initially stayed with friends in Earl's Court until they found the right place to live and the right job. This was a time when, if you had relatives born in the UK, you could live and work in England for up to a year. My adopted grandmother had been born in London, so I easily obtained a working visa before I left Australia.

Our family lived close to one another in Sydney and we always got together on Friday nights for dinner and a singalong. Most of the night was alcohol-fuelled for the adults, and children were assigned to the kitchen, where we played cards and tried to peek through keyholes at the goings-on in the front lounge room. Some nights the adults would dress in each other's clothing or race up to the local Henson Park Hotel to put a bet on the horses before the police raided the SP bookie[4].

My cousin Valda had been in contact with me while I prepared my trip, and now she sent a letter to Lisbon, my last stop before sailing into Southampton.

Miss D Lindsay 'Fairstar' B Deck Cabin 241 C/- Societade Comercial Contandi Ltd. Av 24 de Jalho 126 Lisbon Portugal

Dear Di and Jan,

Well lovies, Mum wrote and asked me to drop you a line and do you have our phone number? Now Di we will definitely be at Waterloo Station to meet you - I will ring Sitmar Line and find out the exact time of arrival, so don't worry if your boat is late or early. We were about 6 hours late, but Helen and Warren found out from Sitmar. Anyhow our

---

4   The 'SP Bookie' (or 'short price bookie') was a way the ordinary bloke on the street could place a bet on the races, without having to go to the Randwick or Rosehill racetracks. A lot of hotels had arrangements with the local police, who would let them know if they were going to be raided.

phone number is 440-1459. If you are ringing from Waterloo add the London area but if you are ringing from Southampton it is 01-440-1459. Ok? Please excuse the awful scribble but I am under the hair dryer. I am having a dinner party tonight, and then we are all going on to a party, so I am worn out preparing everything.

The weather is smashing here at present girls, and I hope it stays this way until you arrive. Next weekend is a big one and we think we will go to Paris - if we can get a booking on the ferry - if not we will go to the Lakes District (North England). If you haven't decided anything definite about sharing a flat with anyone, some girlfriends of mine moved into a big apartment at Highgate, which is quite close to London. They are looking for a couple more girls, so I told them you might be interested. You can decide for yourself later on. I don't know what your plans are, but we have plenty of time to talk about them, and you can stay with us until you're settled.

Hope you are enjoying your trip and had good weather. It makes a difference as you have a long winter ahead. Are there any 'good sorts' on the boat? Have you fallen for anyone yet? Well girls I will close off now and hope this finds you both well and happy - see you soon. Love Valda 44 Windsor Drive East Barnet Hertfordshire UK PS: Be Good! PPS: David's phone number at work is CLE-8422.

My mother had been so upset at me leaving only a few months before my 21st birthday. 'Coming of age', or 'reaching your majority', was a big deal in Australia. My mother felt I had robbed her of the pleasure of seeing me attain the 'age of consent'. But I couldn't wait any longer. I had to get away, and ship fares were much cheaper in our winter than they would be if I waited until after my birthday in November.

Aunt wrote next. She was my mother's eldest sister, and I was closer to her than I was to my own mum. I had run away a few times as a child, and had hopped on the tram to go to her house in Marrickville. She and I were Scorpios; both of us had violent tempers, yet understood one another. We had a strong bond, even though she had moved away from the inner city to be closer to her two daughters in the Sutherland Shire, south of Sydney. I got to know what was going on at home through my Aunt's letters, the first of which follows.

12th August 1968

Dear Dianne,

   Just a little note to tell you we are thinking of you and hoping you and Jan are having a ball. After our tearful goodbye to you we all went to South Sydney Club to wet our throats, which were pretty hoarse after yelling 'bye Dianne, bye Jan'. I tell you; I didn't taste the first 2 middies, I was so dry, but I guess your mother has told you all about it. I saw the photos of you and Lisa yesterday. They came out good and Val is sending you one. Lisa gained 12 oz. last week and Di she is lovely. She goos at her mother and really laughs out loud. I have a faint feeling she might be a redhead. Her hair is falling out and her eyebrows are getting ginger.

   Have you met any nice boys on board yet? I'm longing to hear from your mother all what you have been doing. Your mother misses you. I guess it is too quiet now for her. I haven't much news as yet, but Bev and girls send their love, also Bill. Val is writing to you herself. How is Jan? I guess she misses the children and her mother. Give Jan our love and tell her we all hope both of you have a wonderful time on the boat. Enjoy yourselves for it only happens once in a lifetime. I wish I could be with you.

   Well goodbye Di and if you have any spare time, maybe you will drop me a card just to let me know you are well. Lots of love, Aunt xxxxxxxxxxx

Aunt also filled me in on what my sister was up to while I was away. And I was looking forward to hearing from Aunt's youngest daughter, Val, who was the cousin I eventually moved closer to in my 60s. Val's husband, Mike, became close to me too - it was at his insistence that, three years after my mother Ruby died, Val eventually told me I had been adopted at birth. While I was overseas, Val asked me to be her second daughter's godmother. She gave birth to Cassandra in Bethesda, in Marrickville - the same hospital where I was born in 1947. The hospital was run by the Salvation Army for unmarried mothers, but also nursed married women who were having their babies.

It was Val who suggested I travel with her workmate, Jan, the eldest daughter of a family of 15. I had been planning to escape alone, but the family were worried I would be lonely travelling by myself. I eventually relented, met Jan, and booked our passage together on the *Fairstar*. She was totally different to me: buxom, constantly applying her lippie, brushing her long, reddish hair, and laughing uproariously at the boys' slightly risqué and intentional jokes about her bust and ample hips.

21st August 1968
Miss Dianne Lindsay Cabin 241 B Deck
c/- 'Fairstar' Lisbon

To Our Darling Dianne,

Today has been a very windy and cold day. The Council have dug up the road outside our place and are levelling the road. Tell Jan I received her card and phoned her mother. There was a good article in todays paper by Norman Hartnell. From one basic frock and suit, he gave five different ways one could change frock and suit. Don't forget to leave the belt off the knitted black dress if it is a little short. It will soon drop an inch or so. Hope you are wearing your clothes and not staying in the one outfit. Why didn't you take the white and navy sandals to wear with your slacks on the ship? Beverley is wearing your boots, and those white shoes with the quilting on the front. How did you like Tahiti? Did you have to go through all the formalities before they let you land, and how long did you stay there? Are you eating Australian or Italian food? Those packet foods you used to have, are still in the hall cupboard, and the 'Special Ks' are still in the cupboard too. I'm afraid I'll have to make Dad eat it. Denise has finally broken the Easter Egg and the chocolate is very thick. She takes some to work each day. I told her I was going to increase her board, as she is eating well. Don't forget to send Alma and Vina a card. I will enclose $2.00 in the letter I send to Valda for you about the references. This is to buy cards and stamps. They are going to put the final episode of 'Fugitive' on again, by special demand, as some people couldn't see it last week. Thursday, another windy day, So I decided not to go to Bowls. Have been thinking of you landing in Balboa. How long do you stay in port? Try and cram as much as you can while you are ashore. We had pea soup and meat pies for dinner tonight. I miss you more at dinner time. Hope you demand your dinner like you used to demand it when you were home. We are watching at present 'Dick Van Dyke'. On the news tonight, we saw the invasion of the Russian troops into Prague. It gives one an eerie feeling. Don't forget a card for Father's Day 1st September. When you post your Christmas cards love, make sure you only send them by ship, as the rates are much cheaper. You will certainly have to post them about six weeks before. We moved your bed, bookcase and mattress into the front room last night. I think I will have the bookcase cut in half and put one in each recess beside the fireplace. I painted the fireplace pink, the same as the room. It looks OK. I hope to go to Campsie tomorrow and look at some curtain material. Well darling, I will close now, hoping you are keeping well, and remember Mum thinks of you each night and morning. Love and kisses from Mum xxxxxxxxxxxxxxxx Hello Darling, hope you are having a good time and it was good what you told Mum about church. I hope you get the references we sent to Valda. If you need a job you will be welcome at either one. Lots of love and good luck. I have your insurance on your things fixed, love Daddy.

I don't wear step-ins anymore.

Thursday, 29th August 1968 (Letter 3)

Dear Mum, Dad and Denise,

    I finished my last letter telling you about the preparations for the Pirate Night. Well, it is only 4 days to Lisbon, and I have a lot of interesting news to tell you. The Pirate Night was a great success (I am enclosing photos). I went to the Disco with Tony until 3 am, had a shower and then we all went up on deck to see the coastline of Panama. Coming into Balboa was very similar to the photos you took in Hong Kong. The humidity was stifling and to make things worse I had a giant attack of gastric. I was so tired I slept until 2.30 pm just in time to dress for our trip to Balboa. (I wore the black and white crimplene frock you made me, and everyone thought it very nice). I finally received your 2 letters, one from Aunt and one from Denise. The reason for not receiving your first letter at Tahiti was because you did not write care of the agent. We were sitting in the lounge reading our mail when Jan was called to the Purser's office, and I suddenly realised George Shaw from Balboa, who Jan's Aunt wrote to before we left, must have been at the office waiting for us. We were so excited when we met him as it was hard to believe he had remembered us. He took us first of all to the Tivoli Guest House, which was built over 100 years ago, and was frequented by Teddy Roosevelt and his 'Roughriders' during the civil war. The waiters were negroes and it reminded me of a scene out of 'Gone with the Wind'. (I will be sending photos taken while we were there). Your hair would curl at some of the stories George told us about Panama, and if you saw the things I saw while I was there. When we disembarked, we had to walk about a mile to George's car and I've never seen so many black people as I saw during our 10-minute walk. It is so bad in Panama if you walked down any street at night by yourself, it would be more than likely you would be sold to the white slave trade which flourishes throughout this area! While driving to the Tivoli Guest House I saw slums animals wouldn't live in! Because of the great influx of Costa Ricans, the building of houses and flats cannot cope.

Therefore, most of these poor people have to make do with wooden huts built along the roadside, even quite close to high class areas. The smell was unbearable as sanitation and garbage collection just didn't exist, and the children walked around naked amongst all this filth. To make things worse I saw 2 dogs devouring another dog right on the roadside. Tell Denise she doesn't know how lucky she is living at home! I wish she had seen it as it would make her grow up a bit. While we were at the Tivoli George met 3 other friends and they all took us to Old Panama City founded in 1519 by the Spaniards. The police guard these ruins as there is so much buried treasure still under the ground. We then went back to George's home where we met his Spanish wife Consuela and 2 sons. (George's mother is Spanish, and she lives in Sydney where she has known Jan's family for many years). I will write again soon, but you will probably get my next letter after I arrive in London…lots of love, Dianne xxxxxxxxx

The next letter was written after we visited Curacao in the West Indies. Before we knew it, we had travelled through the Panama Canal, built by Teddy Roosevelt. I rarely got to bed before six in the morning, so I had to drag myself out of the cabin and take a few photos of the locks and the jungle landscape. The next port was an island inhabited by mainly dark-coloured people. Except for the occasional Aborigine in Sydney or the outback, I had not experienced anywhere like this before. I had grown up in a country which had a 'White Australia Policy'.

2nd September 1968

Dear Mum, Dad and Denise,

We arrived in Curacao the following Sunday at 6am. Every port so far has been completely different, and Curacao was more so. If you don't already know Curacao is a Dutch port in the Caribbean, (enclosed is a leaflet). Owing to Dutch influence the houses and buildings are styled in a similar manner as in Holland. The colour

I don't wear step-ins anymore.

scheme was fantastic, and more amazing was most of the population is black. As in all ports, Kris, Jan, Moira (a Scottish girl) and I joined forces and went off by ourselves. We got a taxi into Williamstadt (the Capital) for A50c each and had a look around. Everything was spotless but so expensive (a coke cost 50c each). We were having a look over the Governor's residence when we met 4 Dutch National Servicemen who told us a bit about the place. We were told to go to the Hotel Intercontinental and hire a car. This we did for $A10 between 4 and $A30 deposit. I had the honour of driving a Fiat left hand drive, and was I scared. Not really, I was in my element! We decided to go to the nearest and best beach we could find. We met a Spanish American woman and she let us follow her out of the city on to the main highway. It was funny changing gears with my right hand, but I got used to it after a while and it became easy.

What fascinated us about Curacao was the scenery. I expected to find a lush, tropical place like Tahiti, but instead it was dry and parched with cacti and hardly any trees, more like a desert! We even passed by salt flats as we were driving to Porto Marie (a beach). When we arrived at the beach, we couldn't believe our eyes - the sea was aqua and crystal clear with patches of deep blue. The beach only went for a few hundred yards, and all you could see were hundreds of black people, the women all wearing coloured hair curlers. We found a secluded patch of sand (made from coral) and had 3 or 4 swims during the few hours we were there.

On the way back to the ship we had a flat tyre and the car nearly went out of control. We were just about to change the tyre when some Venezuelans on holidays in Curacao gave us some help, and we just made it back to the town in time to get our rental deposit back, and before the ship was due to sail.[5]

As I am finishing this letter it is only 7 hours until we arrive in Lisbon and I am very excited. Six of us are going to hire a car when

---

5   The tyre blow-out was very scary, as it was a left-hand drive vehicle, and everyone was chatting and laughing while I was trying to keep the car on the road. We came through okay.

we arrive and go to see some flamenco dancing during the night and sightsee during the day. We are due to arrive Southampton on Thursday, and I will be posting most of my other letters there. I've loved every minute of this trip; however, I couldn't stand coming home by ship unless there were a lot more ports of call. You spend too much money in between ports, and get too bored, especially as you see the same people every day. At each port we went out of our way so as not to see anyone from the ship. This is good because we've seen more interesting places than most people on board. Somehow, after seeing these places and living in an entirely different environment, I feel much wiser and more independent. Just think how wise I will be when I get home. Before you receive this letter, I will be in England, and the thought of it is nearly giving me gastric! Thinking of you all, lots of love, Dianne.

2nd **September 68**

FOR MY DAD'S EYES-ONLY P.S. HAPPY FARDERS DAY!!!!!!

To my Darling Dad, I know I always forget important days like birthdays but how could I forget it was Father's Day yesterday.

Hope you scored well with the presos and if you're extra good the fairies might bring you something real special from a far away and exciting country. I miss you most Dad around breakfast time, because it is usually 12.00 noon on the ship when I get to a meal, and I miss the bedside service. Don't let Mum and Denise work you too hard and remember if it gets any worse you can always come over and see me, as long as you bring your own spending money! Lots of love and kisses, Dianne xxxxxxxxxxxx

I read the lines people had written when they saw my mother's photos on the cabin wall. They said that I was the image of her, and I was reminded of how many times I had asked her who I looked like in the family. My sister and I were, as the saying goes, *like chalk and cheese*, but at no time did I question my birth. I spent a lot of time wondering why I was so different. I became the *black sheep* of the family. Many years later, when I asked the surviving older family members about my adoption, they all told me they were sworn to secrecy. Some said my mother threatened to kill them if they told me.

Part 2
Arriving in England

My cousin, Valda, and her husband, David, picked us up from Waterloo Station, and we stayed with them in East Barnet, Hertfordshire. One of the first letters I found waiting for me in England was from my mother. She began to number all her letters, later telling me she did this so it would be easy to follow the order, if I decided to write about my trip one day. I am extremely thankful that she did this. Moreover, she hated clutter, so if she hadn't given me my letters immediately on my return, she may have thrown the lot out.

Friday, 6th September 1968 (Letter 1)

Dear Dianne,

Today's weather has been very pleasant, so we haven't had the heater on tonight. Denise is going out with Allan tonight to see a Show in Town. Last night we went to the 'Doncaster' at Kensington with Uncle Albert, Auntie Betty, Uncle Harold, Aunty Ruby, Robert, Lynne, Denise and Libera. We enjoyed the Show with Ron Fraser and had the table near the stairway at the stage. Noel Brophy was in the audience, and he is not very tall. There was a large crowd. Denise and Libera had their photo taken for $1.50 each. Dad paid her expenses, so I am putting $4.00 away for you, and if you buy something, I will send over a money order. Uncle Harold asked us to go to the new Marrickville RSL Club at Marrickville Station on Sunday night for dinner. It was officially opened this week. <u>Eve Speedy</u> came with us last night. She has lost some more weight and the doctor thinks it is the liver. Her address is 43 The Avenue Hurstville (2220).

At present we are watching 'Bandstand' and Brian Henderson's trip while he was in Spain. Was surprised to see the modern buildings in Madrid. Hope you go and see Spain. What was your impression when you saw the White Cliffs of Dover? Bruce Knight said, the train trip through Kent on your way to London is very nice, but one goes through some slum areas. Where did you meet Valda and David? Denise is going to 'Martins' disco tonight with Libera. Hope Valda hasn't taken you down to local pubs, or has she? Denise bought me 2 bunches of sweet peas today.

<u>Monday</u> A lovely surprise when I went out to the letterbox today. A letter from our big girl. The photos were very nice. Glad to read you enjoyed yourself at the ports of call. You certainly see how the other half lives, as we found out on the trip to Japan. I rang Jan's mother, and her postman comes later than ours. Rang Auntie Betty this afternoon and she received a letter from Valda today. Valda wrote she couldn't sleep one night, as she must have been excited. We were thinking and talking about you and Jan arriving in London. The builder has started on the roof today and the electrician came and put a power point near the door going into the back room, so I can use the radiogram without having to use a long lead. We went up to Hurstville this afternoon and had a look at another stove. It has infrared grilling. Dad was pleased to receive your note, and he was the first to read it. Last night we went to the Marrickville RSL Club at Marrickville Station. It is very nice, and I had a lobster salad and <u>double</u> Peach Melba. They had an Ice Revue and it was very nice and a five-piece orchestra. Well darling, love and kisses from Mum xxxxxxxxx Hello Dianne hope you like England. Did you receive the references I sent you? Thanks for my letter on Fathers' Day. We miss you. Best of everything. Love Daddie xxxxxxxxxxxxxx

I don't wear step-ins anymore.

My mother had an obsession with me sending every relative and family friend a postcard from the 'mother country'. She provided me with the money to post them. What 20-year-old girl, away from home for the first time in her life, wants to spend every waking minute writing postcards? I had barely enough time to write to immediate family. While I was staying with my cousin Valda in Hertfordshire, it took me over a week to settle down, and I finally got around to writing from my new flat in the West End of London.

Monday, 9th September 1968

Dearest Mum, Dad and Denise,
I decided not to write until our accommodation was finalized, and you will be very pleased to know Jan, Kris and I have paid our first week's rent on a lovely flat! It is situated in Montagu Square W1 London (West End One) Telephone No. WEL4182. There is a lovely park in the middle of the square and the houses are over 200 years old. Very close by is Regents Park, Hyde Park, Marble Arch and Madame Tussauds. The actual district is the Borough of St. Marylebone. It is a basement flat, self-contained with a private entrance, living room, kitchen, bath and toilet, hot and cold water, centrally heated, gas, electricity, 3 beds and furnished plus phone. We pay 5 guineas each (pw) plus electricity and gas bills (quarterly). We have to pay 35 pounds deposit for the phone and then only pay for calls each. This is very reasonable because the area is the best in London - part of the West End. We move in tomorrow evening and on Wednesday I am going to B.A.T.[6] about a semi-permanent job. I will write letters to Lawrence Smith and Canning thanking them for their help. It will be best to get a job at B.A.T. as I know the work, and it is very close to where we now live. My fares to B.A.T. Will probably only be 1/- a day (dirt cheap compared to 6/6 a day for Val and David to

---

6   B.A.T. stood for British American Tobacco, the parent company of W.D. & H.O. Wills in Sydney, where I worked from 1963 until I left for overseas in August 1968.

travel from Barnet into London on the tube). We got to Lisbon last Tuesday night 7.00 pm and it was still very light. A truly beautiful city, every footpath has a pattern of black and white cobblestones and the city is crammed with monuments and fountains. We were actually standing on part of Europe! We went to a disco called 'La Ronda' where they played mostly English and Negro records (the Portuguese do not like their own records). About 3am Tony took me to a 'Fado' which is music played by 2 guitarists and a singer - the audience also joins in. The songs are usually very romantic and sad. We arrived back at the ship in time for breakfast, and then Jan, Kris, Ronda and I went back to Lisbon to do some shopping at about 8.30am. I bought a little Portuguese doll, which I may send home if you are nice to me, and I also bought a (brown) suede handbag for 300 escudos ($6 or $7 Aust.). We just made it back to the ship before it sailed at 12 noon. We were so impressed with Lisbon we might go back when we tour the continent next spring.

7pm Wednesday night a very unfortunate thing happened to me. We were resting in our cabin after not having any sleep from Monday until Wednesday lunchtime when Kris suddenly felt sick. I rushed her to the toilet, and as she closed the door, I realized my right thumb was in the hinge part of the door.[7] As Kris had slumped onto the door, I had to push it open with my body. I will not describe what my thumb looked like; however, the pain was unbelievable, and my blood was just pouring out all over me. Thank goodness Leon was in the cabin talking to Jan, because he grabbed me and rushed down to the hospital, pushing everyone aside as we went. I nearly squeezed Leon's hand off as the doctor cut my nail and stitched it up. I was given penicillin tablets and sleeping pills, but the pain was so bad I didn't sleep one minute. The doctor told me the next morning I was lucky to have a thumb, as it was hanging by a piece of skin when he got to it! I went to Val's doctor at East Barnet on Friday, and I am

---

7   My mother was never told the truth about the accident with my thumb. I had been drinking beer after beer with Kris and Jan, and stacking the cans in a pyramid shape on the cabin dresser. We were all pissed. A photo is included, showing the state of the three of us.

I don't wear step-ins anymore.

having the stitches out this Thursday night. The rotten part about it is how inconvenient it has been. I had to carry my bags through customs Thursday arvo, and if Leon and Tony hadn't helped me, I would have pulled the stitches out. It still throbs continually, and I can't even write properly. The doctor told me what a good patient I was, and I didn't scream or anything while he sewed me up. I wish you had of been there so I could have cried on your shoulder. It isn't the same being comforted by friends.

Valda met us at Waterloo at 7.30pm Thursday night and the first thing we did was go to a pub called the 'White Hare' where we met some very nice friends of Val and David. The weather has been beautiful, and we hope to do some sightseeing on the weekends.

Mum you do not realize how beautiful England is. The country around Barnet is hard to describe, as it is so unreal and fairylike. Acres of green grass, black and white cows twice as fat as Australian cows, little country pubs with old style names like 'The Wagon and Horses', where a chap plays old songs on the piano and young and old join in and sing along. Every pub has a darts team, and there is always a great big sheep dog roaming about amongst the tables being patted by the locals or sprawled out in front of the open fire. The people are so friendly and rib us for being Aussies. I drink lager and lime from a pint glass (it isn't very strong so don't get upset).

Val and David have been very good to us and I can't explain how happy I was to see her at Waterloo. David has a moustache and chin beard. He looks very dashing in his bell-bottom trousers and waist-coat. Val is still the same, so much like her mother, but she has picked up a bit of an accent and wears some terrific clothes.

I know now why they like London so much. Everyone is too busy living to worry about mundane things the way Australians do. We waited for Val at Bond Street Friday night and not one person looked at us. In Sydney you nearly get a complex from people staring at you. There are also a lot of dark people in London, but you don't worry about it. To ride in the tube means rubbing shoulders with West Indians, Negroes, Indians and Englishmen. Also, it is quite common to see English girls holding hands with coloured boys and no one looks twice at them. Val and David, Helen and Warren took us to 'The Dive' in Carnaby Street Friday night. It was crowded with Indians, all nicely dressed and all speaking with plums in their mouths. Carnaby Street is an eye opener. There is a shop selling kinky jeans for children (miniskirts, capes, culottes). I bought an imitation full-length double-breasted brown leather coat, for 9 guineas. It is fully lined and waterproof, ideal for wet weather and for work. I am buying a pair of knee length brown leather boots to match. The clothes are dirt-cheap and leave Sydney for dead, fashion- wise. I don't care what you may say but my skirts are going up and I have had my hair cut quite short for 7/6 in Bond Street. I am seriously thinking of colouring it honey blonde. You will not know me when I get home. I have taken off nearly half a stone from all the walking and sightseeing, and I will send you a photo home to show you my new look.

    Val and Dave drove us to St Albans on Sunday, not far from Barnet, and it dates back to when the Romans came to Britain centuries ago. We saw the St Albans Cathedral and I nearly lost my breath; it was so inspiring. It would take 5 years to see all of Greater London alone. I can't wait to see snow and get rugged up in my coat and boots and have snow fights and sing carols at Christmas time. Although I miss you all terribly, if I had not left Australia and seen the other half of the world, my life would have been similar to the life of a jelly fish. You and Dad must have seen how passionately keen I am to see other countries - this is why I am so irrational and impatient when I am at home. I only pray I have it out of my system when I get back to Australia. You don't need money to travel - all you need is the urge and the will to get up and go again, and I know I have it. I am in my element at the moment, and not even a stitched thumb has hindered my burst of energy. I even have blisters on my heels from walking, and I haven't had a migraine since I left home! Right this moment I am sitting in Val's living room. It is 5.30pm and I am by myself after going to London to see our flat. Jan and Kris stayed

I don't wear step-ins anymore.

in town to see a few friends, so I took the opportunity to come back and write undisturbed. I am listening to the BBC, and when I look out the window, I have an unhindered view of Windsor Drive. I can see old houses and their bay windows, gardens of roses in such brilliant colours, and hedges and trees so green. The sky is bright blue and there isn't a cloud in sight. It will stay light until 7 or 7.30pm. In about 6 weeks' time we should be getting snow. If this is England, then the travel posters don't do it justice. Last night we watched TV with no ads and the radio is ad free too. It is quite easy to sit back and listen to Radio France or see famous actresses and actors in TV plays and dramas. While walking around London on Saturday we passed so many live theatres starring such people as Sammy Davis Jnr., Googie Withers, Anna Neagle in 'Charlie Girl', Flora Robson in 'The Importance of Being Ernest' by Oscar Wilde, Richard Coleman in 'Girl in my Soup', Donald Sinden, Leslie Phillips, Rolf Harris, Black and White Minstrels, Laurence Olivier live on stage. You can sit in 'The Gods' for 5/-.

On Friday night Val, Helen, Kris, Jan and I went to an Indian Restaurant for dinner while the boys stayed at the pub. I had Chicken Malaya, rice and Indian bread for 12/6. Indian food is very cheap, however Chinese food is expensive compared to Sydney prices. Today we had ravioli for 4/6 at a continental restaurant in Baker Street after seeing our flat. Val has given us a lot of clues regarding buying of food, and I don't think we will have much trouble with our budget. Later on, we are going down to Petticoat Lane and Portobello Road to buy a few knick-knacks for the flat (it is already furnished, and we were supplied with blankets, sheets, pillows, cutlery, pots etc.). I am buying an electric blanket for 4 pounds before it gets too cold.

So far, I have only spent 40 pounds of my traveller's cheques. If I get a job by next week, I shouldn't need them again until our tour of the Continent. Val has a neat little thing on her bath taps. It is a rubber hose affair with a showerhead, and you can have a mini shower with it. They got so sick of having baths, so they bought one for about 10/- and it is great. We are going to get one for our flat.

We had a ride in a London cab the other day - what an experience. You just about walk into the back, sit down on soft leather seats and there are 2 seats in front facing the back seat. The only trouble is they are expensive to hire, because of the price of petrol. The London cabbie has to go through a rigorous driving test, and know every street, lane and brick of the greater part of London![8]

Dogs are allowed on public transport, in department stores and just about anywhere. I have seen some hilarious signs e.g. - On the escalators at tube stations, 'dogs must be carried on escalators'. In Woolworths where dogs frequent as long as they are on a lead, I saw a sign near the cafeteria, 'in the interests of hygiene dogs are not allowed in this area'. One of Valda's friends, who I met at the 'White Hart' pub, nearly cried while he was telling us how his dog was killed. People take dogs shopping in the heart of London. It is quaint to walk into a huge department store like Selfridges, and watch women and men walking their dogs while they shop. London has terrific policemen. They are nearly all young, good looking and love it when you ask them questions.

West Indian girls mainly work in the department stores, and in the transport system as ticket collectors and station attendants. I noticed something peculiar to most of them - they all wear wigs over their frizzy hair! Some of them are better dressed and have better figures than girls in Sydney. Jan and I waited at Bond St Station last Friday for Val, and I saw some of the weirdest people! Boys with hair halfway down their backs and curled at the ends. Girls with miniskirts shorter than the shortest seen in Sydney. Clothes are the weirdest and nothing could match them anywhere. Leather is popular for suits, coats, trousers, ties, and hats. You can buy stockings with bikini pants attached, and they are so comfortable and easy to wash. I will send Denise some and she can try them out. They only cost 8/6 a

---

8   I returned home in 1970, and met the man I would eventually marry in 1972. He and I both obtained Sydney Taxi Licences. Like London cabbies in the days of no satellite navigation or mobile phones, we had to memorise major roads, hospitals, etc. We had a dream that we would be able to make so much money we could do more travelling. This didn't eventuate.

I don't wear step-ins anymore.

pair, which is a bargain. Val bought a light blue padded bra for 5/- at the markets the other day. They even sell bras and slips joined in one piece. You can buy knitted frocks in Woolworths for one pound, which are nearly as good as 'David Keys'. 'Marks and Spencers' sell thick winter jumpers and knitted frocks for less than 3 pounds.

It is also true about the 'Poms' washing themselves about once a week. You have to stop breathing in the bus and tube, as the body odour smell is so bad. A friend of Leon, who is living in a block of flats at Chelsea, and is the only Australian there, told us he is able to use the bathroom whenever he wants. There is never anyone using it, and the bath is always bone dry!

I am looking forward to seeing my new bedroom - it sounds smashing! Glad to hear you didn't pull out the fireplace as it does something to the room. <u>Do not throw anything of mine out please</u> -I went right through everything before I left and got rid of everything I felt wasn't of use - the rest is the bare essentials. When you store my records could you stand them up because they will warp if they are stacked on top of each other? Also, don't let Denise lend them out. You can play any record you like - I give you royal permission. Long play albums in London are 12/6 so I'll have a bundle when I get home. I go to my first party this Saturday night at East Finchley where Ronda is living. Finchley is very close to Barnet. Most of our friends from the ship are keeping in touch and plan to visit us later on. Tell Denise we are good friends with Colin Cook, the Melbourne Pop Singer. He is a great chap and has a lot of talent. He also plays the clarinet as well as guitar and is a terrific singer.[9]

Give special love to Pop and tell him not to work too hard. Tell him I will be writing a thank you letter to Lawrence Smith and Canning in Sydney and London, thanking them for their help. Tell Denise she must come to England later on, because Sydney is dead. Barry Humphries is raved about over here, and so are the Bee Gees and

---

9   Colin Cook, from Melbourne, was in bands called The Strangers and Thunderbirds; he was on the *Fairstar* with us on the voyage to London.

Rolf Harris. The young girls wear leather waistcoats with sleeves in them and short miniskirts and look tremendous. Lots of love and kisses from your big girl, who is getting more tolerant every day. Dianne xxxxxxxxxxxx

I was so happy to be in London, right next to Harley and Baker Streets. In 2008, I went back to London and retraced my steps through the West End, and in Highgate, where I visited the cemetery and sat beside the grave of Karl Marx. I retraced my steps through Hampstead Heath and thought about the time I went there with a flatmate called Louis in the middle of winter, to see if we could survive a night out in the elements.

When my mum heard about the injury to my thumb, she immediately wrote to me. I hadn't told her it was self-inflicted after a boozy session with friends in the cabin before we arrived in England. Friends had told me I was so drunk that I didn't feel anything while the doctor stitched my thumb without anaesthetic.

Monday, 16th September 1968 (Letter 3)
Flat 1, 18 Montague Square W1

To my Darling Dianne,

I received your welcome letter this morning but was upset to hear about your thumb. Has it healed, and how does it look? I can imagine how it must have felt. Hope you are feeling better now. Dad will write a few lines at the end of the page. We are pleased you have found a flat, and Jan's mother is too. I rang Aunty Betty and she received a letter from Valda on Saturday. She was pleased and excited to see you. Valda also mentioned about your thumb, but she didn't tell me till I mentioned it. I then rang Aunt and gave her your new address and telephone number. Had you also received the small donation Dad and Mum sent you? Let me know, in case the letter goes astray. Today 'The Monkees' arrived in Sydney. There were quite a few young girls at Mascot to welcome them, but personally I couldn't be bothered

I don't wear step-ins anymore.

to even watch the interview they had with them. They looked terrible and this is putting it mildly. Darling, remember when I used to try and get you to lighten your hair? Remember what you said to me? I hope you don't have your frocks too short. Use your commonsense and use your best points. You know some would wear a saucepan on their heads just because someone else did. Don't forget <u>elegance</u> is much nicer than being weird. Have you been wearing your 'Kanga Coat'? The papers said torrential rain hit London last Friday lunchtime. I hope you enjoy yourself in the flat, and glad it is in a nice part of London. I can imagine you taking in all the sights and historical buildings. When you go to Westminster Abbey, I want you to say a prayer for your Mother. Darling, there wasn't a photo enclosed in the letter, but was pleased to hear you didn't gain any weight on the trip over. Dad is going to enquire about the telephone rates, so don't be surprised one morning to have a call from Sydney. Look after yourself, and make sure you eat the right foods. See everything possible and take in the live shows. Darling, I will close now, wishing for next week to hear about the flat and how your thumb is. Love and a special big hug from your Mum. xxxxxx Dianne love if you can get a Doctor's Certificate for all the time you have your finger and send it to me, I can claim it off your insurance. Make sure it is dated from when you did it and when it is better. Your policy covers you for accident and sickness. I am very sorry to hear about it and how you suffered. Hope you are ok now. I am pleased you like London and have such a nice flat and Valda and David helped you. Thank them from Daddy. What's it like to stand at the bar at the old pub? Enjoy yourself and look after yourself. It was so good to hear from you but look after your finger so you can work well when you come home and so you can give me my breakfast in bed. Love to all, Daddy. My darling sister, BOTS - hope your finger is feeling better. Don't work <u>too</u> hard. Love Denise xxxxxxxxx[10]

---

10   My sister's nickname for me was BOTS, and to this day I do not remember why she chose this name for me. Perhaps she was referring to my ample and well-rounded bottom.

My family expected two letters per week, and at this time in Australia, the post was delivered twice daily. But my mum was still insisting I send postcards home, even to neighbours. How I was going to write more, after sending handwritten letters of 10 pages and more?

18th September 1968

Dear Mum, Dad and Denise,

A lot of exciting things have happened since I wrote my 14-page saga last week. Jan and I moved into our new home last Tuesday and Val and David brought our cases down after work. After they left, we were looking through our things and found some chocolates Val had hidden for us. The next day I went out and bought some 'Quality Street' for her and she only has four left (the pig). Kris came about 7pm and after paying a week's rent we were on our own.

Leon, a friend from the ship, and his mate Leigh popped in to see us before they left for Kent where they were hop picking for fifteen pounds a week. Leon is one of the nicest boys we have met and has gone out of his way to help us. He is a professional photographer from Melbourne and has found it very hard getting a job here. When they visit, they always bring us food or coffee, and not many people do this these days, especially men!

Bought an iron for 4 pounds. The shops sell 'Kangaroo' butter and 'Fair Dinkum' bread, hahahaha. The following day we went shopping for food and bed sheets. For an 8 oz. jar of Nescafe we paid 11 shillings and 3 pence. Cheese, eggs and milk are cheap and better than Sydney. The milk has cream inches from the top. You would love it. Vegetables and fruit are very expensive. Over 10/- a pound for muscatel grapes, 1/6 a pound for bananas. The best place to buy fruit and vegetables is at the markets where we are going from now on. Around the corner from our place is a post office, bank, shops galore and an antique store where I sometimes buy a good novel for 2 or 4 shillings. There are 4 Indian restaurants nearby and the smell

I don't wear step-ins anymore.

is out of this world. I eat everything with curry now. The Indian food is divine. All the restaurants are only 10 minutes' walk from Oxford Street, the main shopping area, and Bond Street where Val works. Went to Woolworths to buy a pair of flannelette sheets and another cheap towel. The sheets were marked 19/11 for 1. The shop assistant was Indian and charged me 19/11 for the pair and 5/11 for the towel. You may think badly of me, but I walked out and didn't say a word. If they are dumb enough to hire stupid people who can't even add up, then they can be taken for every penny. Kris bought the same and the guy made the same mistake! We bought a bottle of Spanish wine to celebrate our bargains for 9/11. Kris and I bought an electric blanket each for 5 pounds from Boots Chemist. Those panty stockings are terrific. Even if you ladder the stockings you can cut the legs off and you still have a pair of briefs. I will send some over for Denise to try out. The girls here don't wear step-ins and rarely wear bras - they are so flat chested. I also bought a pair of chocolate brown knee length boots for 7 pounds. They are so warm and have resin soles for the snow. I look like a 'Cossack' when I wear them. Picked up a pair of reddish-brown wool slacks for 3 pounds. They are hipster-style and have a buttoned sailor-type fly front. The latest craze here is those old style short and crazy coloured jumpers and vests. I am positive Dad used to wear them years ago! Denise would go mad if she saw all the clothes. She is just the right size to wear all the latest fashions! I am going to send a box home by sea during October filled with goodies - but don't tell Denise - just send her measurements over! Wigs can be bought for 3 pounds and knitted dresses about 4 pounds. They sell electric rollers in Woolworths for 6/11 each - a bargain. Jan, Kris and I saw 'To Sir with Love' and 'Lord of the Flies' at Piccadilly Circus on Thursday. The theatre was lovely with flowers arranged in a long box right under the screen.

    I met Valda after work Friday night and went to Barnet with her to have my stitches out. What a mess my thumb is. The doctor on the ship cut half my nail off and it must have been in 2 pieces from the look of it. I had 2 stitches one side and one large stitch the other side. I watched him take them out and it amazed even the Doctor how well it had healed. It looks all right except it's black all under the nail and out of shape. It is badly scarred but at least I still have a thumb - thanks to stitches. Val bought us a bottle of Cyprus sherry - she is terrible and even pays the bus fare.

Saturday, some girls from the boat, invited us to a party at East Finchley. It was such a long way from London and Leon and Leigh came back from Kent to go with us. The smell of hops on their clothes was nauseating, but the boys liked their hop-picking job. It was a boring party as we saw the same old faces from the boat. The trains stopped running after 12 midnight and we thought we would have to walk 20 miles home. Luckily a friend drove us home about 4am and we just dropped from exhaustion.

We visited Madame Tussauds and the Planetarium Sunday. I will send a souvenir book home later on. It was very interesting and the figures so life-like. I had tears in my eyes when I saw J.F. Kennedy, Bobbie Kennedy and Martin Luther King grouped together. John Gorton was there. Communist leaders and even Hitler were standing next to British cabinet ministers. Liz and Richard Burton were there and so was Twiggy. The model of Sophia Loren was fantastic. We got a fright when we passed a figure and it moved. Kris screamed and Jan and I ran. It was only an attendant, and I am positive he had been paid to frighten us.

The House of Horrors would have made your blood run cold. They had a guillotine from the French Revolution with blood all over it, and the actual letter 'Jack the Ripper' was supposed to have written to the London Police. It was written in blood from one of his victims and had stains all over it. The Police are positive it is authentic. There were murderers and poisoners on display. We felt quite sick when we got outside.

The flat is lovely - there is a fireplace with bookshelves either side where we have put photos of all the family and souvenirs from all the places visited. Aunty Ruby's Koala bear is sitting up there with Kris's bear. I have called mine 'Big Pinky' and Kris calls her bear 'Little Pinky'. Jan and I sleep on the divan beds - mine is under the front windows, and as they are barred, we can have them open all the time. No one can look in from the street, and it is so quiet and peaceful. When I am out it is so good to get back there. The London air is so grimy you can feel the dirt in your hair, under nails and even in your nose. I have used my umbrella every day. I don't mind the weather though. I can't wait till it snows and everyone walks around in their boots and coats. I passed Maggie Tabberer on Oxford Street yesterday. She was wearing a way-out trouser suit and looked slim and elegant. I think she is over here on holidays.

On Wednesday we went to the British Museum at Notting Hill Gate. The traffic was so thick we walked the whole length of Oxford Street to Piccadilly Circus and on to the museum. It is the most fascinating place we have ever seen and will have to go back again to see parts we missed. I will be sending a brochure to show you some of the exhibits. I saw, in 2 hours, things I had only learnt about at school. We went to the Egyptian rooms and saw mummy cases and the actual mummified bodies of human beings which lived 1400 B.C. There were mummies of cats, dogs, crocodiles and even kittens. In one glassed box there were 2 skeletons of men who died thousands of years ago, and you could still see their hair. They had exhibits of every facet of Egyptian, Roman, Greek, Persian and Cretan life. An exhibit which really was awe-inspiring - to actually see and touch the Rosetta stone dated 196 B.C. and found in the Nile Delta by Napoleon's soldiers. I wish Denise had seen them. The feeling you get when you see an object this old is amazing. This is what I feel every day when I walk down streets like Wimpole Street and Harley Street. I think of how many famous and infamous people must have lived in the houses I pass. As an example, there is a terrace house in a block of shops not far from where we live which has the word 'revolution' on the front window. We found out last night 'The Beatles' own this place and had a Boutique called 'Apples'. It was originally painted white but 'The Beatles' painted it over in psychedelic colours. The surrounding residents made up a petition to close the place. 'The Beatles' gave all the stock away, closed up and hence the 'REVOLUTION' sign. Elizabeth Barrett Browning lived in No 50 Wimpole Street, not far from us, and Lord Byron lived in Cavendish Square, also close by. Michael Faraday, the inventor, lived in Portman Square, just around the corner. These are only a few.

We are planning to see Westminster Abbey soon and I wish you could come to see it. I have just read a bit about it, and you might be interested to know it contains the graves of David Livingstone, Lawrence of Arabia, Neville Chamberlain, Tennyson, Kipling and nearly all kings and queens of England. There is also a museum containing wax figures of people interned in the Abbey.

On Wednesday night we went to the 'Cockney Pride', a pub in Piccadilly Circus. It is styled on Queen Victoria's Era with posters of stars of this period along the walls. The waitresses wear Victorian costumes. It was so crowded we had to stand up for half an hour before we got a seat. I had walked so much this day my feet were nearly numb with pain. Thursday, and it was Laundromat day. I washed my sheets, towels and dried them for 3/6 not bad. We are still discovering little amusing sights every day. We passed an antique shop and decided to go inside. There, in front of us, was a South American parrot talking to us with a proper English accent. We all nearly wet our pants. Last week I saw a young man, who looked very queer, leading a monkey on a chain. The monkey had a huge tail and a funny head. A friend told me he was walking down the Kings Road recently, a favourite haunt of weird people, when he noticed a fantastic Jaguar car go by. What was inside sitting next to the driver? A tame jaguar. What else would you have in a Jaguar car?

Something exciting came in the mail today. My slides of Tahiti, Balboa, the Panama Canal and Curacao. Out of 72 slides only 8 were bad. The Tahiti slides are tremendous. There is one of the 3 of us standing near the Tahiti Village Hotel and I will get a print and send it home. I may post my slides home later and this time I will register them. They are so good I would cry openly if anything happened to them. As we have no projector, and we will be travelling around, I think it would be wise to post them home, and you can see them and show them to your friends. Then you would be able to see just what we did and saw during our trip.

I am enclosing a few newspaper clippings and will write again next week. By the way today we had our first hint of autumn. The trees in the square are shedding their leaves and the footpaths and our steps are like a coloured russet carpet. It has been clear and crisp and not too windy. Give my love to Denise and thank her for her letters. I miss her very much - distance makes the heart grow fonder - I have her photo on the mantelpiece. Tell Dad I love him very much and miss him bringing me breakfast, and especially I miss you and I can't wait to see my new room. Hope you are all well and the weather is getting warmer. Lots of love, Dianne xxxxxxxxxxxxx

No one waiting on me anymore. No breakfast in bed. I was loving the freedom and the excitement of being responsible for myself. I loved how much money I spent, and how much I saved for trips and visits to the theatre and cinema. I even loved the cooler weather, which is probably why I ended up living in the Blue Mountains for nearly 15 years from the middle 2000s.

Re-reading my mother's letters showed me just how much she loved me. Her language was endearing, just like the songs she sang to me when I was a baby. Her favourite words to me were that I was *the three-penneth of the best apple blossoms that ever existed*. She regularly hummed a Richard Tauber song to me - *Girls were made to love and kiss*; and a song sung by Maurice Chevalier from *Gigi*, *Thank heaven for little girls, for little girls get bigger every day*....

Even though my mum told my aunt everything I was doing in London, I still enjoyed writing directly to my aunt as well. She had always encouraged me to see the world, whereas my mother encouraged me to settle down, marry, have the traditional two and half children, and live behind a white picket fence in the suburbs.

Mum and I were averaging two letters per week. Mine were sagas of ten pages plus. Mum crammed the entire history of our village, Earlwood, on one A4 aerogramme.

Saturday, 21st September 1968

Dear Mum, Dad and Denise,

We decided to get up early and go to the markets for fruit, vegetables and meat. Received a letter from you enclosing a lovely green piece of paper with 2 dollars on it (yum) and your photo. Not bad of the old girl! I'll be seeing your photo in the Nola Dekyvere column soon. Kris and Jan were very impressed. Kris and a lot of other people have said how much I look like me old mum, and Kris even thinks I write similar to you. They all agree you don't look 50!!

Anyway, the landlord has a son Robert aged 22 who does all the gas fitting in the flats. Every time he visits, he says - 'can ya spare a cup o'tea and bikkies?' He comes in for a chat and cuppa all the time, and we like him a lot. He reminds me a lot of Ross, but would you believe, he is bigger. I thought my feet were big - his feet are twice my size! He knocked on the door after fixing our central heating system for the winter and took us to the markets at Paddington. I thought I was in Coronation Street. A whole street full of all kinds of stalls selling everything from antiques to jellied eels and snails. We bought grapes, oranges, bananas, carrots, cauliflower, beetroot already cooked, onions, mince for a spaghetti meal, bacon and fresh plaice (fish) from a stall covered in all kinds of fresh fish, and the smell was delicious. Robert told us the best to buy, and we even nipped into an ancient pub and had a light ale, which is only 2/- and not overly intoxicating. We sat next to a group of old ladies drinking their <u>stout</u> and chomping on cheese rolls. None of them had their teeth in, and we nearly wet our pants <u>again</u>. I had a chat with them, and they were sorry to see us go. The three of them must have all been aged over 70. Elsie Tanner and Minnie Caldwell all over again.

I don't wear step-ins anymore.

I have never enjoyed myself so much just shopping. We even bought a Geraldton wax[11] and another potted plant for the flat. Walked out this morning into brilliant sunshine, and an hour later it poured down like a flood. Five minutes later sunshine again. You have to carry your umbrella everywhere.

Tomorrow, Val and David are visiting and bringing their slide viewer. I am dying to see the slides on a screen. I ask everyone I meet if they have a projector. My day will come. We are having fish tonight and my stomach is already growling. I certainly do not eat as much as I did at home - too expensive. Losing a few pounds hasn't hurt me one bit, and I feel much better for it. What I wouldn't do to get my teeth into your home cooked shoulder of lamb, or better still, your fresh mulberry pie and cream. When I start work, I won't have time to think of food.

During Saturday afternoon, Leon and Lee arrived back from Kent. They looked terrible. Leon had a tear in his trousers and they both hadn't washed for over a week. They made a sweet and sour dish, which we ate by candlelight. It was a good evening as they are two of the nicest people we know. Leon is Jewish and very close to his family, as are most Jews. As it was his mother's birthday, he rang her at home in Melbourne. We were so excited, and even drafted him questions to ask. The call was so clear, I could hear his mother from the other side of the room. The first thing Leon said was - 'Is that you Mum, how are ya?' We all rolled around the floor in hysterics. All in all, pretty exciting. He showed us his slides from Italy, and the countryside looks simply beautiful. He loved Venice so much he has been 3 times already and wants to go again. The phone call cost Leon a pound a minute, which isn't too bad.

Monday 23/9 I met Val for lunch, and she had a letter for me from Kerrie and one from Robyn at Wills. Robyn said my boss had

---

11 Geraldton Wax plants have followed me everywhere, and I had forgotten I had one in London! I came across another one in my front garden at Wentworth Falls in the Blue Mountains. I then moved to the city of Geraldton Western Australia in 2019, in order to downsize and be closer to my three grandchildren.

written to the Deputy Manager of Engineering Department B.A.T., Mr D Hughes, who I met recently while he was in Sydney. He said he would like to meet up with me when I arrived in the UK. Robyn from Wills gave me his phone number and I will ring him tomorrow. She also said the office was in a mess since I had left, and I got the impression the new girl is not very proficient. Mr Thompson is going to the USA on business, and I will write to him telling him how I am getting along. I made an appointment for a position tomorrow but will not go into detail until I know more. The basic wage I could get is 20 pounds or more with lunch vouchers. As I am in the West End, I probably won't have to pay fares. The only bugbear here is the high rate of tax. I rang up about a terrific job as Secretary to the Chairman at an Ink and Printing firm dealing for H.M.S. (Her Majesty's Service). They wanted a girl with driving experience but had to know London pretty well. It would have been good, but there are thousands of jobs out there waiting to be applied for.

Tuesday 24/9. I gave Mr Hughes at B.A.T. a ring. He recognised me straight away and was glad to hear from me. He has invited me to his home in Ascot and wants to show me the Ascot racecourse and Windsor Castle. I nearly lost my voice when he asked me. If I don't have any luck at this interview tonight, I might ask Mr Hughes about a job. Jan and Kris have gone to the O.V.C. about jobs, but I preferred to do it on my own.[12] I also cleaned through the flat while they were gone - it is impossible cleaning when Jan is here, she is so untidy! It is a beautiful day; plenty of sun and blue sky but the air is quite crisp. It gets very humid in London, and things get quite sticky no matter how cold it is. Would you believe Special K's are cheaper here and you can buy a large size? I have Special K's and Glucodin every morning and it is just like home. I found out recently a Lady and Colonel are living in our building. Very high class I must say. About 8 houses up the square on our side is a basement and first floor owned by Ringo Starr from the Beatles. We are pretty sure John Lennon and Yoko

---

12   I think the O.V.C. was a jobs centre, similar to job-finding agencies in Australia.

I don't wear step-ins anymore.

Ono are living there right now. Can't get near the place because of security.

Val and I saw wigs in a Department Store selling for 4 pounds. Denise would be in her element! Kris and Jan came home about 5.30 and Kris bought a hairpiece for 5 pounds - very nice. I walked all the way from home to Marble Arch, and down Park Lane to Hyde Park Corner for a job interview, only to find the person interviewing me was at a Board meeting! I was quite mad, but as nothing could be done, I made an appointment for 10 am tomorrow, and I won't tell you anymore until after. Mr Hughes rang tonight and said he and his wife want me to come down this Sunday. I have to catch a train from Waterloo to Ascot. It only takes about 40 minutes, and I am really looking forward to it. I mentioned I was job-hunting, and he said he would like to talk to me about jobs.

Wednesday 25/9 a good day. I have a job working as secretary to the Managing Director of Abbotts Wines and Spirits Merchants. The firm is a small concern situated in Knightsbridge. I will earn 18 pounds a week with 3/- lunch vouchers each day. It takes me 30 minutes walking to Marble Arch then through Hyde Park and past the Serpentine. Val has given her approval. Jan is working for a catering firm about 10 minutes' walk away and earns the same as me. Kris is working as a clerk at the Blind Society for 13 pounds a week and lunch vouchers. As rent is only 5 guineas a week and food about 2 pounds, I might be able to save a bit seeing I have no fares to pay. I am glad in a way I didn't go to B.A.T., as I wanted to get right away from a job similar to the one, I had in Sydney. My new wage is in Australian money approximately $40, which is much more than what I slogged away for at Wills. We all got out of bed at 8 am this morning and it was wonderful outside. The air was very crisp, and when you breathed, mist came out of your nose and mouth. As I walked through the Park, I saw a man galloping along on his horse, and lots of people walking their dogs. (I saw one huge white dog with a poodle clip galloping along like a great big white polar bear), and also saw a 'Bobbie' on a 2-wheel bike! I just had a look at the map, and where I work is just around the corner from Buckingham Palace. I'll be able to have lunch with the 'Old Girl'! You must write to the British Travel, ASL House, King and Clarence Street, Sydney, and ask them for a map of London. You will then be able to see where I live and work, and when I write about places I have visited, you will be able to look at them on the map. I may have left a map amongst my papers, so have a glance through.

I received a parcel from Canning at Watford today. I told you I had written to Mr Masek telling him how much I appreciated his help. Well he wrote me a letter saying - 'I have just returned from holidays and your letter of 10/9 awaited me. I am glad to hear you are now safely in London and you have found accommodation. You will find London is a large and exciting city with an enormous amount to be discovered. I was born here and am very fond of it. I hope your stay in England is a great success. Yours sincerely, E.L. Masek, Director.' Mr Masek also enclosed a Red Guide to London. I am sure you agree how nice a gesture this was, and I am going to reply and thank him.

My thumb is much better with the stitches out but looks all scarred. I will have proof of this misfortune for the rest of my life. Tell Dad I can get a Doctor's Certificate, but I didn't have to pay for anything. Val's doctor didn't even make a claim for it!

You and Dad would adore London, so come before you get too old. If you don't stop pulling walls down, and changing the house all the time, you will never get there. I will say a prayer in Westminster Abbey but tell me who's grave you would like me to stand at when I say it. Enclosing the Entertainment Guide from the Times. Hope you are well and happy. Will write again with more news. Lots of love and kisses Dianne xxxxxxxxxxx

Now I had a job - the pick of jobs. The Poms loved the young secretaries piling into London from the colonies, as we had an excellent work ethic and were never late; and I was a perfectionist in most things I did.

I don't wear step-ins anymore.

24th September 1968 (Letter 5)
Love and Kisses to Di from Denise xx

Darling Dianne,

Aunt rang me late yesterday to tell me she received a letter from you, also Valmai received hers. Today has been rather warm, but there has been a warm wind, which wasn't too pleasant. The lounge room (where the television is) has been lined and the plasterer is coming tomorrow to patch up the walls in the kitchen. We had a baked dinner tonight, jelly and cream. Dad went over to ask Mr Cohen would he like a baked dinner, and the old chap has been sick for three days with the gout. We sent over a pot of tea and biscuits straight away, as he hadn't a thing to eat because he couldn't get out of bed. For a change Denise is staying home tonight. On Thursday morning I received your welcome letter. We are pleased you are settled and like your flat. Darling, I was a little disappointed about the episode of the sheets. I could have taken the lady at the mannequin parade at Bardwell Park for $1.00, but made Alma take it back to her. Always remember to do unto others as you wish them to do to you. Went to Mansours at Roselands yesterday to pick up your curtains. The lady, who served us, came from England, so I asked her what it was like at Montagu Square, and she said it was very nice. Dad also bought a very nice bedspread for you. Similar to mine, but a pretty dark blue, and a green shot through it. Your new mattress came tonight (Friday), and when the new dressing table comes next week, I will be able to finally finish your bedroom. Was speaking to Jan's mother and she said Jim will be 2 on 3rd November. We are going to watch 'Mission Impossible'. Remember when it is 9 o'clock in the morning in London, we are starting to watch 'McHale's Navy' at 6pm. Today I washed the walls in our bedroom, washed Dad and my bedspreads and my blankets. The weather has turned cool the last couple of days, so we had to put the electric blanket on. Tonight, we will have to put it on again. Eve Speedy rang me today, and said you sent her a card. Have picked the colour for the lounge and we are getting it made. Dad is buying a black armchair for himself. It is $100.00, but it is lovely to sit in. Our lounge is $540.00 in the shop. Denise has gone out with Russell. She has been out quite a lot. I cut out her blue frock yesterday and will have to find time to make it. She has taken Allan's photo out of the frame. I hope you are eating the right food and have vegetables as much as you can. Give my love to Jan and Kristine, Valda and David. 'May God watch over you and keep you safe'. Love and big hugs Mum xx Hello Love, Glad you like England and your flat is a beauty and your finger is going ok. We are still working but getting extra closer to finishing. Good you wrote to those people. Enjoy yourself, best of love to all, Love Daddy xxxxxxx

As I was being told about my new bedroom, at no time did I specifically ask my mother what she was doing with all the things I had left behind. Things like my stamp collection, the books and magazines I had collected, and letters from my pen pal in Japan. Later I found out that my dad had grabbed important things and stored them in the garage roof for me; otherwise I would have come home to a completely new environment. My mother did toss out my schoolbooks, and all my childhood toys like teddy bears, which I would have liked to keep.

30th September 1968 (Letter 5)
18 Montagu Square London W1

Dearest Mum, Dad & Denise,

Jan is worried about the slow delivery of her mail, so would you give her mum a ring and assure her Jan is writing every week? Something is going haywire between London and Sydney. It may be, tell her, Post Office changes here are playing havoc with deliveries, as I myself have just received your letter 4 dated 25/9 today (5 days to deliver). As I think I said in my aerogramme of 28/9, it has been 7 days since receiving one letter and it nearly drove me crazy. Thank God you rang, or I may not have lived through the weekend.

I don't wear step-ins anymore.

Somehow, I had a feeling you would ring as I did not sleep for many days and kept having weird dreams about home.

What is this I hear about Denise & Russell? I cannot keep track of all her beaus (boyfriends to all you lowbrows). Anyway, it is good to hear she is <u>getting out</u> and <u>not staying at home</u> all the time! When is Dad going to take some photos of the new house you moved in to? If you pull anymore walls down the roof will cave in! Fancy Souths winning the Football!!! - They are a pack of film stars more than footballers, and if I had of watched it on T.V. like Dad and Denise, I would have cried.

You seem worried about my chances of employment - don't. The job I thought I had fell through simply because I stupidly told them I was only going to work until Spring and then tour the Continent. I will not make the same mistake again; I can assure you. There are jobs a' plenty and I am progressing. Seeing I was lucky to spend so little on the ship I am in no trouble at the moment, but I have no intentions of staying the way I am and will have a job shortly. (Keep this to yourself - Valda had to say she would stay 5 years to secure her present position, and I did not know this before I went for an interview). By the way, Jan started her job today, but to my surprise came home shortly after - she was politely told they did not need her services and was handed 20 pounds (sufferance pay I suppose). They had not asked her for any address or phone number so they are now 20 pounds in the red. Jan, and I are therefore both visiting the Employment Agency again today, and what will be will be.

Enough about jobs, and onto more important things. I cannot wait to see what you have done to the homestead. Why don't you talk Dad into taking a few flash photos of the finished work and send me some prints? Here I am trying to picture how palatial it must look not realising father can actually take living photos of it all, especially when I have spent so much time teaching him how to use his camera!

You want to know whom I have written to? Well I will list; On the ship I wrote postcards to Beverly, Valmai, Aunt, Aunty Betty, Ruth and Kevin, Aunty Ruby. From London I wrote to Mr & Mrs Porter, Mrs Massey, Mr and Mrs Speedy, Aunty Dora, Aunt, Aunty Betty, Valmai, Mr Hood, Sandra and a few of my friends. As you suggested in a previous aerogramme I will try and send one postcard each few days. I have also written thank-you notes to Mr Masek at Canning (Watford) and the other gentleman in Birmingham. Also, Mr and Mrs Hughes for having me yesterday. I will tell you all about yesterday presently.

Saturday night Tony and I met Val, David and 2 of their friends, Lloyd an Australian whom they met coming over, and his Canadian girlfriend Dianne (a well-chosen name don't you think?) for dinner at the Norway Food Centre in Brompton Road Kensington. I am certain when you read the enclosed leaflet from the Norway Centre your mouth will water, knowing how much you like smorgasbords. Val, as usual, made a pig of herself, but I admit it wasn't hard for me to keep up with her. After your phone call I found it hard to eat, and therefore thoroughly enjoyed every morsel. You cannot imagine how funny it was to see 6 people pile into a Fiat fastback going home. Me and my long legs - my head nearly making a dent in the roof, and David not being able to change gears. Nevertheless, we got home quite early, but talked for hours and naturally I didn't finally get into bed till 3 am. Sunday was Ascot day and getting up at 9am was quite an ordeal. Leon and Leigh came around to say goodbye as they were leaving for Germany for a Photographer's Convention in the morning. Leon and Leigh are 2 of the best friends we have made since leaving home. They are real mates and not boyfriends. Both are early 20s, wear long hair and beards (Leigh uses hairspray would you believe) are professional photographers, wear way out gear, do not smoke or drink (now and again) and visit us all the time. They both come from Victoria by the way. We met Leon on the ship and Leigh was meeting Leon on arrival in London. For the past 3 weeks they have been hop picking in Kent so as to save some money for their trip to Germany, lasting about 3 weeks. They are really 2 of the nicest people we know and when they visit, they never arrive empty handed. They brought

I don't wear step-ins anymore.

a dozen eggs from the farm, cook up meals for us (sweet and sour eg.) and shout us to the movies. I am sending a few photos over soon so you can see what we all look like now. Leon looks like 'Our Lord', and everyone who meets him cannot help commenting on this. When you see his photo, I think you will agree. He is in the Pirate Night photos, but all the boys were wearing makeup and it is hard to tell what they look like. Leigh on the other hand gives you the impression he is effeminate, but after talking to him for a while, you realize he is very shy and modest. (Very uncommon in most men). He has a steady girl in Melbourne who writes regularly and so has Leon, but for the time being we are their favourites. Leon was with us when I hurt my thumb and nearly carried me to the hospital where he stayed while the old Doc sewed my thumb back on. Tony also came down and for the rest of the night they had a shuttle service of coffee and food brought down about 4 decks to my cabin. Tony and Leon both helped me with my cases through Customs as well as carrying their own. They are what I call real good friends. It is peculiar the only real female friend we have from the ship is Kris, the rest being boys. Mainly because the girls were very catty and talked about everyone behind their backs. One friend from the ship, Jeff Preston is an Opera, Pop and Ballad singer, at the moment trying to get a recording contract. He is flatting with Colin Cook and Marty Kristian (Denise will remember them). Colin and Marty, from Melbourne are pop singers and have been on most T.V. Musical shows. They sang at our Discotheques on the ship and had their passage paid for doing so. We see them quite a bit and may get an invite to their parties. At the last one the guest list included Cliff Richards, The Shadows, The Easybeats, Olivier Newton-John (a Sydney model) The Bee Gees and a few others.

Now I will tell you about my day at Ascot. I left home about 11 am and had to get a taxi as I was running frightfully late. Lucky I did get a cab because the driver took me right past Buckingham Palace. If I hadn't been in a hurry I would have stopped and had a sticky. The Grenadier Guards were just about to do a parade and change the

Guard. It just looked like what you see at the movies, only this time I was in London watching with my own eyes. Wow, the red and gold and those bearskin hats - very impressive. Queen Victoria looked very regal standing outside the gates like she was guarding the Palace! I passed Westminster Abbey and went across Westminster Bridge with The Houses of Parliament and Big Ben nearby. Arrived Waterloo Station, got out and paid 5/- (not bad) and went inside. Thoughts went through my mind of the night we arrived and saw Val and David on the platform. I also remembered the beautiful film 'Waterloo Bridge' but didn't see anyone as handsome as Robert Taylor. As usual I was in a state of utter confusion, nearly missed the train and then someone had to close the door of the compartment for me (I couldn't figure out how it worked!) Read the Sunday Times all the way - it only took about 40 minutes or so. To make matters worse I made an ass of myself opening the door. I nearly knocked myself out falling - the only way to get off I always say! Mr Hughes was waiting and nearly shook my hand off. He is about 40, tall and wiry and has a ginger mo. - typical English with pucker accent. Works as Deputy Manager of Engineering, British-American Tobacco. Their home is a bungalow style with 3 bedrooms upstairs and bathroom with carpet and heating throughout. Even the towel racks are heated. I expected to sit down on a heated toilet seat but to my dismay it wasn't. Mrs Hughes was very charming and called her husband 'Darling' all day. I brought down a box of choc mints for Mrs Hughes (after dinner type). They have a 15-year-old daughter Jan and 10-year-old son Nigel, who both attend boarding school. They have a beautiful garden, which I imagine looks superb in spring. Tall birch trees and firs surround it. For lunch we had a type of melon for an entree, roast beef, peas, beans, potatoes, Yorkshire pudding and cherry pie for dessert and coffee. They have 2 gorgeous welsh corgis; one is a female and the other her male offspring, and I naturally got quite carried away patting them. The female one is very intelligent and when Mr Hughes said 'Die for your Country' she fell down and played dead. Mrs Hughes father was once a keeper of Windsor

I don't wear step-ins anymore.

Castle, so when they took me there, they were able to tell me quite a bit about it. The countryside in Surrey is magnificent. I have never seen such beautiful scenery; a hedge, which is dead straight all along the 500 acres. The Windsor great park is 4,800 acres! The castle was founded by William the Conqueror and in St Georges Chapel lay the bodies of George III, George IV, William IV, George V and Queen Mary. Unfortunately, we arrived just as the chapel closed for visitors and I must go again. We went through the State Apartments where there were paintings by Rubens, Rembrandt, Van Dyke and others. Everything was on a grand scale, huge chandeliers, tapestries, antique furniture, paintings on the ceilings, armory, statues of famous people, fantastic gold and silver ornaments. A guide told us the Persian carpet in the Queen's Ballroom takes 50 men to carry it. There were chairs used for royal ceremonies and many other things. The actual village of Windsor is very small and mostly occupied by people concerned with the castle. I could have spent a whole day there, but we had a thunderstorm, which made it impossible to walk anywhere. You can see Eton College from the Castle and the Thames, which borders the park on 3 sides. Queen Victoria and Prince Albert are buried in the grounds and I will have to make another trip back to see it. Also saw the famous Ascot racecourse - not impressed. It is only a snob's turn and another boring Royal Trademark. I would like to see the fashions and the horses though - may get an invite if I am lucky. Had a lovely afternoon tea, talked a bit more about my chances of employment at B.A.T., and left about 7pm. I was so tired when I got home, I just fell into the bath, nearly fell asleep and got to bed at 8.30 - but tossed and turned all night as I have done for the past week.

It is 4am Tuesday and the 3 of us are still writing and getting very hungry. Kris is in one of her crazy moods and we are all chatting about old times and planning a trip in the country this coming weekend. We may go to Stonehenge in Salisbury or Isle of Wight, but probably won't decide until Friday anyway. The central heating comes on 1st October. The weather isn't too bad and really one doesn't have time to notice whether it is running or not. I hear the Sydney climate is getting rather sticky - another long hot summer.

I was so glad to hear you would show your hospitality to Cliff Carrington from Balboa. I have written to him giving our home telephone number, and unless he changes his mind, he plans to arrive after the New Year. He and George Shaw made our stay in Balboa a memorable one, so he would love to see you. I will write more about him after he replies to my postcard. So far, the people we have met at different places have welcomed us with open arms, and it really is good when you think we are strangers. This is the most noticeable aspect of travelling. People go out of their way when visitors approach and help so much. Some Londoners are terrific, but then so many people in London are tourists. I myself have been queried many times by tourists who thought I was born here. Saturday night while Tony and I went to meet Val at Norway Food Centre, we shared a cab with 2 other people. I said, 'are you going near Kensington?' and one of the passengers said, 'what part of Australia are you from?'

Please don't say I write measly letters - I could go on for at least another 20 or so pages, but it is after 6 and I feel like a few hours kip. Only about 3 hours to wait for postman and maybe another letter. Our mail seems to bank up and if only it stretched over the week - I would have a letter a day. Will write again soon. Lots of love and kisses from your 'big girl' Dianne (slowly diminishing) (Don't send money, send a shoulder of lamb, potatoes, veggies, gravy, a homemade mulberry pie with cream or strawberry jam and cream – oh, the agony). Love you always, Dianne xxxx

My Aunt Betty, Valda's mum, wrote to me, filling me in on some of the family goings-on. Around that time, I had a break-up with my two flatmates in the West End flat. I still got on with Jan, but Kris was getting out of hand, bringing guys home and having sex with them in her curtained-off bedroom. Jan and I had our beds at either end of a large room, so there was no privacy for us at all. This was a basement flat in a semi-detached house, which meant open plan living,

I don't wear step-ins anymore.

except Kris bagged the curtained space for herself. I went to stay with my cousin Val until I found another shared accommodation in London.

Monday, 30th September 92 degrees
Miss D Lindsay from 'The Land of Sunshine'

Dear Di,

Well old cheese, here I am again with a little bit of news on the home front. Everyone here is quite well. I wasn't really surprised to hear you were staying with Val, as I don't think a threesome ever really works out. Di, you will always find one bitch around. Not to worry pet, you will work something out, and I won't say a word to anyone about it. Your Mum would only worry. It would severely interrupt her painting, and this would never do. Your dad would catch the next jet to London! We had a night out at the Marrickville RSL last night, and your Mum and Dad were present. We all had a good time. Everyone finished up a little tipsy, except your mum, who consumed a large amount of tea, and 3 helpings of sweets. She then gave us all a sermon on the evils of drink. We all replied, 'We'll drink to that', and then polished off a few more middies. What a scream. I am enclosing some money for you pet, to buy yourself something nice for your birthday, or else just go out and get sloshed and all sing 'freeza' (strine meaning 'for he's a jolly good fellow). The present is from Al, Rob and me. We were so pleased to hear you have a good job, and I do hope things work out for you. Have a smashing birthday. We will be thinking of you. Love Betty xxxx

At the beginning of October, I sent my mother a short note complaining about her requests to send postcards to family and friends. I told her I was happy to send letters to close family and the occasional friend or neighbour, but it was taking a toll on my personal time, especially now that I was working full-time. She responded on the 5th of October, crossing out endearing salutations and ending her aerogramme on the first page, leaving the last page blank.

Saturday, 5th October 1968 (Letter 8)
Miss D Lindsay Flat 1, 18 Montagu Sq. W1

~~To Our Big Girl~~ Dianne,

Two months yesterday since you and Jan left Australia. The plasterer finished the lounge ceiling yesterday and I put the first coat of paint on the kitchen ceiling. Friday was a nice day, but this morning, when I got up at 6.30am, it was very cold and today has been one of those bleak days. I put a second coat of paint on the kitchen ceiling and Dad washed the lounge walls down to get rid of the white stuff the plasterer had splashed. I painted across the back of the house this afternoon, and Dad had a barbecue tonight. Ross came in this afternoon.[13] He came home this morning at 5am. He didn't go to Wagga on account of the weather but is going to Bateman's Bay tomorrow. Ross had his tea with us. Dad cooked 12 sausages, 4 steaks, 4 lamb chops between the four of us. We thought of you while we were eating. We also had a large apple pie and cream between us. Ross actually wiped up for me. Tonight, I took up your linen skirt. Jan's mother rang this afternoon to tell me she had received a letter from Jan. Denise went to Town this morning and bought a white dress, and bone pair of shoes and black bikini. She bought me two bunches of white carnations with a red one in each bunch. They were very nice. Denise bought Dad two bags of eucalyptus lollies. We are watching on TV 'Homicide'. How are you going at work? Are they easy to work for? Send xxxxxxxxxxxx a Christmas card. Darling, I am very tired as I am sitting in front of the TV listening to the news. We went on the Harbour Cruise today with

---

13 Ross was the son of our neighbours, Alma and Gerald Seymour. I got on very well with him when we were growing up, as I was a tomboy. We would play cricket on the wide road outside our houses. Prior to my leaving for overseas, he, my sister, her boyfriend Allen and I drove to the snowfields near Mt. Kosciuszko for a few days.

the Church. God was good to us, as it turned out a lovely day. This morning at 6.30am I went out to get the paper and it was spitting rain, and it was overcast. By 8 o'clock it started to clear up and we had a very nice day. We left Circular Quay at 9 o'clock, went around the Harbour, down under the Spit Bridge, down Middle Harbour. By lunchtime we came to Shark Island and had lunch. I had a sleep in the sun, and then we came aboard and went to the Gladesville Bridge and were back at the Quay by quarter to five. During the afternoon we saw the new submarine come up the Harbour and watched it land at the Submarine Dock. We also saw the 'Himalaya' depart on a cruise. Mrs Bernays from the Church went on it with her daughter and granddaughter. Yesterday was a cold, windy day. Denise went down past Nowra yesterday with Russell and she is out today. Don't forget xxxxxxxxxxxxxxxxxxxxxxxxxxxxxxxxxx

I received your <u>Personal</u> letter this morning Tuesday. I will respect your wishes. As you know I have never given to either you or Denise without the other one knowing. What I sent to you was only what I have given to Denise. I have sent some money to Valda for your 21st birthday. If I had received your letter earlier, I would not have done so. I am not a good letter writer, Dianne, as my news is only within the four walls of my own home, and my afternoon occasionally at Bowls. It is six weeks since I have been to Aunt's place and seen Beverley and Valmai. Don't feel obligated, you have to write such long letters to me dear. After all Dianne, your mother has always been a bit of a 'loner'. Hoping Jan and Kris are well, Love Mother xx

Prior to receiving this poignant letter from my mother, I had written an extremely long letter on small notepaper, totalling 18 pages.

Monday, 7th October 1968

Dearest Mum, Dad and Denise,

    Before I get on with more important talk, I hope my previous letter didn't upset you too much, but I was so mad when I saw all those addresses. It just didn't look like a letter from home. A lot of things have happened since last week. Firstly, Leigh unexpectedly arrived back from Europe (Leon stayed to see a bit more of the Continent) so the 4 of us decided to hire a car for the weekend. It only costs 7 pounds 8 shillings between 4, 10 pounds deposit and 380 miles free, then 4 pence for every extra mile. We pay for petrol at 5/10 a gallon!

    Before I go any further, I finally have a job with a small firm 10 minutes' walk from home. The office is in Welbeck Street, between Harley and Baker Streets. (Sherlock Holmes?). I work for Mr Barton and Mr O'Dell, who chain-smokes Rothmans cigarettes, and both seem very easy going. There is also a young junior called Tina who is only about 17 and she is telephonist, typist and coffee maker. The firm is a property consultant's office dealing with clients who wish to buy property. I get 17 pounds per week plus 3/- a day luncheon vouchers. My work is quite easy as secretary to both men, but as they are out most of the time, I have to run things by myself. I start at 10 am until 5.30pm so I don't have to get up till 9am!

    Now I will tell you where we went on the weekend. Left about 6pm for South Wales and Kris did the driving first. We put an Australian flag on the front of the car (a new Cortina) and everyone thought us diplomats, so we gave them a royal wave. You would not believe the traffic in London until you see it with your own eyes. The highways are phenomenal, and 60 mph is the minimum speed a car must do. Frightening at first, but one gets used to it after a while.

    We drove until 8pm then stopped for fish and chips just past Oxford. We were all ravenous and had 2 courses each. By 12 midnight we were in Wales, (I was driving) and decided to stop off the road and sleep. It wasn't very cold, so I slept in the boot and had a good rest. Was woken by bleating goats about 7.30am and

I don't wear step-ins anymore.

couldn't believe what I saw. The countryside was like a patchwork quilt of greens, browns and russets. The farms are sectioned off with hedges and it is very pretty indeed. The sun was just rising behind the hills and looked like a furnace. After 10 minutes or so the sun disappeared behind another large cloud. We had bread and cheese sandwiches for breakfast and Leigh drove on.

The country was too beautiful for words, with houses made in Tudor style. I took quite a few photos so you could see how pretty it was. Leigh had a pen-friend in Hereford (in England but very close to the Welsh border) so we decided to visit them. Arrived in Hereford about 11am driving the wrong way into a one-way street. We were met by a policeman. He was very nice and understanding towards us, found us a parking space, stopped traffic for us and had a chat. We asked him if we could take his photo and he said it was against the rules. He then decided to walk casually past so we could snap him. Jan, Kris and I sat on a bench in the square and as the Bobbie walked past Leigh snapped the camera. As usual everyone thought we were proper nuts, but we couldn't care less. Leigh rang his pen friend and they arranged to meet in the square about 12 noon.

Leigh's pen friend, Sheila Townsend, is going to be married next year. Her parents are very nice (her father was awarded the MBE recently). Sheila's fiancée is a surveyor and knows a lot about Hereford's history and took us for a tour of the city. We were told the history goes back as far as the Norman Conquest and there are even sections of walls built to deter Oliver Cromwell and the Royalists. The cathedral dates back to 1200 and has beautiful stained-glass windows. I try to buy a pamphlet from every place I visit, so when you receive my parcel by sea you will find about 20 pamphlets enclosed. I will write on them so you will know what they refer to. Please keep them for me so I will be able to look back over them on my return home.

David, Sheila's fiancée, showed us a shop with an old Tudor House on top. He explained how it was moved it its entirety to the square, rendered to a better condition and then re-assembled over the shop, which was completed while the old house was in the square. David told us the story behind a church with a slightly bent steeple. The builder fell to his death while completing the structure, so it was left as it was. Perhaps an English version of the Leaning Tower of Pisa?

Mr and Mrs Townsend insisted we come for lunch, but beforehand, David and Sheila took us to their favourite pub. It was very small and decorated like a horse stable. The owners had picked flowers and were putting them in vases. It was so lovely we just sat and gazed in amazement. You and Dad would love them - they are so quaint and full of history. All the locals shook our hands and blessed us for being Australian. The country folk are very obliging towards strangers, but we have found some shop attendants rude and not helpful at all.

Mr and Mrs Townsend gave us a lovely lunch, which consisted of chops, sausages, pies, mushrooms, potatoes, apple crumble, cheese, bikkies and coffee. It was so good to fill our poor empty tummies, seeing we hadn't had a good nourishing meal for so long. Left about 3pm after many happy goodbyes and decided to head for Cardiff, the capital of Wales.

On the way we passed through coal mining districts, and what a depressing feeling it gave us. Rows and rows of Victorian semi-detached dwellings stretching for miles. We were in the same area as 'Aberfan' where landslides occurred after heavy rain, and children were killed while attending school. I remembered asking myself how people could live in this type of environment. The air was thick with coal dust, and the people suffering with lung complaints must have been very high. We were so glad to get to Cardiff, however as it was about 8pm, we didn't get a good look at it.[14]

We continued on to Bristol, then Bath, where we camped for the night. I slept in the boot again and woke up about 8.30am to more beautiful landscapes. The countryside is magnificent in autumn, and

---

14 Memories of driving through this coal town have haunted me all my life. I recently saw a reference to the Aberfan disaster on television in the second series of *The Crown*. I worry about my grandchildren's future, if we don't phase out using fossil fuels and convert to renewables.

I don't wear step-ins anymore.

I am amazed it isn't very cold at all. Bath is gorgeous, like a European city and most of the buildings date back to George I, plus the Roman ruins are dated B.C. As Bath has mineral springs the Romans had steam baths which are still there. We were not at all impressed with the way the town had preserved the ruins. They had built a building around it, therefore the ruins looked ridiculous.

Had cheese and bread for breakfast at about 11am, a long stretch between meals. We then went on to Salisbury (Stonehenge is close by). On the way we stopped to take photos of sheep along the roadside. We actually tempted an expectant ewe with biscuits. I took a photo of the ewe eating a biscuit while Kris held the biscuit between her fingers. What a scream!

Stonehenge was a big disappointment, as it was too commercialized and fenced off with barbed wire, which made it hard to examine the stones unless one paid for an inspection. We decided to buy a pamphlet and view it from afar. I will send the pamphlet home together with numerous others. Afterwards we drove back to Salisbury, a pretty town, where we had lunch of bread and cheese and half a tomato each. Then on to Windsor passing some beautiful scenery. We got into London about 8pm, had a Chinese meal and went to bed early for a change.

Monday and Tuesday 7th and 8th October. Started work at 10am so I left home 9.50am and walked the short distance from Montagu Square to Wellbeck Street. The young junior Tina tried to put it over me at first, but I put her in line. These pommies do not know what the word 'WORK' means. She answers the switchboard, makes coffee and posts my mail. That's it! She reads magazines and listens to the radio for the rest of the day. Mr O'Dell and Mr Barton are terrific, and I get a lot of shorthand from both. They are out of the office a lot but keep me busy. Tina nearly dies when I work over the 5.30pm mark or when I stay over the lunch hour. It is a thing I was used to in Sydney so what the heck. I leave the office singing and people must think I'm mad. It is just because I am happy and contented with what I am doing. I am left alone most of the time and Tina is gradually coming over to my way of working. My bursts of energy made her type a list of addresses for me today. I had complained about having to ask her for addresses, and her conscience was pricked into action.

Tina is about as big as the 'Little Tart' and her skirts are so short. One has to look the other way when she bends over, as her panties show![15] I feel like a grandma when she raves about pop stars. I'm more interested in finer things now. I don't listen to much pop music except The Beatles, The Stones, Aretha Franklin and other coloured singers. Last night I picked up Germany on the transistor radio and listened to 2 hours of old Beatles tunes. Brought back memories!

Do you remember Tony Hunter, who I went out with the whole voyage? Well, I still see a lot of him as he is staying with relatives in Essex about 20 miles out of London. He is very nice, and I must admit, I am growing fond of him. Did I tell you he is an Interior Decorator? He plans to settle in Australia after a while, so you may get to meet him. Since leaving I haven't been out with any other boy. We just get along so well together. Val and David have met him and think he is marvellous. Suddenly I feel more mature since I have been away for 8 weeks, probably as you are not waiting on me hand and foot anymore. I know my capabilities and limits, and as I am nearly 21 it is about time! I hope you have replied to my aerogramme and wasn't too upset, but I was mad when I read your letter after waiting a week for mail. I only exist waiting for letters from you and the family. At dinner, Kris, Jan and I read our mail out loud as we enjoy them so much.

Had lunch with Val today and she told me about your letter to her and the 20-pound postal note. Val thinks you are millionaire, throwing money around like this! I want only to hear your voices for my birthday. What are you doing to my bedroom? I certainly won't be used to such luxuries after sleeping in car boots. Leigh is going

---

15   'The Little Tart' was one of my affectionate names for my younger sister, Denise.

I don't wear step-ins anymore.

to ring you from Sydney Airport when he arrives and before he goes to Melbourne, so he can tell you how we were before he left. Jan's mother will also get a call. Lots of love, Dianne xxxxxxx

I was so pleased to receive another crazy letter from Valda's Mum, Aunty Betty. She had written this letter before a previous letter posted earlier. It didn't matter if it contained old news, as I was just desperate to hear from home.

2nd October 1968
Miss D Lindsay Flat 1 - 18 Montagu Square W1 London
England Land of Sunshine and <u>no rain</u>

Dear Di,

Well old cheese, I am replying to your earlier letter at long last. Thank you very much for letting me know how you thought Val and David looked, although I thought it was most tactful of you not to say Val was fat. Your flat sounds just smashing, and I do hope everything goes along just fine for you all. We all went to Marrickville RSL Club Sunday night, your Mum and Dad included, and we had a great night.

The old Rube Girl was tut, tutting about you robbing the salesman over the flannelette sheets and I had a good chuckle. I really thought she would get up on stage and preach a sermon any minute. We will really have to slip this girl a Vodka. How are you enjoying the food over there? Your leather coat and boots sound just great and as for the hemlines rising, I am not surprised at this. How is your job-hunting going? I told Aunty Ruby about the koala bear and she was very pleased. I do hope the heating has come on for you now or you will freeze to death. It was a shame you hurt your thumb. I suppose the true story was a steward was chasing you around the cabin and trod on your thumb. Not to worry, it could have been worse.

Tell Val if she buys any more pots and pans, she will need the Queen Mary to get home on. Is London as exciting as you expected it to be Di? Don't forget to go and see Buck's Palace, will you? We were relieved to hear Val and David are not talking like those bloody Poms. I couldn't stand this accent in my earholes. We went up to see Lisa and Valmai last week Di, and you wouldn't believe how much she has grown. She is a living doll and Valmai is so happy with her. Since you left home your Mum has been painting like mad, and we have lost count of how many plumbers, carpenters and other tradesmen they told us have been through the house. They will probably extend to the church grounds or the terminus. Well would you believe the end of the street. Well my pet, will close now and remember, not too much smoking. Remember Joan of Arc's famous last words when she was tied to the stake; 'I'm smoking more and enjoying it less.' Lots of love xxxxx Betty

My mum had continued to send letters, but without the requests that I write postcards to everyone who lived in Earlwood. She was also unsure where I was now living, so she posted aerogrammes to my 'place of business', as she called it (one did not work - one went to business). This following letter from her also documented the terrible bushfires raging in Sydney. Some of my family lived in the Sutherland Shire, and I was always concerned for their safety.

Friday, 25th October 1968 (Letter 13)
D Lindsay c/- Ronald O'Dell 55 Welbeck Street W1 London

Dear Dianne,

We received your letter by this afternoon's mail. I was beginning to worry in case you were sick. From next week we will be only receiving one mail a day. The sign of progress. Today has been a shocking day with 55 mile an hour gusts of wind. Six fires were out of control during the night. They started from the Blue Mountains to Berowra and raging bushfires at Woronora to Engadine destroying one house. On TV news tonight we heard one young woman pleading with one fireman to save her home. All the women and children were evacuated from certain streets. Tonight, the wind has dropped, but we

I don't wear step-ins anymore.

had to keep the back door closed all day. Snowfalls were reported in several outer Canberra suburbs, and snow covered the ground at Oberon, 30 miles east of Bathurst. The temperature was in the low 60s. Where do you go to get the 'Map of London'? You told me in another letter, but I have put them away, so you can let us know in the next letter. The tiler finished the shower room and it looks nice. We took the tiles out, and had these tiles put into the same height as the brown ones. We have got a regulated tap, which cost over 15 dollars, so the water should be at the temperature you want. Today, Monday, has been a very hot day, and at 4 o'clock the temperature was 27 degrees above average. There was a very warm wind and it was one of those sickly days. Denise went swimming tonight with Russell, Marilynne and David. About seven o'clock a southerly came up and it is now quite pleasant. From today we only get one mail a day. There still are fire dangers, as far down as Wollongong. Yesterday, Sunday, we went to Church and the Rector passed a remark he missed me at Church the previous Sunday. I am glad some people notice me. Today I took my electric blanket off the bed and got into my summer nightie. I put your stripe sheets on Denise's bed today. The electrician came and put the lights up today, and I will be glad when everything is back in order. The news flash said the southerly made two fires uncontrollable, and threatening Bundeena; a lot of people are evacuating from there. They are showing films of them, and the fire is threatening Engadine shopping centre. They are the worst bushfires on record, and all roads south of Heathcote have been banned to motorists. Auntie Betty rang me this afternoon, and she received a letter from Valda today, and you, Carol and Valda were flying to Scotland for the weekend. Hope you enjoyed it. Today was another train strike, and David took and brought Denise home. Today Tuesday, the chap brought our new kitchen blinds. They are white background with lemon and orange pears and light and green bands printed over it. I am pleased with it, and it cost over $19. I also have two new venetians as you come in the side door, and we had wire sliding doors where your windows used to be. Today hasn't been as hot but the bushfires are as bad. Three died at Springwood through the fires. A five-million-dollar shopping centre was opened at Hornsby yesterday. Hope you are keeping well, remember me to Jan and Kris. Lots of love from Mother xxxxx Well Dianne by the time you receive this you will be a big girl now. How was your birthday? Hope you enjoyed yourself. How are you going with your job? Hope you received my present in time and your 21st key for luck. It must be starting to get cold now your tracksuit is on the way. How are Valda and David, Jan and Kris? Give my love to all and hope they enjoyed your party xxxxxxxxxxx Daddy

When times were busy at work and home, I could only struggle to write an aerogramme to the family. It was also getting close to my 21st birthday surprise night out with Val and all my friends. I was so happy to be in London, initially in Montagu Square W1, then in Archway at the bottom of Highgate Hill in North London.

25 October 1968

Dear Mum and Dad,

   Please forgive the formality of a typewritten letter, but I had to hurry this out before the weekend. I have a few things to tell you which may upset you both, but it has happened and at least I am telling you. Since arriving here things haven't been sailing too smoothly in the flat. It turned out Kris didn't have many morals, and I have been fighting with her for the past 6 weeks. To make things worse, Jan has said nothing about these arguments. She has been content to live in her little corner and not contribute a word. What I disagree most of all with Kris, is on many occasions she has wanted to let male friends stay overnight, in her curtained-off section of an open plan living and sleeping area. Even though I told her no and never, she has made it her business to make my life at the flat unbearable. Val and David know about this, and last Saturday night when I walked out of the flat never to return, they asked me to stay

I don't wear step-ins anymore.

with them until I found another place to live. After a week of looking, I finally found a flat last night near Highgate with 6 other girls. 2 are English, 2 are Welsh and I am not sure of the other 2. I share a room with an English girl who works in a fashion house in London. The room is very large with a huge open window, fireplace, washbasin and large wardrobes.

The flat consists of 2 floors, and on the whole is very large and roomy. There is a T.V., bathroom, separate toilet, telephone ARC 1604 (ARC is the district code and if it is any easier when you telephone, please ask for ARCHWAY 1604). As I don't leave for work until after 9am, if you rang 11pm Sydney time you would get me at 8am! You may not have to book the call, but to be sure ring the O.T.C. and they will tell you what has to be done. The address, by the way is 6 Archway Road, Highgate, N19, London, and I am moving in this coming Monday. I hope you understand these things happen, and as I wasn't happy, the only thing to do was find another flat and start again before winter set in. 3 guineas per week, electricity and gas paid quarterly, so it will probably only cost me 4 pounds to 5 pounds a week to live.

Now, more exciting news - Val, Helen and I are going to Scotland for the weekend. We are flying to Glasgow 11pm tonight and staying with Helen's mother. Saturday we are going shopping, and Sunday we may go into Edinburgh, and then fly back in time for breakfast Monday morning. Helen and Warren just came back from Los Angeles where they stayed with Helen's sister, who she has not seen for 14 years! Helen's mother is very old and lives in Mary Hill, a poor part of Glasgow, but if you know some people there, it is a great place to visit. Glasgow itself is very poor and industrial, but to see the worst part of a country makes you appreciate the beautiful places.[16]

---

16   I had one of the best New Year celebrations of my life in the very poor area of Mary Hill, Glasgow. Everyone got totally sloshed, and we were all dancing on tables to genuine Scottish music, including the bagpipes. The people we met were so down to earth. There were no airs and graces that night.

I am meeting Val and Helen at Bond Street Tube and we are going to the 'Shakespeare's Head' pub in Carnaby Street for a few light ales, and naturally a hearty meal before we catch the bus to Heathrow and the plane. You cannot imagine how excited I am about this, seeing I haven't been in a plane except for the time Dad took me on a Joyride around Sydney at night. It was ages ago - does he remember it? For the last week I haven't managed to get much sleep with all this walking around looking at flats, and I have seen some crummy places during the time. Last Tuesday night I had to have my shoes heeled as they were worn down - I seem to walk miles every day. I know the tube system practically off by heart and am a veteran at pushing and shoving my way on the escalators.

My job is terrific, and I wouldn't part with it for the world. It is a joy to go to work and I miss the place over the weekend. I get a great feeling of satisfaction out of finishing letters and knowing I have contributed something. I take down shorthand every day, and it usually takes me the rest of the day to type it back. As the work involves buying of property for shop development in all parts of London and the country, I am learning a lot about the area, and a lot about the legal side of it. I have about 3 cups of coffee a day. Tina makes it for me, and I am becoming an addict.

It is certainly coming into winter, and most people think London could get a white Christmas! The reason being it snowed in early November last year, and by the time Xmas came around all the snow had melted, and the streets were one slippery mess! As I don't leave for work until late, at least the daylight has broken through. For people who leave for work really early, they usually don't see the day at all! For the past few days it has been very misty in the mornings and quite cold. You can definitely feel winter coming on. I am finishing this at the airport terminal, and we saw a movie earlier this evening called 'Interlude'. It was a beautiful love story set in London. If it gets to Sydney please see it because most of the scenery is in London and parts of the country. Will write again next week and tell you all about Scotland and look forward to your

I don't wear step-ins anymore.

letters. Hope you understand about me moving out from the flat. I had to do what I wanted to do, and it looks like I am on my own from now on. Love to all of you, Dianne - 6 Archway Road Highgate N19 London

Finally, I had moved from a situation I did not like. I found accommodation in a shared house on the outskirts of London, close to Hampstead Heath. I had also taken off my step-ins and thrown them in the bin, vowing never to wear them again. I was thrilled I had informed my family of this action of personal and intimate freedom. I was nearing my 21st birthday. Before my birthday, I wrote a very personal letter to my Dad.

Thursday, 31st October 1968

Dear Dad,

I wanted to write to you personally because at the moment I am feeling rather depressed. Just before I left, we became closer to each other than we had ever before. I am sure Mum has told you by now about me leaving the flat and finding another one near Highgate. This was mainly brought on by Kristine Chapple, who Jan and I took on as a friend too soon. In my opinion, we shouldn't have asked her to share a flat with us in the first place. On the ship she was always bringing men back to the cabin, and on one occasion I had to tell one gentleman to leave so I could get some sleep. Jan, on the other hand always went to sleep straight away, so she had no idea what was going on. Kris knew I was onto her and all her tricks, so she made it her business to make me feel quite miserable. 2 weeks ago, when I had enough of it, I just walked out and went straight to Val and David's place, taking only my overnight bag with me.

To make things even more miserable, I only just broke off with Tony who I met on the ship about a week out of Sydney. I found out he was a compulsive liar. He told me such gigantic stories, and naturally I believed them all. The only people I have been able to turn to are Val and David, who have been terrific while all this has been going on. I stayed with them for about a week until I found this place at Archway. I have been here since Monday night. I wrote in my previous letter about it. The thing worrying me most is what am I going to do about Jan? She didn't say a word to me when I left, and it's such a shame to end a friendship like this. Kris seems to have cast a spell over Jan, telling her what to do and what not to do.

I have to start all over again and make new friends. I feel so lonely it just seems so morbid. The girls at the new flat are all very nice, but as they are nurses and on shiftwork, I don't see much of them. The girl I share my room with is exceptionally nice, but she is going steady and again, I don't see much of her either. Most of them go away for the weekend, and if it wasn't for Val and David asking me to a party on Saturday night, I probably would have gone quite mad sitting here all alone.

I am really looking forward to hearing from you and the family next Monday morning, so much so I have been tempted to ring you myself. Each time I get this feeling, I say to myself you may not be home, or you won't know what to say to me and spend the 3 minutes saying hello. I know I am capable of doing everything I came here to do. I have already seen more than most people could see in the time I have been here. I have a job with money coming in every week and I have 300-pound tucked away in the Commonwealth Bank for when I go onto the Continent next spring. I will no doubt be able to put more into my account to make it even more than what it is now. <u>I can save money if I want to and I definitely want to!</u> Living and looking after myself doesn't worry me much now, but of course I would love to be waited on hand and foot like I was at home. I know when I come home again, I will appreciate it more than I did. The comforts of home are a thing to look forward to, and the hardships I am experiencing now only make them look more promising.

I don't wear step-ins anymore.

I only know Dad, in my heart, I want to see a lot of this world. if I don't, I will come home and be just the same old person I used to be, moaning and groaning and being hateful towards people who try to help me.

I appreciate you and Mum more than ever now I haven't got you with me. I need you and Mum more all the same, especially your guidance, even though it is only in a letter. I must be able to correspond with you both, or else I have nothing left to look forward to because nobody else writes to me.[17] Dad, I think you know more about me than anyone - I realised this before I was leaving and I think we are very much alike. It has been my fault moreso than Mums that she and I have never been able to talk about much. This is why I am so withdrawn and introverted, need people, someone to talk to or I will go mad. Please write to me and give me your opinion about this - I need help so badly,

I hadn't ended my letter with kisses. Nothing, just a comma. I'd say I was smoking the 'green stuff' while writing it. One day after I sent the letter to my father, I had to ring my mum and tell her about leaving the flat, before she received my letter. She wrote and sent a letter straight away.

Friday, 1st November 1968
PS: On the money order I have put Mr O'Dell's address

Dear Dianne,

I certainly got a shock when you rang this morning and told me you had left the flat. I do hope everything works out for the best. I rang Jan's Mother later, and she knew you had left the flat, but didn't know the reason. I told her and she said Jan had never mentioned it

---

17 Not true. Aunts, cousins, neighbours, friends and workmates wrote regularly. I had too many letters to include in this book, but in any case I wanted to keep it mostly between my mother and me.

to her. She was upset you had both separated, and said she wished you and Jan had only been together. I remember when Eunice went away, another girl wanted to come with them, but she said no, because three never get on as well as two. I was a little surprised when you took Kris with you in the flat. After all you and Jan had known one another's faults, but you didn't know much about Kris. I would contact the Post Office to see if you could direct your mail to your business address. I hope you have a happy 21st birthday, and after all Dianne, God works his wonders in strange ways, and these things often work out for the best. There are a lot of things money can't buy and self-respect is one. Denise has gone out with Russell, and she is going to a wedding tomorrow. She is wearing the outfit she wore to Lisa's baptism. Today has been a lovely day, but since we have got into our summer nightwear, it has turned cold in the night. Dad said he might go back to his winter pyjamas. We are getting a sliding glass door out in the shower room. It will cost about $58 (Dad's price). You won't know the old home. The bushfires are still going. Yesterday someone rang South Sydney Hospital and told them a bomb was going to go off before ten o'clock in the morning, and they had to evacuate the patients out into the gardens. Some were scheduled to go into surgery. It certainly takes all kinds to make a world. Hope everything will be OK. I will be thinking of you. Happy Birthday. Love and best wishes from Mother xxxx.

Hello Love, hope you are OK. Sorry to hear about you leaving the flat but I don't blame you. Why didn't you get rid of Kris from the flat or did Jan want to stay with her? Tell me all about it in the next letter. Hope your birthday went well and you received all your presents. Look after yourself and keep yourself respectable and keep your chin up in the air. How is your job going? Are you doing a good job? Hope Val and David are well and doing all right. The house is going well. Got rid of Builder, Plumber, Electrician and Tiler this week. Got to get the carpets down now and get the new lounge and chairs in. I have fixed your insurance for all your belongings, so if you lose or have anything taken report it to police and then let me know so I can claim. Missed you very much for your birthday. It was lovely to hear your voice on the phone. Mum was very upset about the news, but I know you will do all right and look after yourself. I sent you a cheque so you could put it in the bank till you want to go on your trip. Best of luck, love Daddy xxxxxxxxxxxxxxxxxx

I laughed out loud. Mum was still signing her letters 'Mother', but Dad kept up the 'love Daddy' with double the kisses.

I sometimes got a chance to write a proper letter to the family while I was at work. I didn't start until 10am, and my two bosses travelled a lot. When they returned from trips, they would either dictate letters or put them on a dictaphone machine, to be transcribed while they were away. Mr Barton and Mr O'Dell had very long lunches.

7th November 1968

Dear Mum, Dad and Denise,
    (Please forgive me typing this letter, but I rushed it out during one of my not so busy days.) It is now Thursday morning about 10am, the boss isn't in yet and I think it is about time I wrote you all a letter. Since last Thursday I have been in some sort of a daze, and completely incapable of doing anything properly. I have had a truly wonderful birthday thanks to Val and David.
    On Saturday afternoon they gave me a birthday dinner, and Helen and Warren came along too. I was thrilled with the key you sent me. Did Dad make it? They had a cake for me, and shortly you should receive a corner of it wrapped in foil. I hope it will still be fresh. On Saturday night we all went to a party at Swiss Cottage in a flat owned by Americans. It was a beach party of all things, and during the night we had a 'cold snap' would you believe, so things got pretty chilly. Monday morning, I found cards from the other girls in the flat just before you rang, and when I finally arrived at work, a stack of cards and presents were on my desk. Tina gave me a Cussons gift pack of powder and bath bubbles, which was very

nice of her. Helen and Warren gave me a record voucher to buy the soundtrack from 'HAIR'. I will endeavour to send thanks to all the people from home who sent me cards and presents. I will tell them what I am going to buy with the money orders, probably clothing as it is so cheap and good quality.

I received your letter and money order on Tuesday afternoon, just as I was leaving work, and was so happy with the way you took the news about me leaving the flat. Thank you for feeling I am doing the right thing. I know myself things will run more smoothly now I am away from Kris, but one thing is worrying me; Kris has her boyfriend from Australia coming over to join her this month or early in the new year. I am worried she may run off with him and leave Jan to her own devices. Jenny, my roommate, and a terrific girl gave me some advice – I should ring Jan on some pretext and find out what the situation is. What is more, Jan not only lives with Kris, she also works with her. If Jan moved out, she would also have to throw in her job, which by the way, will probably only last till after Christmas anyway! I could not, for any money in the world, live with Jan again, because we have nothing in common, and are not really close friends. Jan is aware of this, but I don't want to see Jan get hurt by such a two-faced Mata Hari like Kris – time will tell though. Jan has my telephone number at work, so it is a question of letting things lie for a while and being patient on my part.

The cheque you sent me is in the bank, and I can assure you it will go towards my trip on the Continent next spring. What I must do now is make some good trustworthy friends, and I may have a chance since meeting the girls in the flat. They are all very nice and friendly. We all eat quite well too. I had lamb's fry for the first time since leaving home last night, and it was delicious. We have vegetables nearly every night, and plenty of eggs, but too much coffee (about 10 cups a day, and I am slowly getting addicted).

Last Tuesday night was Guy Fawkes night, and Judy, Sally and I went to Hampstead Heath to watch the people blow their money up in smoke – some skyrockets sell for 5/- each or up to as much as one pound. The Heath is one of the loveliest villages in the London area,

I don't wear step-ins anymore.

and is only a 1/- bus ride from where I am living. Some of the fireworks were terrific, but as usual we had some idiots who threw bungers amongst crowds of people. It was good to get all rugged up in hope it snows soon. I am really looking forward to seeing London at Xmas – it is so much nicer than eating Xmas dinner in 100-degree heat!

Mr O'Dell came in for half an hour and has just gone out to lunch and probably won't be back for a couple of hours. Tina accidentally dropped her typewriter about a week ago, and he decided to get a new one, which Tina thought would be for her. As I do most of the typing I got it, and I do feel bad about it as Tina had her heart set on it. By the way, it cost nearly 90 pounds!!

I was very upset to hear Nixon got the presidency – It won't be long before America ends up like Britain - the English don't have compulsory voting, and they don't seem to care about their situation. They always seem to moan and groan no matter who is running the country. One of the girls in the flat told me a bit of scandal about Wilson. Her family mix in political circles, and they found out Wilson is having an affair with his secretary. As soon as he finishes his term as PM, he and his wife are getting a divorce! What do you reckon? Saw Ted Heath on the TV last night – he is the leader of the Conservatives - he looks about as insipid as the rest of them, so I don't see much hope for the Poms now or ever. So glad George Wallace didn't get into the White House – he could have lined up all the Negroes against the nearest wall and let the Klu Klux Klan go to town on them. Cliff Carrington, the American I met in Balboa Panama, wrote recently saying how disgusting life is in America at the moment. He also said their way of life is so false and over-rated. I know I couldn't live there.

The bushfires sound pretty bad over there – wish we could give you some of the rain we are having presently. Mr O'Dell asks me all the time about Australia, and everyone I meet seems very interested in the lifestyle. I sit up most nights telling the girls in the flat about living in Australia. Some are thinking of going there when their term in hospital finishes here.

I don't know whether or not I told you? Tony and I have broken up. All the things he told me about being English and doing a stretch in the Australian Army in Vietnam - all lies! He also lied to me about his age and is really only 20! In the end I thought I was going to crack up, so one Saturday when he came down from Essex to visit, I told him to get lost. He put on a big act and I thought I was going to burst into tears. I do feel better now I am free once more. Sometimes I wonder what is going through their heads. What is the use spinning stories - you only get caught in your own web of lies eventually.

In the next couple of weeks, Jenny and I are going to see Canterbury Tales - it is an adaptation of Chaucer's story, only with more comedy and some music thrown in. All the critics are raving about it, but at the moment it is hard to get tickets. Val and Helen want to take me to see the ballet when the season starts again. Never know I may get a chance to see Nureyev! Every Thursday night on TV is 'Top of the Pops'. You think our pop stars are way out! Well, you should see them here! Denise will more than likely know who I am talking about when I list a few stars like Lulu, Miriam Hopkins who sings 'Those were the Days, My Friends', and other singers who look as if they just landed from Mars.

Did I also mention about having a male student in our flat called Lou Pocock. He has his own room naturally, away from all us girls and he is very nice. Whenever one of us comes home he makes us a cup of coffee, and usually goes out of his way to help. He gave me a birthday card and takes off my Aussie accent all the time. Everything I say he mimics, and one of these days I will end up bashing him. At the moment he is in Denmark with the Army Reserve until after the weekend. It will be quiet without him. Lou is studying economics at the College near St Pauls. He is a very good debater, and a couple of nights ago Jenny and I argued till way past midnight on the subject 'Do human beings still have free choice'. We still haven't come to some mutual agreement, and it looks like it will continue when Lou gets back - more late nights!

I don't wear step-ins anymore.

I rang Val last night and she informed me my parcel arrived with a letter. I am meeting her at lunch today to pick them up and will also be going shopping with her tonight – the shops stay open until 9pm every Thursday, and it is a crush trying to get from A to B in the city. Most of the big stores have their Xmas decorations up, and it should look terrific in the next month or so. There are still a lot of foreigners in London at the moment, especially Americans. Next door, but one to work in Welbeck Street is the 'Londoner' Hotel. Just about every nationality walk in and out during the day. You would think, now it is getting colder, the tourists would be leaving. Then again, some could be here on business. I seem to be looked upon as a typical Londoner by most of them, maybe as I wear boots, short skirts and have short hair. Maxi wear is the rage too, as well as knee length, and some of the girls look fabulous. I must say the English girls who walk along Oxford Street during the lunch hour would put Sydney girls to shame – fashion-wise and complexion-wise too. 9 out of 10 girls wear hairpieces, and the old-fashioned style is coming back. So is the 20s look. Overcoats and suits are out of this world and look so tailored. Mum, you would have a field day here, and probably make poor old Dad, a pauper. If I hadn't put the 100 pound in the bank the day I got it, I would have spent it on clothing. There is just so much I could buy, and most of the fashions suit me too! Val, I am afraid, is going to make me spend quite a bit tonight, but I don't care. Marks and Spencers sell knitted dresses of Scottish Wool for 2 pound up to 4 pounds, and the quality is just amazing. Underclothing is dirt cheap, and men's woollens are the best.

Just now Tina is composing a poem to all her friends, and the radio is playing a 'Supremes' song. Isn't it disgusting? When I get back to Sydney, I won't know what work is! One day this week when Mr O'Dell was out, Tina invited her 4 mates around for afternoon tea. We had bread, cheese spread, chocolate cake, biscuits and coffee. They are all around 18ish and complete nuts. One of the girls, Frankie, works in Carnaby Street in the TV studios, and wants to eventually join a theatre group. She is very talented and an extrovert. The clothes these girls wear would make you gasp, so way out. At the moment the craze is huge arm watches with great big dials and bands. They look great but never work. Tina's watch loses half an hour every hour!!! They all go out to a disco every second night, belong to so many clubs around London; they must pay a fortune in membership fees. Much better social life than Sydney. Denise would be in her element.

Just got back to the office after meeting Val and picking up the jumper. Whew, does it smell of mothballs! I am glad you sent it over though, as it is getting rather cold, and I will need it. Mr O'Dell has been gone over two and a half hours, so he must be having a lovely lunch. I usually buy brown bread sandwiches or rolls in Marylebone Lane for lunch, and the queue is over 10 deep at the tiny little shop I go to. It is worth the wait because they taste just like homemade sandwiches. To give you an idea how cold it is, when I breathe, great big clouds of steam emit from my mouth and nose. My face, hands and knees freeze. What is it going to be like in a few months' time when winter really settles in?

It was so good to hear from you last Monday morning. If it had of been an hour later, I would have left. When the girl said, 'Sydney calling' and Dad started talking, I just burst into tears. I didn't expect you to ring again, not after speaking to me for 6 minutes the Friday before. Val thought you would ring, but I didn't believe her. Lots of love, I think of you always, Dianne

My mother seemed to be over me moving away from Jan and into another flat outside London. She now called me 'Dear Dianne' and ended her letters …'your loving Mother'. Dad was still 'Daddy' and he put lots more kisses!!

I don't wear step-ins anymore.

Letter 18 - 16th November 1968

To My 'Dear Dianne',

    When we arrived home from Town at lunchtime today, Denise found your letter in the mailbox. Jan sent me a lovely card for my Birthday. It is a little early, but I have put it on the shelf where I put the Christmas cards. The shelves are different now, the same wood as the cupboards are made of, and I have pasted a lovely paper on the back of the shelves. (I will enclose a sample of the paper). I was very pleased to read you were going to ring Jan, as I was going to suggest to you to phone, and then it would be up to Jan to see what she would do. Ross came in when we arrived home, and I asked him to sit down, but his jeans are so tight, he couldn't. The fly part of his trousers is starting to come apart, and I am sure this can't be too comfortable. I bought Denise a lovely shade of pink linen, to make a straight frock and a jacket for Christmas. She bought a nice Tootall navy material, with a satin stripe, and a navy slip to be made for Russell's birthday 7th December. She bought a pink and blue check for the beach, and a nice crimplene similar to the chilli colour of your David Keyes dress. Today the temperature went to 85 degrees and tomorrow they predict 95. I took Denise over to Robyn at Hurstville this afternoon to have her hair permed. It turned out nice, and I had to go and pick her up at 5 o'clock. She has gone to a 'drive in' with Russell. I received your other letter on Thursday. The chap came yesterday about the lino, and we are getting it laid on Monday. Hope you get a lot of wear out of your blue jumper. Grace Bros at Broadway has its Christmas decorations up, but I haven't noticed anyone else. We went over to George's River Sailing Club, and met Aunt, Uncle Bill, Mavis, Perc, Uncle Albert, Aunty Betty, Uncle Harold and Auntie Ruby. They received your 'Thank you Cards'. It was a nice smorgasbord, and I had 5 pieces of apple tart, but you must remember I don't eat bread or potatoes. The entertainment was very good. Denise went swimming at Stanwell Park. I played the poker machines with $4.00, but just came out even. Today,

(Monday) the temperature reached well in the 90 degrees. Tonight, I cut out Denise's slip that she wants to wear for Russell's birthday. Aunt brought the photos of Lisa's baptism, and they turned out nice. Valmai is sending some over to you and Valda. The ones Dad took are still in the camera. Our Christmas bush is starting to turn red, and the smaller tree is shooting up. Denise received your letter today, and she never gives it to me to read, but always reads Dad's and mine.[18] Hope you enjoyed your party last Saturday. Well darling, I will let Dad write a few lines, hoping you think of your Mother now and then. I am enclosing 'The Text of the Week' which appears in the 'Sun' paper. Love and a big hug from your loving Mother xxxxxxx Hello Darling, hope you are going well, and everything is OK. How is your job going? I suppose it is getting cold now. Soon will be snow. You will be able to have a good time building snowmen. Is Jan still living with Kris? It will soon be Xmas and all the presents and cards coming in. Did you get your cartoon and your track pants? I sent them to your first address (Montagu Square). We will miss you on Xmas morning when we open our presents, but we miss you all the time. How are Valda and David? Hope they are well. Give them my love and thank them for your birthday party. We had a good time over here for you. Hope you are looking after yourself and eating well. We are getting near knock-off time for Xmas holidays, December 17th till January 13th. I will have a bottle of wine for you and say it is for Dianne. Well love, keep your chin up and don't let anybody put it over you. Give my best to the girls, Love Daddy xxxxxxxxxxxxxxxxxxxxx"[19]

My mother wrote to me practically every second day. On the other hand, I was now writing weekly, or even fortnightly, and on aerogrammes. My mother was loudly complaining about my lack of

---

18   The reason my sister wouldn't let my mother read her letters, was that they were probably the 'R-rated' version of my stay overseas. I have asked my sister if she still has my letters, but she cannot remember where they went, or if she gave them to my mother for safe-keeping. Heaven forbid!

19   My Dad was the biggest flirt. When he eventually visited me in London, he would kiss all my female flatmates. He also adored Tina, with whom I worked, and her young friends.

I don't wear step-ins anymore.

writing to her and hinting about my sister not letting her read any of my letters to her.

27th November 1968 (Letter 20)
6 Archway Close Highgate N19

Dear Dianne,

Today has been a lovely day. The bushfires have been pretty bad up at Springwood, as we need the rain badly. Last night I saw 'Tiny Tim' on T.V. and I am sure he must be a bit queer. His hair hangs over his shoulders, and he sang 'Tip Toe through the Tulips'. Haircuts have gone up for males to $1.00, and the price of sets and perms are going up today. Talk about England with their taxes, we are getting as bad. Does the increase in taxes affect you? Our garbage wasn't collected on Tuesday, as some of 'the garbos' are out on strike. Dad had to burn some of our rubbish in the barbecue tonight. Aunt rang last night, and Uncle Bill was home three days last week as he had the flu, and he has to go back on the heart pills again. Aunt said he looked shocking. Tonight, on the news we saw the starting in London of the big car race. Have finished your room. The curtains and bedspread are all out, and Dad is making a table beside the bed. We are going to buy two lampshades and it will be completed. Any time you want to surprise your dear old Mother, your room is ready. Thursday Darling, on T.V. Tonight it was tragic to see the bushfires up in the Blue Mountains. Today 120 homes were burnt to the ground, and at least two people are dead. It is cooler now, but early this afternoon the sun had a big red ring around it, and most of the sky was very hazy. There is a complete ban on all fires to be lit in homes or anywhere. They predict another hot day tomorrow. Denise has gone out with Russell. The chap for the curtains came today, and I have ordered white drapes similar to the other ones. The carpet is to be laid on Saturday, but I have changed the colour from gold to a neutral green. I have practically finished painting. Only a few odds and ends to be touched up. Treasure, I haven't had a letter since 16th

November. When Denise receives a letter, she never lets me read it, and I respect her wishes. Had to smile to myself this morning. I was hosing the front lawn when a taxi pulled up. It was waiting for at least 5 minutes when Ross comes out and goes to work in it. Alma told me he went to a party last night and didn't arrive home till 2 o'clock this morning. Hope you are enjoying yourself, and have you gone to any new shows? A news flash just came over the T.V. asking people to help the 'Fund for the Fire Victims', and another 2 people are reported to be dead. Well Darling, hope there is a letter from you soon. Would love you to make me a cup of tea now and then, love and best wishes from your loving Mother xxxxx Dianne love, hope you are well and enjoying yourself. It is Mum's birthday on 13/12/68. I'm taking her out for dinner to RSL Marrickville, which just opened. It's a lovely club. Giving her usual present - dough.[20] Hope David and Valda are well and your nurse friends. We knock off work on the 17th December for Christmas holidays. Won't be long. Keep your chin up xxxxxxxxx Love Daddy xxxxxxxxx

During the month of November, I turned 21 and moved to another flat in London, sharing with three English girls and one male student, who had the top floor attic room. Lou was handsome and looked like Errol Flynn without the moustache. He had a habit of running up and down the stairs naked and reciting the poems of Byron, Shelley or Wordsworth. He also had a tuft of hair growing on his lower back at the base of his spine, similar to a horse's tail; and all of us girls had fallen madly in love with him, me the most. He would come into the room I shared with Jenny, naked, kneel beside my bed and talk of writers like Joyce or Hemingway.

I was probably smoking a lot of 'green stuff' when I wrote the following letter to my family.

---

20   'Dough' was a slang term for 'money'.

I don't wear step-ins anymore.

Wednesday, 27th November 1968

Dear Mum and Dad,

These past few weeks I have been unable to write properly to you and have now decided to try and tell you why. To give you a clear picture of the situation, it is necessary for me to lead up to the gist of the story, by way of a few pages explaining what preceded all this, so please stay with me.

I have told you about moving away from Jan and Kris, how I stayed with Val and David for about a week until I found a new place. I also told you how happy I was, but I don't think I mentioned the fact my happiness was due mainly to Mr Lou Pocock, the male member in the flat. Lou and I began a very sound and sincere friendship about 2 weeks ago, based on mutual understanding of each other. Lou is a student at Westminster College, and will then go on to University and his bachelorship. His subjects are philosophy, logic and his main interest is psychology, which he is teaching me about.

Mum and Dad, you have given me a body that is healthy, a mind, which Lou informs me has potential equal to most other human beings. I've had a good Christian upbringing. Yes, I do believe in God, a Supreme Being, a Creator, but not necessarily the Gods most people worship, and seek forgiveness for their sins. I am one better than the majority of people swarming over this tiny Earth – I have been given sensitivity. I feel so much it gives me headaches. To walk down a street to most people, is a normal mundane task with no meaning, a thing most people do every day. When I walk down a street, I could relate everything I see to you. When I listen to a piece of music long enough, I have the uncanny ability of being able to hum or whistle the whole piece, no matter how long, anytime I want from then on. Remember my music teacher, Mrs McGeaghie used to test me, and I could pick the right note each time she played it. This is why I wouldn't study because I preferred to play by ear. Oh, how

I wish I had never given up the piano.[21] Sometimes I crave to sit and play for hours. Lou's girlfriend, Juliana, an American girl from college plays the guitar. She is not yet 18, but so nice and with such a love for living. We sit for hours. She plays and sings, and I join in. Maybe I will learn the guitar if she is willing to teach me. She used to play the piano too and knows just how I feel.

Mum and Dad, you do know how much I love you for giving me my life? God only knows how much I will be indebted to you both for this gift. I have been alive 21 years, but only now forming a meaning, making all the things you have done for me, justifiable and appreciated.

London is the city in this case, a cosmopolitan melting pot of all races, creeds, colours, thoughts, the rich and poor. I have never, in all my 21 years, seen so much life in the few months I have spent in London. I know what an Aborigine feels like, because I have just commenced my Walkabout, my epic journey. My guiding star is made up like any star - millions of pieces of matter. All the gifts you and Dad have given me, all the lessons you have taught me, the difference between right and wrong, my morals and my love of life.

I went for a walk through Hampstead Heath last Sunday. The Heath is only about a mile from the flat, and I cannot find words aptly describing the beauty and life abounding there. To see the trees changing colour during autumn would thrill you. It reminded me so much of a sunny winter's day in Sydney. How I miss Sydney sometimes, the house, and most of all my family. But everything in this world so far is beautiful, worth seeing, experiencing and loving.

It is nearly 5pm, and seeing the Boss is away today we will be going home soon. Lou is cooking dinner tonight, and it should be very funny. We are having a party at the flat this Saturday. We only

---

21   I began learning the piano at the age of seven. My teacher initially lived in Campsie, but later moved to Bardwell Park. After my father died in 1984, I found a two-year diary, where he documented taking me to piano lessons twice a week before he went to work. I did many exams at the Railway Institute and Conservatorium, gaining High Distinctions. When I got home in 1970, I found that my mother had given our pianola away to my Aunty Betty.

I don't wear step-ins anymore.

decided last night, and the unexpected always turn out best. I will write again very soon in the same manner, because I cannot write any other way, only from my heart. Love to you all forever, Dianne

I wrote another aerogramme on the 6th of December.

Dear Mum and Dad,

I received your letter 20 and I wish you wouldn't get so worried about me not writing so often. I have been planning and doing so many things these past couple of weeks, but I know it is not good neglecting writing home.

This week has been marvellous. Jenny, my roommate asked me on Monday night if I would go to Paris with her sometime in January, and what is more, Val might be coming with us. Should be great fun with just the 3 of us. Will probably fly over just for a couple of days and look over the city and nightspots, which are supposed to be very good.

Last night I borrowed Tina's membership card and went to Samantha's disco in New Burlington St off Regent St. Two of the girls from my new flat met me there at about 10 pm. I have never seen such a place in all my life. We walked downstairs and were blinded by flashing psychedelic lights. It was so hot I was glad to be wearing one of my new short sleeve dresses, the black one. I felt very groovy with my hair cut short and I had just lightened it the night before, so it was very blonde. It was so crowded we could not move more than a few feet and most of the people were French or Danish. Most were all dressed in weird clothes and doing all sorts of funny dances. We were entitled to a free glass of champagne. It took us about half an hour to get through the crowd to the bar which was right near the band. The music was so loud I vibrated from my head down to my toes. I found a seat next to an American chap called John and we started talking. He is in the Air Force at Cambridge. I found out he turned 21 a week before me and was able to go home to celebrate with his family. He asked me if I would like to go to Westminster Abbey the next day. As both bosses were away, I had the morning off and Tina had the afternoon off. We arranged to meet at Piccadilly Circus at 9.30 am.

It was freezing in the morning, and even at 7.30 am it was pitch black outside. I put the washing in at the Laundromat where the lady does it for me personally, so I can pick it up in the evening after work. She likes me, and does it save a lot of trouble and time. The Abbey was very beautiful, and I bought a book to send home to you, which has a lot of photos of some of the tombs and architecture. It was so peaceful until a busload of Yanks invaded the place. As it was 11 am and I had to get back to work we left. I have a loathing for guided tours. They are so noisy and make a sacred place look like an amusement park, which I feel the whole of America is. I must have walked about 20 miles from the Houses of Parliament, past Downing Street, along Whitehall to Trafalgar Square. I nearly forgot to walk past Queeny's house and catch the changing of the horse guards at the Barracks. It just felt like I was watching it on television, only this time it was real, and I was standing about 5 feet from the whole event. I nearly had a chance to pat the horses! To walk through London is so lovely. It is the most beautiful city in the world even when it is cold, and my feet have blisters covering them. Even if you only walk one street, there are so many old and historic sites to see or fascinating people to watch. I get a fantastic joy just walking from one spot to another in London. I cannot compare it to any other city I have seen so far.

Saturday night I am off to another party for Frankie's birthday. She is Tina's cousin and all the people they know are very nice. I am told I will be the only Aussie there amongst all the foreigners, and it should be very interesting. They all live in Tottenham where the Hotspurs soccer team comes from. I hardly talk to any Aussies now except for Val and David or her friends, which is good because I am making a whole lot of new acquaintances every day. Sunday morning, I am catching the train from Euston to Macclesfield Cheshire to visit Betty, the tea lady from Wills. I will be gone for a few days and do get around. I won't be coming back until Tuesday, I think. Had lunch with

I don't wear step-ins anymore.

Val during the week and the girl gets madder each time I see her! We enjoyed ourselves so much I nearly forgot about work and was away for 2 hours! We spent about half an hour in a card shop near Bond Street laughing at all the funny cards. I will be writing again soon after I get back. Love Dianne

It was getting close to my mum's birthday on the 13th of December, so I rang her early in the morning. She wrote to me immediately afterwards.

Monday, 16th December 1968

To My Dear Dianne,

Thank you Darling, for helping to make my birthday a happy one. On Thursday, you were on my mind all day, and on Friday morning I got up, made my bed and was coming into the hall, when the phone rang. I wasn't even worried when the chap said, 'London was calling'. Although you are 12,000 miles away, you were the first to wish me a Happy Birthday. We went to City Tatt's for dinner and then to the Barclay Theatre to see Katherine Hepburn and Spencer Tracy in 'Guess Who's Coming to Dinner?' I thoroughly enjoyed it. I am enclosing $5 for you to have dinner and a show for my birthday. I won't guarantee you will have the same as Denise had, large plate of oysters, T-bone steak with salad and strawberries and ice cream with coffee. Denise bought me an Estacel suit, similar to the navy blue I have. It is in a taupe shade. Also, she bought me a cream jumper and cream and taupe stripe twin set. Russell sent a large sheath of flowers. Beverley gave me a bracelet, handmade (which is very nice) and an orange and white check tea cozy. Valmai gave me perfume, Aunt, two slips, and of course I got the usual from Dad (money). Did I tell you; I am going away for a weekend to the 11th Annual Central Convention at Stanwell Park? There are about 16 women going from our Church to hear speakers from California, and we are hoping to rent a house for the weekend. Valda sent me a nice birthday card and today I received your card. Darling, did you pick this card on account of the 'Tea-Service' on the cover? Denise gave me a lovely card with a story 'What is a Mother?' Don't forget to ring at Christmas and reverse the charge. It would be easier for you to catch us than for us to contact you. Hoping to hear from you soon. Love and big hugs from your ever-loving Mother xxxxxxx

I managed to send my family a longer letter typed at work, documenting Christmas and New Year plans, and boyfriends.

17th December 1968
6 Archway Close N19

Dear Mum, Dad & Denise,

The last few weeks have been filled with joy, and of course misery. I think I like getting into a black mood, as when I eventually get happy, it is a marvellously euphoric state of happiness. I don't like telephoning as I never say what I want to say, and I get so tangled up inside before the call is due to come through. To be truthful I don't think it worth phoning at Christmas, and I also have a feeling the G.P.O. is fully booked for overseas calls. Have you received my parcel yet?

My new hair style and colouring has done wonders for my morale – I have 2 male admirers at the moment, and whenever I go to parties, which is every Saturday night, I get more and more popular. It has done me good, as I now mix much better with people than I ever did in Sydney.

Last Friday night I went to Val's, and she is in bed with an allergy caused by something unknown. We cracked a bottle of Cyprus sherry, and watched David Frost by the fire. David was away, so we had a couple of laughs reading letters from home and talking. I stayed the night and didn't wake till noon on the Saturday. Val became worse, so David dropped me at the station in case she was contagious. It was so cold, it seemed as though it would snow, but it was only frost

I don't wear step-ins anymore.

so thick it covered everything like a blanket of white. Lou was home, so we chatted in front of the fire for hours, and then got ready for a party at Richmond near Kew, south of London. Jenny, my roommate and her boyfriend Robin, had asked Lou and I to a 21st and on the way it snowed! The party was terrific. Lou, John (a friend of Robin) and I didn't get home till 4.30am, and we then had a lovely cup of hot chocolate. John asked me out this week. He phoned twice last night, but I was at the local fleapit seeing 'Charly'! He sounds very keen!!

I didn't wake until 2pm on Sunday, and Adrian rang to ask me to a Disco in Bond Street called 'Hatchetts'. Adrian is a friend of Tina and Frankie. I met him at Frankie's birthday party a few weeks ago. We have been out about 3 times to Discos like 'Birdland', 'The Habana' and now 'Hatchetts'. Adrian and John both own cars, so it is nice to be driven around London, instead of bussing and tubing, which can be a real drag late at night. Every day I receive mail, and Jenny gets tired of running up the stairs with it! I was thrilled to get your card with the paper clipping of Sydney, and the jokes from Dad. Thank you too for the postal order – I have put it into my cheque account and will buy some clothes when I go shopping next with Valda. She is my good luck charm for shopping! I can't wait to get home to the flat, and skite about our lovely harbour, and rub them the wrong way with the cartoons.

Both of the bosses were away today, so I didn't have to get in to work until 11.30. Lucky too, because I didn't get to sleep until 2am this morning talking to Lou. I slept in until 10am. I am still at the office typing this letter, and it is now 5.40pm. I don't mind because the buses are so crowded around this time, and usually get quieter after 6. It is so congested in London at the moment. I dread walking down Oxford Street, as it is so busy. Mr O'Dell has given us all next week off, except the Monday. I plan to laze around doing nothing but sleeping, reading and writing. Most of the others in the flat are going home or are on duty at the hospitals.

We are all going to Covent Garden Friday morning at 4.30am, to beg for fruit and vegetables for the patients in the hospitals. It will be a lot of fun. It has been raining solidly for over 24 hours, but it hasn't been cold. We are having a party at the flat on New Year's Eve, which will start at 11pm and finish in time for work the next day. All the people are staying until the morning and going to work from the flat. We have to borrow some heaters, because it is a pyjama party. It is going to be a bit chilly in the middle of winter, dancing around in our pyjamas while it is snowing outside. I am in the grip of a monster cold, and each morning it gets worse. Am taking these beaut tablets that seem to be doing the trick, but this weather doesn't help. I am enclosing some clippings from the papers for your enjoyment. Will write again very soon. Love Dianne xxxxxxx

At the end of 1968, my mother told me Dad was enquiring about airfares to England.

Tuesday, 31st December 1968 (Letter 26)

To My Darling,

New Year's Eve love, and we are staying home, as we have had two late nights, and I can't take too many. At present I am watching Channel 7 for 'Year Out - Year In'. It is a news review for the last 12 months. Denise has gone to Sans Souci for a party with Russell. I made a navy-blue linen over-blouse, and she looked nice as she went out. Kept Russell waiting well over half an hour, trying to put on those false eyelashes, and finally had to leave them off. One of my Christmas presents was a 'Breville' hair curler. They are an American product. I have used them once, and Denise used it tonight. Yesterday (Monday) we went to Austinmere Beach down the south coast. Dad has quite a sunburn as it turned out to be a lovely day. Last Sunday we went to Kogarah, and it was one of the best shows I have seen. There were four acts; each one was very good and entirely different.

I don't wear step-ins anymore.

As usual I had prawn cutlets and enjoyed it. Lynne and Aunty Betty's Robert came, and Lynne is a nice lass. Robert receives over $90 per week. Ross from next door had another increase of $30 dollars per month and earns as much as his father. I saw him tonight, and he is going to a party at one of the work's properties at Sylvania Waters valued at over $80,000. I think he is growing bigger. Haven't received any presents yet, and the postie told me this morning lots of parcels haven't been delivered. Said there were more cards and less parcels this year. Auntie Betty hasn't received her presents from Valda yet. You won't believe me, but the boyfriend is going to town on Thursday to enquire about the airfare to England.[22] Reckons if it is reasonable, we can spend about four to five weeks touring in the UK. Wonders never cease! Hope you had a lovely Christmas, and a white one. Was thinking about you. Did you enjoy Mother's birthday dinner? We are tired of eating pork, ham, and tonight we had a nice grill. Well darling, love and kisses to you and hope you are keeping well. Your ever-loving Mother xxxxxxx Hello Darling, thanks for the slippers I found under the tree. Hope you have a good time for New Year, and you received my Post Box with your tracksuit and Foster's beer xxxxxxx sent to the old address xx Love Daddy xxxxxxxxx

My first letter of 1969 was to my family in Sydney. I loved the new flat, the new flatmates, and my job in Welbeck Street W1, close to where I had first lived in Montagu Square.

1st January 1969
6 Archway Close London N19

Dear Family,
Another year is here, and this coming Saturday I have been away from home for 5 months. When I think back over 1968, I realise it was the most exciting year of my life, and a turning point. Christmas here

---

22 'The boyfriend' was a pet name my mother called my father.

was very different, naturally. Tina and I both got a 10-pound bonus, 2 week's pay, champagne and smoked salmon sandwiches for lunch. We gave the bosses travelling kits, which they thought delightful, especially as they do a lot of country tours for property business. We got a week off over the Christmas and Boxing Day holiday, and I spent most of it with John Scott (my current admirer), hopping from one pub to another, meeting his friends. We saw the movie 'Till Death us do Part' the day before Christmas, and Lou and I went to St Pauls Cathedral on Christmas Eve. The service had been changed to the Church of the Holy Sepulchre near the Old Bailey, so we walked there. It started snowing in the late afternoon on Christmas Eve, and I was so happy I felt like flying!

The Holy Communion service was beautiful, and Lou and I both sat enraptured. John had managed to get an hour off work (he is a telecommunications expert at the Post Office) and met us after the service. He couldn't take us home, so we hitched a lift just about to the door of the flat. It was snowing quite heavily, and we skated along the pavement on the ice. 2 Negroes asked us directions outside the tube station, and we were so high in the clouds, the four of us stood around wishing each other a merry Christmas and Happy New Year!

I didn't get to sleep until around 4ish, after chatting with Lou in front of the fire for hours. I spent Christmas Day with Val, David, Helen, Warren and Lloyd at Barnet. I have never felt so exuberant with the snow all over the countryside, the house, and every conceivable thing on the ground. The English friends of Val and David are so warm and likeable, and I felt so at home with them. Val bought me a blanket with the money you sent over – it is lemon, so lovely and warm. I also received a light brown polo neck jumper, scarf and makeup from them. Helen and Warren bought me some powder, soap and an address book (a black one to put all my beaus' names in)! I gave Val a bright orange button down collar crepe blouse with long sleeves, and I gave Helen the same in pink. David and Warren liked the Benson and Hedges cigarettes I bought for them, and I

I don't wear step-ins anymore.

gave Lloyd a miniature pewter beer mug. Helen made a terrific turkey dinner, and I ate and drank so much, it took most of Boxing Day and the next day to recover.

John spent Xmas with his mother in Southampton but telephoned on Christmas Day to wish me a merry Xmas. We went on Friday night to a farewell for a Melbourne friend of his, who was going back to Australia via India. It was quite a nice night, but men are men when they get together for a farewell, and it dragged on till the early hours of the morning. By the time we took Peter back to Earls Court, and John drove me back to Highgate, it was 5am when I finally crawled into bed. John was back at 8.30 to tell me it was snowing a blizzard outside. In a way I was pleased to be awake, because I wouldn't have missed the snow for anything. We went shopping around 9.30, had breakfast, and then I felt terribly tired, irritable and depressed by it all. We were supposed to be going to the Airport to see Peter off. I didn't have it in me to go, so I let John go by himself. Moped around for the rest of the afternoon cleaning the flat, which was a mess from previous celebrations. Lou raised his head, and actually got out of bed around 3 in the afternoon. He wanted to finish a movie film, so we went into London to the West End, and generally caused a riot in Grosvenor Square at the American Embassy. I took a photo of Lou standing on his head in Grosvenor Park with the American Eagle on the Embassy at his feet! He caught me on the film just standing around. He then took a photo of the both of us standing in front of the Roosevelt memorial with the 8-second timer on my camera. We then walked from the Marble Arch end of Hyde Park to the Knightsbridge side past the Serpentine, looking at the tramps, watching the ducks and just talking about everything. The park was covered in snow. I felt so lovely with my boots, woollen slacks, rollneck jumper and kangaroo coat on! We had a look in the British Museum in Cromwell Road, and then had a peek inside a second-hand bookshop, when the owner gave us a lecture on the decline of the English (not the British!) for half an hour solid. All the while Lou felt very agitated. Lou looks so English, with his moustache curling up at the ends, and he seems to get picked on by anti-English fanatics like this man in the bookshop. We then had a bit of nosh at a hobo-frequented snack bar, and finally got the tube home to a warm cosy fire, hot chocolate, soup, steak and scrambled eggs.

Nobody was home. The nurses, Sally, Jane and Maggie were working, and it was bitterly cold outside. The snow had stopped. It was now icing up, and the sky clear and cloudless, which is typical of pre-snow weather. Lou and I had previously discussed surviving in the open, with just the clothes one was wearing. Tonight, we decided to prove or disprove this point. We dressed as warmly as we could in as much clothing as we could put on, had another huge meal, and took a survival kit just in case we got lost. We then proceeded to hike up to Hampstead Heath, which is about 4 miles from the flat up Highgate Hill. We started out about 9pm and reached the edge of the Heath around 11ish, and quite warm from the gruelling walk. We decided on a spot deep in the forest, sheltered from the wind coming up the valley. We then fashioned a shelter from leaves, snow, birch and fern. We used nothing else except what we could find around us, and at 12 midnight crawled under our shelter and tried to sleep. It became so cold I thought I would turn numb. We would have stayed till morning, but the damp began to seep through our clothing, giving us the shivers. At about 1am we felt it hopeless to stay, so hiked back to the warmth of the flat. My legs were aching, and every part of my body was exhausted, but we trudged on and on while the wind turned my hands and ears blue. I didn't wake till the doorbell started ringing at 1.30 Sunday afternoon.

To upset me even more, Lou came bounding down to tell me to get ready for church at St Pauls. I nearly believed him when he said it was 6.30 in the morning instead of late afternoon. Friends of Jane had decided to visit from Suffolk, so 2 obnoxious girls, who caused me to react in a very sarcastic manner to every remark they made, invaded the flat. I was the only person who had bought food for the weekend out of my own money, and Jane expected me to feed her friends! I was in no mood for jokes after the previous night's exhaustion, so in the end they forked out for Chinese meals from the restaurant across the road. To make matters more obnoxious, their boyfriends (American servicemen) decided to pay them a visit at our flat. We were lumbered with this typical Texan called Tex (naturally!), who wore 2" high heel boots, a Stetson hat, huge buckle belt, and would you believe, a lovely pair of thin-rimmed goggle glasses! He spoke with a fabulous Texan drawl, proclaiming to one and all, the potential of Texas as the land of the wealthiest people on this Earth. In fact, he made us all feel quite sick. I personally felt like pushing his face in! His pal was christened Slick (typical!), but his real name was Bill - how unusual. His only asset was he had been endowed with a great sense of humour, so at least we had a few laughs. Then, to our surprise, they went across the road to the Archway Tavern, and came back with 14 bottles of light ale, 2 bottles of cider and grins from one ear to the other smeared all over their ugly faces. This went on until 2am, when I decided to have a nosh of mashed eggs. When I got up the next morning and looked at the lounge room, my blood rose and nearly popped out of the veins in my head. Even Lou was disgusted with their behaviour. I promptly made a vow to revenge my wrath on the lot of them when I got back from work.

Most of the girls came home on Monday night from staying with their family over Xmas. When my roommate Jenny saw her things all over the place, from when the youngest girl had slept in her bed, she nearly tore the flat down! I was annoyed Jane had not mentioned anything about her friends visiting. She had let them sleep in beds not being used, had nearly drained my food supply without giving me a penny towards it, and let them use our flat as they wanted. Jenny and I let it be known to both of the girls they were not welcome. Thank God they had to leave Monday night for home, or someone might have been murdered in their sleep. Julie came over for dinner (Lou's girlfriend), and she brought her guitar. As we did quite often, Julie and I had a singing session in front of the fire. Naturally, Judy and Cathy (the 2 horrors from Suffolk) plagued us, interrupting us continually, which did leave me with a temper that could have turned me into a maniacal killer if they hadn't of left when they did.

I spent New Year quietly with Maggie, Sally and Jane at the flat as John was working. In a way it was pleasant. I didn't get to work till 11ish today, after dragging myself out of bed this morning at around 10. Tina has spent most of the day on the phone talking to one of her numerous girlfriends, with her feet on the desk and listening to the radio. When her favourite pop tune came on, she put the phone to the radio so her girlfriend could listen to the music. I must admit I get a great kick out of working with her - she has such an infectious manner, so like Denise in some ways. She has the same boundless exuberance, and with a great attitude, which seems to be the present-day outlook of most teenagers. Listen to me talking - I must tell you this attitude is no longer with me. I am getting older and more mature as each day goes by.

I must explain the situation at the flat - most of the nurses are leaving for other hospitals in late February, which means they will be moving. Jenny, my roommate, who works in Great Portland Street at one of the many fashion houses wants me to join her in another flat, as she has been at this one for over a year and would like a change. Lou may join us too, which would work out fine as he gets on well with both of us and is more like a brother to me. So, it may be moving time again for me in the next few months. Jenny and I still plan to go to Paris early February for a weekend with Val, we hope. Betty wants me to visit her in Cheshire next spring. This all means I may be stationed in London until next year. Another thing that may keep me here till then is my job, which is one in a million. I may not find another one like it if I leave. All this is for the future. I cannot say much until a while yet, but I wanted to put you in the picture, even though the view may be a bit hazy at the present time xxxxxxx Dianne

Simon and Garfunkel's music played over and over and over again in our flat. Their song *Homeward Bound* was a teary favourite, and the movie *The Graduate* was out in cinemas and loved by everyone.

I don't wear step-ins anymore.

My mother and father would probably have no idea what I had been going on about in the previous letter. The following letter was acknowledging my parents' news. They were planning to visit me in London while doing an overseas trip of approximately six weeks. I was over the moon with excitement and trepidation.

10th January 1969

Dearest Mum and Dad,

What a wonderful piece of news you sent me this week, so exciting I still haven't settled down to normal. All the people I know are just as thrilled about your trip, and Jenny plus the other girls at the flat send their regards.

The best time to see London is late April/early May, because the Spring has just commenced. The weather at this time is pleasant all over the British Isles, and the most important thing is the city and the countryside isn't too crowded with tourists. If you came in June or August, it would be quite impossible to walk down Oxford St. without being trampled by the masses. The weather at this time is quite good, and even though the mornings and nights are cold and crisp, the days generally are quite sunny. Don't leave your visit any later than May, or you both may not enjoy it. There is nothing worse than to visit a famous place and find it overrun by Americans. I find them ostentatious, loud and having no regard for the sanctity of a place such as Westminster Abbey.

Don't book any tours in London - I will take you around. After 5 months here I know London so well I could take out a Taxi Driver's licence. Remember too, most of the people I know are English, and they are quite looking forward to showing you some scenery and nightlife. There is a fabulous restaurant in London called the 'Contented Sole' which only serves seafood, which I know you and Dad will have to visit. I will be about to take some of my holidays soon, so I will have the time to take you around. I enclose a few photos taken of London from the air, which I know you will love.

I must do some work now because I have been typing this letter all morning. I will write again in a few days but had to get this one off to you as soon as I could. Give my love to all and sundry. Take care and hurry up and book your flight. See you very soon, Love, your daughter Dianne

I had to write a few days later, after telling my cousin Val about my parents' proposed trip.

14th January 1969

Dear Mum and Dad,

Had lunch with Val yesterday, and between mouthfuls of food, we spent most of the time talking about the marvellous time we are going to give you both when you arrive. The news made Val so happy she decided to ring her mum during the night, which is unusual for her to do, as she gets very emotional about it. I haven't seen Val for over 2 weeks because she has been in Glasgow with Helen and Warren for the New Year, and they go out so much I can't keep up with them. We had a look in a few shops after lunch, and as usual Madam used her gentle art of persuasion in helping me write a couple of cheques. There was a sale at a handbag store, so I bought a gorgeous mustard casual leather bag for 4 pounds and a hessian type blue, red and bone carrier bag (good for all the small parcels one accumulates during the day) – only cost 2 pounds. We then had a few laughs in the card shop selecting birthday cards for Valmai.

Fantastic news! Cliff Carrington, the American guy I met in Balboa Panama, wrote me saying he was arriving in London on February 3rd for 2 weeks, prior to arriving in Sydney in March. His ship is having repair work in Rotterdam, so he is spending the down time in London. He is a first-class person and so friendly and obliging. He also has unusual interests like car racing and going on

I don't wear step-ins anymore.

expeditions to the South American jungles. Rather exciting, don't you think?

You would be amazed at how many English girls have decided to go to Australia, especially after listening to my ravings. It is wonderful when the girls in the flat start asking questions and cut clippings out of the papers about Australia and pin them on the wall. One of the nurses brought home a clipping last night, showing the amount of beer cans left after the 3rd test between Australia and the West Indies. It was so lovely, I pinned it on the wall straight away.

Poor Tina has just come back from the Dentist and has had the whole nerve taken out of one of her teeth. 25 needles to deaden the pain!! Which reminds me I must go for a check-up. Tina also sends her love. The boss just left and will be away for the next 2 days, so all is lovely. Will write again very soon. Love to all, Dianne

A week later my mother and father sent me details and dates of their travel plans. They would be arriving at the beginning of May, so there were only three months for me to prepare for their visit.

Friday, 17th January 1969

Dear Dianne,

Today the humidity was over 88 degrees, but tonight it is overcast, and it is very pleasant. We have the front door and the sliding doors open, so there is a nice breeze coming in from Botany Bay and the airport. We went to Town this afternoon and saw the chap at the Bank. The itinerary at present is 11.15 am Leave Sydney Friday 2nd May, arrive in London 8th May.

Have 3 days in London, then depart 11th May for a tour on the Continent (14 days). Seven days in London from 24th May. Nine days touring Scotland from 31st May. Arrive back in London 8th June, then 5 days in London before flying home to Sydney. Haven't made any bookings for accommodation in London. Have you any suggestions?

I am only buying an overcoat. Do you think it will be best to wait until I arrive? Tell Valda to keep her nights free when I am there. Denise bought sunglasses, a navy-blue purse for work, a white blouse and one of those gaudy dress rings. Denise has gone to the beach with Russell. Can't remember the last night she was home. Hope you have been keeping well. Received your letter last Tuesday. Will be counting the weeks, darling. Love and kisses from your loving Mother xxxxxxxxxxxxxx

Well Sweetheart, you are going to see us sooner than you thought. Mum has given you the dates, so you can show us London. She is so excited to think she is going to see her big girl Bots.[23] We had a nice Xmas and went swimming. We are going to the Marrickville RSL Club to see Alf Garnett next week. Dianne, if you want anything brought over let me know. It won't take long for the time to come for us to be on our way. We are getting so excited. Denise is going to stay with Aunt, so everything is OK. Keep your chin up. See you soon. All my love xxxxxxx Daddy xxxxxxx

It was so wonderful to receive aerogrammes from family and friends. Sometimes I would arrive home and find half a dozen waiting for me to read all at once. The other girls in the flat were jealous and loved listening to me read the letters out loud.

Tuesday, 28th January 1969

Dearest Mother & Father,

I have 2 aerogrammes, one, which I received on Saturday, and the other this evening. Your news from home raises my spirits to heights unknown. I exist each day knowing I will be seeing you both in about 3 months' time. I had a simply super but quiet weekend. On Saturday, Jenny and her boyfriend took me to Portobello Road, which

---

23   'Bots' was an affectionate name given to me by my sister, and I'm pretty sure it was a reference to my ample bottom.

I don't wear step-ins anymore.

is one of the liveliest markets in London. We had a Pub lunch at the 'Perseverance' first, which is gorgeously decorated in 18th Century style. The walls are literally covered in brass, silver and pewter.

I bought 3 second-hand books for 1/- each. Looked at tons of antique jewellery, which is all the rage here, and finally found what I have had my heart set on - a Turkish Puzzle Ring. It is silver and made up of 4 separate rings fitting together into one whole piece. I now know how to put it into one piece, and it looks fantastic on my hand! I also bought a tiny Book of Prayers for you and will put it in with this letter.

On Sunday, Maggie, Sally and I went for a 7-mile tramp across Hampstead Heath. If there is one place I love in London, it is 'The Heath'. You must see it when you are here. By the time you arrive, all the trees and flowers will be in spring bloom, and I cannot imagine how beautiful the Heath is going to look then. Even now in the middle of winter, I feel awe inspired as I walk along its many paths. Have not seen so many dogs and owners walking in one place. The English are such animal lovers. It is not uncommon for me to have a chat with numerous strangers about their pets, whom they coax along the tracks so patiently. I feel very melancholy and wish I had a huge dog to walk and race with too, however I will have one sooner or later, when I finally settle down.

I received a letter from Denise this morning. I think the name 'Russell' was mentioned at least 50 times. He must be keen to put up with her!

I had the busiest day of my life today at work! Tina had a sickie today so she could go for her driver's licence. She phoned me to say she had passed, and her father has promised to buy her a car. She is as spoilt and petted as I was, and as Denise still is. When I look at Tina, she reminds me so much of me when I was her age. I feel quite old and mature when I say something to her, because what I think about things now is a lot different to what I used to think - thank goodness! We have been on a strict diet at work and home. When one has to buy food for oneself it becomes a chore to cook, so what I do regularly is go out Saturday mornings (shops are open all day) and get provisions like a dozen eggs (I eat these in 3 days usually), sausages, bacon, cheese, butter, Brussels sprouts (would you believe), a few Vestas and at least 4 tubs of yoghurt. I rarely buy meat. It is too expensive and is not good quality. I eat a lot of grapefruit and usually consume 10 cups of coffee a day. At work, Tina and I mostly take turns and buy on our way to work with our luncheon vouchers (3/- per day) a loaf of slimming bread, fruit, cheese, sometimes eggs, and of course, yoghurt. I must eat on an average, 2 tins of yoghurt per day. I look and feel very healthy, although the thought of your cooking makes me homesick quite often. My face is so clear, which is due mostly to the non-existence of strong sunlight and super cold air. I am sure you and Dad will be shocked when you see me. One thing I am very proud of is I don't wear step-ins anymore, just stocking tights, bikini pants and a bra-slip. Which reminds me, Denise's gift for Christmas was a BRA-slip not a dress! Does your suit fit you? It will be perfect for your trip. Did Dad like his jazzy cufflinks and Scottish WHISKY POURER? I bought this and the shortbread in Glasgow.

Getting on to more important things – I am so pleased you have decided to make your stay in London for a certain length of time, and not broken as was before. I will be able to get my holidays from work, so I am at your disposal day and night – can you stand it?

At the beginning of March Jenny and I will be looking for a new flat, and by the time we move out at the end of March we hope to have one already. When you arrive Jenny and I insist you stay with us. Valda has a double fold-up bed and mattress which you can have, and Dad can have my bed. Jenny is just as excited as I am and can't wait to meet you. I read all your letters out loud and they all think you're both terrific! You can certainly count on me to join you on your trip around Britain – it will be just the right time of year to go.

My friend from Balboa, Cliff, arrives in London next Monday, and I can hardly wait to see him. It will be exciting meeting him again after

I don't wear step-ins anymore.

such a long time. He will be in Australia before you leave, so please make him welcome if he visits you, which I know he will.

In the beginning of March, Val, Jenny, Linda (a workmate of Jenny and a new friend of mine) and I are going to Paris for a rip-roaring weekend. We are flying over on the Friday night and coming home Sunday night. We are all looking forward to it very much.

The weather has been truly marvellous, and from all accounts it should mean an early spring. The birds and animals are already mating. The squirrels in Hampstead Park haven't even hibernated for the winter!! We naturally get some drizzly days, but I haven't felt exceptionally cold at all. In fact, I wish it would snow again!

When Cliff leaves London, I am going along to Evening Classes at The City Literary Institute. It is about time I did something with my mind. I read so much these days but must put my brain to some use. What I am aiming for eventually is some sort of educational learning, and possibly the opportunity to put this to good use. My ability to understand Russian novelists like Tolstoy, Dostoyevsky and English poets like Wordsworth and Lord Byron, who I am reading now, tempts me to satisfy my hunger for understanding.

It is nearly 12 o'clock Tuesday night. I am sitting here madly writing whilst the trucks thunder past along the North Road just outside our doorstep. We have the tubes pass right under the flat, and this place is going to fall down one of these days. I am used to it though and will miss this place when I finally pack up.

Do you remember the film 'Anna Karenina' with Greta Garbo? Well, I have nearly finished the book by Tolstoy, and it is so sad. I have never liked a writer as much as Tolstoy. His vision of human motives and feelings gives me the power to visualize each character as I read their story. I still would like very much to visit Russia one of these days.

Today (it is 1.30 am Wednesday), I am going to lunch with Jenny and Linda at a Vegetarian Restaurant in Carnaby Street called 'CRANKS'. As the bosses are away up North today and tomorrow, life will be very pleasant. Tuesday was hectic as Tina was away. I had to work a switchboard with one hand, take shorthand with the other, type with one foot and make coffee with the other foot! Therefore, I didn't have a minute to scratch myself, which is why I am writing this letter. The big boss is off to Switzerland next week for a skiing holiday – lucky boy! I had to make all his bookings, which gave me a great experience in these matters. To be truthful and even egotistical, I could, and do, run the place! Tell father I will accept a partnership in his firm, when new blood is needed? Mr O'Dell is quite a businessman, and exceptionally ruthless in his dealings. Some of the loopholes he pulls to evade income tax would astound you! As they say, 'All's fair in love, war and business.'

Most of Mr O'Dell's 'little helpers and comrades' are Jewish. You would be amazed at how big a hold English Jewry has on property and fashion houses in London. Tina is Jewish, and after having dinner at her home last week, plus being good friends with her family, I am accepted as one of them. I admire and respect the Jewish community. Their family life is so close-knit and completely different to any race on this earth. Tina's father narrowly escaped the Nazi Purge and lost his entire family in the Gas Chambers. He came to England with nothing, and now has a thriving clothing business. The family wants me to have a Jewish meal with them soon. Tina asks about you and Denise and sends her love. Lots of Love, Dianne xx

It was nearly the end of the first month of a new year, a year promising me a visit from my parents. I was so hoping my sister would come over to London with them; however, she put supposed future marriage expenses before trips to exotic countries.

I loved getting letters from home. My mother jammed aerogrammes with mundane information, telling me all about visits to Town and even what she or my dad created for dinner. Yes, my father watched *Joe the Gadget Man*, and purchased all those little gadgets to make vegetables and fruit into works of art! He created the most awe-inspiring salads and mixed them with only the best and juiciest seafood, which at this time in Australia, was cheap and plentiful. We would eat Hawkesbury River oysters collected by him personally. After shucking and cleaning the oysters, he would put them back into their shells, add sauces and chopped bacon. This is what I missed most about living in Sydney.[24]

Monday, 3rd February 1969

To Our Dear Dianne,

Today we went into the Vaccination Clinic, Medical Centre, Australia Square. Had two injections in one, and the first injection of the flu. We have another injection on 17th February, and the second flu injection in four weeks' time. Tonight, they are a little painful. We went to the Bank and finalised the trip, so I am sending the Itinerary. What do you think about the accommodation while we are in London? I can't believe we will be seeing 'The Boyfriend' with Barbra Streisand. You know me, won't get too excited, in case my plans go astray. Was speaking to the lady in Town, where I bought a bone pair of shoes today (Nannette Shoe Shop). Her son has been in London 12 months last month. He earns more over there than he did in Sydney. She said I was lucky to be going overseas. Do you realise it's 6 months tomorrow (Tuesday) since you left home? Phyllis Diller is in a series starting on TV at 11 o'clock in the morning. Tonight's TV review quotes, 'If any housewife happens to be feeling dowdy or depressed around 11 am, then we recommend 25 minutes of Phyllis Diller to remedy both conditions.' She fixes her hair with the aid of a screwdriver and a cold chisel, mirrors crack when she looks in them to put on her make-up, and short-sighted visitors confuse her with the floor mop. We hope to go down the South Coast next Sunday for a picnic. How did you like the family photo? Last Thursday I went to Bowls, the first time I have played since the first week in October. My

---

24   'To shuck' was the term used to loosen an oyster with a specially shaped knife with a large wooden handle. There was an art to opening an oyster shell and freeing the oyster within. Dad would fill a hessian bag with oyster shells and bring them home to open and clean.

legs were aching on Friday. Frank Ifield arrived in Sydney last week. He is reported to be earning $6,000 a week. Not bad for yodelling! Must write to Betty, after she was kind enough to write and tell me how you are going. I would like to see her if it is possible when I come over. I want to see as much as possible. Another ship loaded with young soldiers, went to Vietnam today. They are replacing another unit, who are due to come home. Well Treasure, another week has passed. Hoping you are keeping well and think of your dear old Mother occasionally. The text in tonight's paper is, 'Your hands have made me and fashioned me, give me understanding, that I may learn thy commandments.' Darling, love and big hugs and kisses from your ever-loving Mum. xxxxxxxxx Hello Love, well we have finalised and booked our trip to see you at last. We had our first needles today and Mum is so excited about coming to see you. Hope you are going well and enjoying yourself. Hope Valda and David are well and what do they think of us coming over? Well love, the time won't take long to go. It is 6 months today since you left home (think about seeing Ireland with us). Best of luck and love Daddyxxxxxxx

While I was living in Archway, our flat became a place to stay for the friends and relatives of the five people sharing. I had met Cliff Carrington in Panama City, where he had shown me around. It was now my turn to reciprocate.

Wednesday, 12th February 1969

Dear All,
    Cliff from Balboa arrived last Monday week, and out of the goodness of my heart, I let him bunk at the flat. This proved disastrous and very inconvenient, after the novelty of having him for the first couple of days or so. Now I am counting the days until he departs.
    I have shown him all over London nearly every night of the week. Last weekend we went up to Val's where we stayed until Sunday

night. Last Friday night we saw 'HAIR' at the Shaftsbury Theatre. I enjoyed it so much the second time, I intend seeing it again before it finishes. When we came outside a blizzard was raging. There was at least 6 inches of snow on the ground and it was blowing very hard. Everyone was running around in it, laughing and singing, and the tube was a joy to ride in, the people were so gay. I can't describe how beautiful London is when snow is falling, and how wonderful it is to be covered with the stuff. After changing into warmer clothing at the flat, we went back into London and got off at Piccadilly Circus. We just started to walk up to Leicester Square and Soho. Found a super Chinese Restaurant, and I had a glorious meal, which consisted of Chow Mein, rice, chicken and almonds, fried shrimp, bamboo shoots, vegetables, Chinese white wine and Jasmine Tea (a whole pot of it)! We then walked all over London, helped an old man who had slipped over on the icy footpath. By the time we decided to make for home, the transport had grinded to a halt which meant finding a taxi (impossible!), thumbing a lift or hoofing it. We walked in the direction of Highgate and tried thumbing as well. Got as far as Mornington Crescent, 5 miles or so from London, with more than 5 miles to go. A kindly Swiss Italian man stopped for us and took us right to Archway Station. Lou and Julie were home, so we finished the Chinese Wine in front of the fire and thawed out.

During the week, Cliff and I had a Greek meal in Soho, which was also very super, and then we saw 'A Space Odyssey'. The night before we did a walking tour of the city, and I showed him some of the best Pubs around, like 'The Cockney Pride Tavern' in Piccadilly, which is decorated in Victoriana and Music Hall records are played. Valda informed me last week the Pub is a great hang out for queers! We had a look in at the 'Shakespeare's Head' and went downstairs to 'The Dive Bar', which is like a cavern. It is covered in groovy photos of Pop Stars and has a jukebox. We also popped into a pub next door to Scotland Yard called 'The Clarence', and I swear it was filled with Policemen in plain clothes! It was a very old Pub with decorated columns, old style furniture, and the women's powder room was very plush and antique. Walked along the Victorian Embankment, saw Lambeth Palace where the Queen Mother hangs out, Waterloo Bridge, Big Ben, The Houses of Parliament and Westminster Abbey. Got the Tube at Charing Cross after walking along the Strand and seeing Nelson's Column in Trafalgar Square.

After the snow all Friday night, the rest of the weekend and Monday was glorious weather. I have never seen such blue sky, even in Sydney, and the sun was very warm. Did the usual shopping Saturday morning, then mucked around listening to records until David arrived to pick us up. Valda made a lovely dinner for us, and then we went up to the 'Wagon and Horses' Pub. Came back to George and Francis's place, where Val made her call to her Father. It was very exciting, and Val was so happy about it. She let me have a word with Aunty Betty, and I must say she sounded so well on the phone. I only just realised how long ago it was since I spoke to the rest of the family.

The week before Cliff arrived, I was hit with the flu on the Wednesday, and it got so bad the girls called the doctor.[25] Lou also was sick, with terrible pains in his abdomen and nausea, which the doctor thought was appendicitis. It turned out to be colic from eating too much bad meat. Lou had to stay in bed and take this horrible medicine. I was told to stay in bed the whole weekend, and the doctor also gave me some horrible medicine to take. I don't know what was in it, but it left a green stain on the spoon, which made me wonder what it was doing to my insides. I ached continually for 6 days and had to take sleeping tablets to sleep. I lost half a stone in weight and could feel every bone in my body. The girls in the flat were marvellous. Maggie came home from the Hospital one day just to make sure I was okay. Val and David visited, and all I could do was laugh at Val, who kept making eyes at Jenny's boyfriend Robin. He is an absolute dish, very tall, dark hair, handsome, wears really conservative clothes and was once a male model. You will more than

---

25   For some reason, I was constantly being mowed down by a cold or flu.

I don't wear step-ins anymore.

likely meet him when you are here. Valda thinks he is a darling, and even flirts with him when David is around - good job!

Val wants me to go along to Elocution Classes. The girls at the flat keep telling her how nice she speaks with her Aussie accent, but she hates it and wants to talk posh! I was amazed at the way the Aussies threw Warren Mitchell out of Sydney. The words he says are nothing to what the average Englishman says. I cannot see 'HAIR' getting past the censors in Sydney without being cut to shreds. Nearly every second word is a swear word, and most are very rude for Australian standards. The word starting with 'F' is used continually in Plays and Television here, and of course by the English socially. It doesn't have an offensive meaning here at all and is the same as saying 'bloody' in Australia.

Mr O'Dell, the big boss, left for his skiing holiday last Friday. The office is very peaceful and making me so lazy. Whenever someone asks me my occupation, I have to tell them truthfully 'Living' is my occupation and 'Work' is a pastime! I learn so much just listening to Tina raving all day. Last night I had dinner at her friend's office in Green Park. There was Tina, Paula, Linda and Frankie. These girls all have good jobs and do nothing all day. The office where we had dinner is in a block of apartments, fitted with 2 bedrooms, shower and a lounge. Georgette Heyer, the writer, lives downstairs, and some chap who owns most of the shops in Carnaby St. lives next door. Very posh!

The other boss, Mr Barton, came into the office yesterday wearing Wellington boots with his good suit! In the afternoon he took them off and padded around in his socks! We had a super lunch of fish and chips, ice cream and lager and lime in a can. For the past 2 days I have worn my trousers to work, as we have had quite a bit of snow, and more is on the way. I wouldn't swap all the snow for anything. The cold and snowy weather seems to make one feel like putting effort into living. One is also so acutely aware of the sun and blue sky after the cold has broken. I appreciate the warmth and comfort so much more than I ever did at home. I more than appreciate the convenience of a car, when I walk miles until my feet ache!

Valda wants you to see the Ballet and some plays too, so we will book some seats when we definitely know the dates. There is also a great restaurant called 'The Elizabethan Rooms' in London, where you sit at a huge wooden table, eat off pewter plates and are served by girls dressed as wenches. Dad will like this place very much. David said to me last weekend he is sending Valda out of the Country when you arrive. He is frightened Val is going to drain the money resources when we take you shopping. She gets great delight in spending money on clothes, and helping other people spend their money too. I'll put some clippings in with this letter from the papers again. Hope you like them, and they give you an idea of what it is like here. Please write soon, until I see you, Lots of love Dianne xxxxx

My mother had a wonderful way of describing every meal she ate, especially the meals eaten at the many RSL Clubs she frequented. Here I was in England, unable to afford meat and seafood, which I would normally consume three or four times a week at home in Sydney.

Wednesday, 12th February 1969

To Our Big Girl,
Today the rain has eased, and only showers this afternoon. It has been raining since Sunday. We were going for a picnic on Sunday, down the Coast, but ended up at Kogarah RSL for the afternoon show, and had dinner later on. Mum's Special, Prawn Cutlets, Side Salad, Ice Cream cake with caramel flavouring, and another sweet, Strawberries and Cream. The Show was a good one, and they had a big crowd, on account of the weather. Monday, I had to go into Macquarie Street to see Dr Treloar for a Glaucoma Test. The Doctor was very pleased. I don't have to take any drugs but have to have a periodic check-up. Don't faint, Denise is home tonight, and also was home on Monday night! I am enclosing the two trips we have booked. Instead of staying overnight in Edinburgh, we are staying at North Berwick. Our seat numbers are 13 and 14. My birthday 13 and

I don't wear step-ins anymore.

Dad's birthday 14. I hope we can see the gardens of Balmoral Castle. We depart on this trip 4th June. How do they appeal to you? Tonight, on the news, we saw New York, snowbound. How are you getting on? Uncle Albert said you are wearing those miniskirts, and you are a real blonde. The only thing I wanted you to change was your impatience, and not to be too hasty in your temper. We have another train strike, which started at midnight, so Dad had to drive Denise to work, as David was leaving at 6.30am. He also had to bring her home. They think the strike might affect the food and milk coming to Sydney. Saw the shortest mini frock in Farmer's. The lass had a baby in a stroller, and I am not lying, the skirt ended where her legs started at the top. Even one saleslady said to me, 'where has modesty gone with some girls?' Last night I made curry prawns, and they were lovely. We opened a packet of 'Rice Riso'. The packet had been there since you were home. I bought a pound of frozen mixed vegetables in Coles on Monday, and used them with some water, milk, curry and flour. I got the recipe out of the Sunday paper a couple of months ago. My text for you today, 'Hold fast to God, with one hand, and open wide the other, towards your neighbour.' Well Darling, another week has passed. Hope you are keeping yourself warm and eating the right food. Love and big hugs and kisses from your loving mother. xxxxxx. Dear Dianne, well I said last week another week closer. Well this is another one. Mum has started making her dresses and new coats for the trip. She never stops telling everyone she is going to see her big girl. You can now arrange a trip to Ireland in the fourteen days we are in London for the three of us. Find out about a car to see England and Wales. We are looking forward to it and seeing our big girl. We have another train strike. I take Denise to work and have to pick her up too. It took me 50 minutes to get to Darlinghurst from Earlwood. Give my love to Jenny, David and Valda and Miss 'short dress' in the office.[26] Look after yourself and keep your chin up. I'm another year older on Valentine's Day. Love Daddy xxxxx

---

26 'Miss short dress' - my father was referring to Tina, my workmate, whose skirts began at the top of her thighs.

I had a dream job! It was situated in the middle of the West End of London. My hours were 10 am to around 5 pm, and these were very flexible if the bosses were away. My work colleague was a 17-year-old, micro-mini-skirt-wearing Londoner from Tottenham, called Tina. She adored working the switchboard, buying lunchtime sandwiches and making delicious coffee for us all. She had a mouth on her and was extremely opinionated, but I loved her and so did the bosses.

Tuesday, 18th February 1969

Dearest Mum and Dad,
   I got your latest letter this morning dated 12th February. At the moment I am in very great humour because Mr O'Dell is in Zermatt, Switzerland skiing, and Mr Barton is in Surrey, probably never to return, as the snow in his neck of the woods is pretty gruesome. Tina is deeply involved in sketching, and the radio has been playing continuously for hours. I have just finished reading one book '1984' by George Orwell and are now in the throes of 'Animal Farm' by the same author.
   A few of Tina's friends are visiting for lunch, so about half an hour ago we got some provisions from the local delicatessen. We bought French rolls, cheese, hamburgers and three cans of lager and lime from the off-licence in Marylebone Lane. The cans and cheese are on the window ledge keeping cold, and the rest is on top of the radiator getting nice and warm. What a super, beautiful life we are living here, and how it suits my temperament.
   I had lunch with Val yesterday, and we talked about your trip. Val and I both came to the conclusion you should try and be in London for a set time. We will be able to arrange some nights out, and you will also have a chance to rest now and again. I will be able to take time off to spend the days with you doing some leisurely sightseeing and shopping. Val is also planning to take a few days off. One day we could take the barge up the Thames to Windsor and Kew

I don't wear step-ins anymore.

Gardens. It is one of the most beautiful trips and very relaxing in the springtime. It is also historically interesting, and fantastically scenic and colourful with the open countryside and flowers just blooming. At night we can see 'Funny Girl', some stage plays with actors like Leslie Philips, who is always doing a show in London, or the Ballet. If you want to try food, there are so many different types of restaurants of all nationalities. One could spend a year trying a different one each night. There is no doubt, in either Val's or my mind, once you see London, you will want to spend some time here. Whatever you do, don't limit your stay to a few days, or you both may regret it. On top of this fact is the other point – We have not seen each other for over 6 months, and after you leave it may be quite some time until we see each other again.

With regard to hiring a car and going to Ireland and Wales, this is a great idea and very economical and easy to do. The transport authorities in this Country have travelling to Ireland down pat, and this can be arranged in one go. After your stay in London and during it, we could arrange all this. Actually, Val and David are going to Ireland in April by car, so I will find out all about it from them. Friends have told me of some super places to see there, and I always feel that when you tour a small country by car, your time is your own and you can stop whenever something catches your eye.

One suggestion I must make, and Valda agrees – Why don't you do your tour of the Continent on the way back to Sydney? So, fly to London as planned. Spend a few weeks in London with us. Hire a car and visit Wales and Ireland. Do your tour of England and Scotland. Leave London on Continental tour. Go home from somewhere on the Continent.

You aren't going to Rome, the Eternal City?? Haven't you seen the Sophia Loren shows on TV yet? When you do, nothing will stop you visiting this Ancient and Holy City. I notice you have some time off, so take every opportunity of getting away to other places that aren't frequented by the Tourists.

I love the way you are flying from Sydney, and stopping at Athens, Bangkok and Amsterdam. This is very good, but as for the guided tours, I can see some more places by better ways. This is my opinion. It is your tour. Val is writing on this too, so you may get some helpful hints, as she has at least been to a few places in Europe.

Cliff left London on his way to Sydney last Friday, after two solid weeks of exhausting me. We went out nearly every night, so last weekend I caught up on my sleep. I've already told you about me having the flu a week before Cliff arrived. I forgot to tell you I didn't have to pay for the doctor to visit me at the flat. Up the British National Health!!! I was in bed from Wednesday night to the following Monday. Maggie, one of the nurses threatened to bring a bedpan home from the hospital – ugh. I never felt more home-sick from lack of attention. The girls were marvellous to me, and Tina even wrote me a letter from work, but it would have worked a miracle just to have you sit by my bed and hold my hand. Love you all, Dianne xxxxx

Sometimes my Mum would dash off an aerogramme and forget to write on the back part. At Christmas, the Post Office would sell aerogrammes with pictures of waratahs. My mum thought she should not write over the picture, so she left it blank. I didn't care how short the aerogrammes were, as long as I kept on receiving these gems from home.

Thursday, 6th March 1969

Dear Dianne,

I know this aerogramme bears last Christmas Greetings, but Denise bought them last month. Yesterday was colder than it has been for a while. We got on a bus taking us to Market Street in the City. One girl on the bus (pardon me if you could call her a girl), was wearing the shortest mini I have ever seen. In fact, you could see where her legs

I don't wear step-ins anymore.

joined her body. What price is modesty? Guess where we went for lunch? 'The Summit', at Australia Square. We had our last flu injection then went for lunch at 1.30pm. The view is fantastic, although today wasn't the best. The meals are very pricey, but I had the most lobster I have ever had. The dessert was $1.50 for a small slice of chocolate with cream, but I enjoyed it. Another week has passed Treasure. Don't forget to let me know if you received the photo, as I had put some money in it. Well Darling, love, hugs and kisses from your ever-loving Mother xxxxxxxxxxxx

Invariably, our letters would cross paths on the aeroplanes going back and forth between England/Australia and Australia/England. When things were quiet at home or work, we continued to churn out two letters a week to one another. My mother would chastise me if she did not receive at least one letter per week from me.

Monday, 10th March 1969

To Our Dear Dianne,
   Must tell you the big news. Val and Mike's Lisa is going to have a playmate next October, when she will be 16 months old. I rang Aunt this morning and she told me the news. Valmai is having Dr Segal for the confinement and she is going into Bethesda Hospital in Marrickville. Tonight, I have been sewing, and brought the machine out in front of the TV. Tonight, Dad made me a large salmon and crab salad, and it was delicious. Watermelons are still in season, and I make a guts (pardon the expression) of myself each night. Dad bought peaches for me to take away to Wollongong, and they were 15 cents each. Hope Valda and David are keeping well. Darling, I will close now. One more week closer. Big hugs and kisses from your loving Mother xxxxxx Hello Darling, well 8 weeks to go before we leave to see you. Hope all the cold weather has gone, and you have some

sunshine for us. Mum and I went for a trip to Wollongong yesterday. It was a beautiful day. Well, I hope Tina, Jenny, Valda and David are well. Best of luck, keep your chin up, Love Daddy xxxxxxxxxxxxxxxxx

I was so missing the sunshine of Sydney and the plentiful supply of fruits and vegetables. London during winter was unbearably damp, especially if one lived somewhere like our three-storey flat in Archway, which was in an old building with no damp courses and totally inadequate heating. This winter was unusually cold, and for a longer period.

11th March 1969

Dearest Mum and Dad,

I received your letter and must say how much I enjoyed reading it. We seem to be on a better wavelength now, even though 12,000 miles of ocean separates us. I have started taking vitamin pills each day, but would you believe I have caught another rotten cold in the head and have woken up hardly able to breath. I blame the dampness of the flat. It is so easy to get colds if one moves from a warm room to another without preparing for the drop in temperature. I am so looking forward to getting another place with Jenny and Linda. Going to Jenny's home in Hertfordshire for Sunday lunch this week. Her mother wants to meet me. I am sure Jenny and Tina will love the bracelets you are having Bobbie make.

I sent Ross a very rude get-well-card, which I know will pick him up no end. Sorry to hear he has an infection. He will have to look after himself now and start thinking of his body as flesh and blood, and not as a machine, as he tended to treat it before. If one's body is healthy, then half the battle is won, don't you think? I can do so much; it sometimes frightens me. I get bursts of energy at the wrong time, and it makes me so frustrated. You have enough to do without knitting me a cardigan, but to compensate you may help me choose a few articles of clothing while you are here!

I don't wear step-ins anymore.

I had a super weekend with Howard, who is currently my companion. We went to 'The Spaniards Inn' at Hampstead Heath on Friday night, and Lou and Julie came too. There we reclined in antique chairs near a huge log fire in the 'Dick Turpin' Room, sipping 'Pernod' (aniseed liquor) and discussing various topics of interest. Most enjoyable, especially when Howard has a racing car and plenty of the green stuff![27] Saturday morning I was up early, and Sally and I went to Chapel St. Markets close to Camden Town, where we rubbed shoulders with the other half (all colours and creeds). Bought some pineapples. They cost 2/6 each (A$50 cents). Before Howard came to escort me to the disco in the night, I slowly gnawed my way through a delicious piece of rump steak, costing me the equivalent of A$1.50, plus grilled pineapple. Satisfactory sustenance for body and soul. Howard and I poured along the road through the West End like hot molten lava in his little Porsche sports car. Our posteriors were separated from the road by a slim 4 inches of metal and we finally squeezed into a neat parking position in Regent Street. We then made our way to 'Bart's' - Lionel Bart's Discotheque. I had a super time grooving away to the current records and mixing with the toffs. I wore Spanish-style black evening trousers, flared from the knees, and a super black and white Tricel long sleeve, roll neck top, plus my greenstone, Danish silver ring on one hand and my Turkish puzzle ring on the other. I felt elevated to the highest extreme! Danced until about 2.30am, and it was a blissful night charging along, breaking the speed limit in the now deserted West End. I scraped myself out of bed around 9am, as Howard was taking me to the car races at Brand's Hatch in Kent. His car reached 110 miles per hour on the Motorway. On the way home we went through the City of London, passing St Pauls, The Tower of London, Tower Bridge and the Roman Wall. Every time I see London like this, my heart attaches itself more and more. I feel as though I belong to the whole huge fantastic creation that is London. Everyone sends their love, especially me. Dianne.

---

27   When I first read 'the green stuff' I thought I might be referring to hash, but now realise I meant money.

I had not sent a letter home for over two weeks. I had written letters but not sent them, because of dramas at the flat. My next letter to Mother explained what was going on.

Saturday, 15th March 1969

Dearest Mum

I have told you an awful lot about Jenny, but she is in such an emotional state, I must say more. She has been dangling her fingers in the fire at work for too long. i.e. she is emotionally involved with a married man, plus has a steady boyfriend, who tags after her like a puppet on a string. To top it off, she still has eyes for Lou (our flat mate). Her girlfriend Linda, who is staying at the flat, is engaged to be married this June. She is also having a gay affair with a married chap at work, and his wife is threatening retribution via telephone calls to Linda's mother! 'Oh, what a tangled web...'

Jenny left work yesterday. When I got home around 7ish, she was standing at the window gazing intently at nothing. 'To Dream the Impossible Dream' played in the background. It certainly looked like a scene from a Greta Garbo movie. I could see right through the play-acting and couldn't give Jenny any sympathy. She just wanted attention. I can't be with people who live in a state of false surroundings.

When I think like this, it seems to me how much you and I are alike. As I do things, I remember you doing them, and the resemblance is excruciatingly similar. There IS something other than flesh and blood between us, isn't there?[28] Love, Dianne.

What kept me going was the constant flow of letters from my family; and even though I had bad days, which sometimes stretched into weeks, I eventually came through the fog. My mother's reply to

---

[28] While reading this letter, I am blown away. I now know that I was adopted at birth and brought up by Ruby and George Lindsay, my adopted parents.

I don't wear step-ins anymore.

my distraught letter about the goings-on at the Archway flat was so comforting. I was very homesick, and it was now only six weeks until I would see my mum and dad.

Friday, 21st March 1969

> To Our Big Girl,
> Received your Letter this morning, and I think you must have been a bit homesick. You must remember, love, when you live with people you see both sides of them, and a still tongue makes a wise person. I could have arguments with Aunt, but I hold my tongue. When I was talking to her on the phone this week, she wasn't in the best of moods. Some of my friends tell me things because they know I don't repeat. You have to accept people as they are, as long as you don't do the things you don't like them doing. Even Denise comes home and tells me things she doesn't like about the people they go out with. I tell her you can always find some good in everybody. Remember Mrs McKnight? She was always having arguments with people, because she couldn't mind her own business. Sometimes a kind word will go a long way. Hope you are feeling much better and burn the letters that mention anything about the flat, as you never know who might read them. Cliff got his new car. He rang me on Wednesday. Judy, (a lass he met coming out from England) rang me to leave a phone number where she is staying in Newcastle with her sister. He seemed to be happy when I told him Judy rang, and was going to drive to Newcastle after lunch. Today a letter came from the bank for him. Not very long, Treasure, before we see you. Love and big hugs and kisses from your ever-loving Mother xxx Hello Love, hope you are well and keeping your chin up as always. Go to church on Sunday and you won't get lonely. It won't take long now before we see you in 6 weeks. Love Daddy. xxxxxxxx

Things at the Archway flat were now settling down, and we had a new lease that stupid me took on, because no one else would. At least I now had three months of security in my living arrangements.

24th March 1969

Dearest Mum and Dad,

Have some super news to tell you - I have kept the flat at Archway by signing a new lease for 3 months, and this means I do not have to move at all. Sally and Louis are staying on as well, and at present Jenny is undecided. We are putting an advert. in the paper tomorrow morning for some more people, and I am not looking forward to interviewing. Very convenient the bosses are away for the next 2 days. On top of all this I may be going on a 9-week tour of the Continent myself which leaves London 18th June, but this will not be definite until the end of this week. I think I may explain this all to the Boss and if he needs my expert services, he may be willing to put a temp on while I am away. One never knows.

If the Boss decides he needs me for next winter, I may find it necessary to stay at work until 24th May - meaning I may not be able to meet you at London airport. Customs usually slows up arrival times, and by all chances you may not eventually get into London until late afternoon, and then I will be finished work. Also, of course, when you have gone through Customs, the best thing to do is phone the office at 01-4865991 before 5.30 or the flat 01-2721604 after 6.30. (Only use the 01 prefix if phoning out of London and delete it if from the London area).

Mum - can you bring me a flannelette night shirt (not pyjamas) and another pair of those lamb's wool slippers? I have nearly worn both out and presently sleeping naked, because the night attire is so crappy here. Please get me a nightshirt very plain and any colour. I would really appreciate this. Also don't forget to bring in your allowance of cigarettes and spirits by duty-free, (these are extra expensive) and I must at last admit to you Mum, one of my pleasures is smoking.[29] The only other request I make is you both arrive in good health, having an open and unprejudiced mind and prepared to accept your very different eldest daughter!

I finally have a steady male companion. It is Howard with the Porsche sports car of course, and you may have the great honour of being driven around in the thing, if you can learn how to bend your body in 4 places to get in it first. Lots of love, Dianne

My next letter to Mum and Dad documented the goings-on in the Archway flat and the arrival of new flatmates, who turned out to be sisters from Wagga Wagga. Helen and Liz were hairdressers, aged 24 and 19, and very friendly and funny.

Sunday, 30th March 1969

Dearest Mum and Dad,

Yesterday and Friday, the weather was typical of our spring. It was heaven compared to two previous weeks of cold and dullness giving me a great feeling of depression. It is amazing but true, how weather plays such a great part on one's frame of mind and body!

From tomorrow there will be 6 of us in the flat at Archway. Jenny, me, Lou and Sally are staying plus two Australian girls we all met last week. Helen and Elizabeth are sisters from Wagga Wagga. I must admit, their Aussie accents embarrassed me when they came to see the flat. Every second word was 'beaut' and even Jenny commented how different my accent was to theirs. I seem to have lost a lot of my accent from being with Tina all day, and also being with other English people. Even so, people still have a tendency to ask if I am Australian on the 'phone. In shops, I get caught up in long chats with complete strangers, about their friends and relatives who have

---

29   I actually admitted to my Mother that I smoked and drank alcohol - so I could ask her to take advantage of things she could bring through Customs in London.

gone to the colony! Jenny and I have a strange relationship for roommates. We only see each other briefly during weeknights and she goes home on most weekends.

Val and I have started shopping together on Saturday mornings. We don't see much of each other these days, unless for lunch during the week. She has a nasty habit of buying food for me. She must think I don't eat, which is partly true, although I refuse to admit the fact. I am really looking forward to our Paris trip on 30th April. I will only be just back, and you and Dad will be here – Hell, it is not far off! Did I tell you Jenny's parents are going on the QE2 maiden voyage? Her father worked on the development of the ship, so they go free of charge – blimey! Well dears, I received a letter from each of you this morning at work – what joy. So, you watch 'Laugh In'? I saw it at Tina's last Sunday night, and tears rolled down my face from laughing. We see episodes that haven't reached Australia yet, but I rarely watch it at the flat, because we are usually listening to music or having arguments.

Our 2 new girls are marvellous, and so full of spirit and humour like most Australians who visit England. Liz is 19 and her sister Helen is 24. They are nothing alike but show each other's good points to the full. Lou hasn't got a chance now there are three Australians to three Poms. Last night we drowned out the TV with our laughter. We annoyed Lou so much, it reminded me of Dad putting up with you, Denise and me, and telling us to shut up. David Frost was on last night, sending up the countryside. Lou nearly missed all the best jokes, as we were talking so much. Then we did keep-fit exercises in the lounge room and talked until 2.30 am about every conceivable topic. Definitely off our skulls! Thank you for the money Mum – I have had to buckle down of late and do some serious saving. Living in London isn't easy at times, and as usual I have big sprees at the Record Shop and Bookstore. I am a compulsive listener and reader, moreso than eater and sleeper!

I spent today playing silly B-s at the office as Bill and Sir were away. Tina's friends, Paula, Linda and Frankie came to visit. The office was turned into a discotheque/lady's room, while I watched in fascination at all the antics? Will write again very soon. Lots of love, Dianne xxxxxxxxxx

My mother wanted to be taken around London in my boyfriend's Porsche, which proved to me what I had always thought - she had another side to her and was a secret rager!

Wednesday, 9th April 1969

Dearest Mum and Dad,

I wrote you a lousy letter yesterday because I was in a lousy mood, but this morning my week brightened when I found a letter from you plus 2 from Valmai. On top of all this good news, the days are sunny and beautiful, very mild and it stays light until 8pm. I get confused about the time.

The bosses were out all day yesterday, extending their Easter holiday without telling us, so we casually left about 4pm. I got all my dry cleaning done when I arrived home, and had a very slimming dinner of oranges, cheese and a glass of creamy milk. Then one of Jenny's admirers phoned. He is an absolute scream and reminds me of Bev's Bobbie. He said he was coming over to see us and bringing one of his friends. By the time they arrived the flat was full to overflowing with Liz and Helen sprawled all over the floor, talking to one of their pals off the 'Orcades', the ship they came to England on. Julie, Lou's girlfriend was here, just back from skiing in Austria, and tanned like a 'darkie'. Lou was back from his Army jaunt, begging for money because he was too lazy to get up and go to the bank. The record player was blaring with everyone singing along in completely different keys. Only four of us went up Highgate Hill to the 'Crown' Pub, and sat outside in the gorgeous warm night, drinking lagers and limeade. When we got back, we attacked Liz and Helen in their beds, and commenced to tickle them all to near death. Fred's friend, Eddie, asked me out this Friday evening. He is really super to be with, so I have accepted. Howard is supposed to be taking me to Rugby this weekend. He hasn't phoned yet to confirm, so things will be somewhat sticky by the end of the week!

Glad to hear you have accommodation booked. When you know the place, please tell me, and I will check the joint out to see if it is suitable to your tastes. If this weather is any indication of what summer is going to be like, I definitely would not bring any heavy woollens or coats. Just stick to light clothes because it does get very humid here during the middle of summer. The weatherman has said, England is going to have better weather than the Continent. This is the second week of fine weather, and there hasn't been a cloud in the sky for weeks, even at night.

Still nothing to do at work – the Bill and Sir arrived around 10.30, suntanned and smiling, and informing us they are going away tomorrow on a trip for this very short week. I am going to ask their advice about second-hand cars, as the Sir owns an E-Type Jaguar – lucky Sir.

So, you have the nerve to say you want to go touring around London in Howard's Porsche sports car! If you are serious, start doing some morning exercises in preparation to get in the car. The secret is to put your bottom in first and swing your legs up and down like a monkey, without showing your breakfast to passers-by. I am a veritable veteran at getting in but cannot master the feat of getting out in a lady-like fashion, so I wear trousers. Will write very soon, lots of love, Dianne

My mother's next letter began by documenting how hot their weather had been in April 1969, the hottest on record. At one stage she even talked about an article she read, documenting how England had experienced the hottest Easter for 45 years. I loved how my mother put PS at the beginning of her aerogramme, in this case letting me know my friend from Panama, Cliff Carrington, had called in to see her and my dad.

I don't wear step-ins anymore.

Friday, 11ᵗʰ April 1969
PS: Cliff called in on Thursday. He was going back to Newcastle.

To Our Dianne,

    The time is 8.30pm and the temperature is 82 degrees, 15 degrees above normal[30]. We have the fan on, and the 2 sliding doors, plus the front door open. Yesterday the temperature went to 90. It is the hottest April on record. Denise has gone out in her white sleeveless frock. Saturday, we have had the back patio painted green, instead of the different colours, and it looks very nice. I have done quite a lot of Denise's suit coat and hope to finish it this week. The days are still very warm. We received your letter this morning. Sunday, Russell came to Church this morning with Denise, Dad and me. They went out afterwards. Today has been another warm day, although a breeze has been around. Saw a piece in the Sunday Telegraph, where England has had the hottest Easter for 45 years. Seems it is worldwide. Our lawns are looking very well, and Dad cut them yesterday. Dad told Mr Laycock today we were going to England in three weeks' time, and he asked Dad if he could water or do anything while we were away. Well love, I will close now, hoping you are keeping well, and look forward to seeing you soon. Love and best wishes from your loving Mother. xxxxxxxxxxxx Well Darling it is 18 days to go. Won't be long now. Mum is having Eve, Alma, Florrie, Valmai, Betty and Dilda for lunch today, and I am running around getting everything ready. Looks like I will have to book the aerodrome. All the boys are ganging up for a send-off party. Hope Tina is well and Valda and David, and you of course are extra well. Keep your chin up. xxxxxxx Love Daddy xxxxxxxxxx

---

30   Temperatures were measured in Fahrenheit while I was overseas. A Metric Act was introduced in June 1970, and official use of metric was adopted in September 1972.

I quickly sent off a short aerogramme, telling my Mother I had split up with Howard. I knew she would be terribly disappointed that she may not be having a tour of London in his Porsche sports car. It didn't take me long to be introduced to another guy, called Eddie, who was a friend of my roommate, Jenny.

Wednesday, 16th April 1969 about 11.30

Dear Mum and Dad

I hardly got any sleep last night, what with tossing and turning, and thinking about how soon it was I'd be seeing you both. Thank goodness, the bosses are out today, or it could have been very touchy.

Our gas main has clogged up and we have no hot water. Since Sunday it has had to be a stand-up bath pouring boiled water over oneself after a good soaping beforehand. I was talking to Lou this morning, just before I left for work around 9.15 (disgusting, isn't it), and he is really looking forward to meeting you both, especially you Mum, after seeing some photos. He reckons you're a good sort, so watch it, because Louis is very charming when he wants to be. He is on holidays from College and may ask you out!!

I have been asked to a wedding on the 14th June, which is the Saturday before you arrive in London from your England tour. You remember when Jenny's friend stayed in the flat not long ago, and I told you she was getting married? The wedding is going to be one of those great social events. Hopefully we will have time to look for an outfit for me to wear to the wedding.

You will be very interested to know Jenny is Showroom Manageress for a dress-designing firm in the West End. She will be able to give you many hints on the best buys in London. Her firm specialises in simple styles, beautifully cut, and they sell to firms like Selfridges.

Jenny is really getting into deep water with her male friends. She has been going out with this gorgeous chap Robin for 4 years. He

I don't wear step-ins anymore.

persists in asking her to marry him, when she has no intention of marrying for years to come. At the moment Fred, a friend of Lou, is taking Jenny out. He is a fireman and is super lovely. I have been out with his friend Edward, (Eddie) who I am just waiting on to phone me again. Last Friday, Eddie took me to Bayswater for an Indian Curry. I am proud to say I can eat a Vindaloo curry which is the hottest curry made and didn't have to drink one drop of water. I must admit, I didn't taste the 2 cups of coffee I drank afterwards, but what an effort. One tends to get addicted to eating curries, even though they may be murderous to the stomach next morning. Each time I go out my taste buds water when passing a curry shop. Must take you to one when you're here.

We then went to see the movie 'Where Eagles Dare' starring Richard Burton. It was fantastic, but the film broke down 6 times. A rare event in London. The movie house was really packed, and as people can smoke in the cinemas here, everyone was chain-smoking while they tried to fix the film. It was one of the funniest happenings I have ever witnessed. When the movie ended, we just had enough time to get about 3 tubes home, and nearly missed the last one at Camden Town.

I had the most embarrassing morning of my life last Saturday, when I had to go to the Women's Clinic at London Hospital. I have been having trouble with the waterworks, so the doctor sent me along for a complete examination. One has to be so careful about personal cleanliness when sharing a flat with so many people and using the same toilet. The doctor at the clinic said I had an infection they cannot trace but gave me penicillin anyway. It was awful Mum when I had this examination. I couldn't even drag Val along with me because she was in Ireland. I just sat there turning a deeper shade of red as the morning progressed. The nurses even drained me of some of my rich, beautiful red blood, and I have to go back this Friday for the results. The only good thing about it all, is it didn't cost me a penny! One has no time to be colour prejudiced either because the nurse was black as black, but one of the nicest people I have yet to meet and very efficient. I didn't get back to the flat until 2.30, when I had to then go shopping with Liz and Helen. We had an hilarious time in the supermarket, buying food for the 'kitty' and each other. In all, we had 1 pound 10 shillings to spend on general all-purpose stuff for the flat. When the shop girl told us, it was only going to cost 1 pound 5 shillings, we all burst into screams of laughter, and everyone just stared at us like a lot of dumb sheep.

About 9.30pm, and with nothing to do, we dragged ourselves together, and got the bus up the hill to Highgate Village. Popped into the 'Flask' public house, which was built in 1600, and is so tiny one has to bend their head to walk in the door. Liz wanted an advocaat and cherry brandy, so we thought OK, but when the chap asked for 15 shillings, our jaws dropped, and this really depleted the cash reserves. To our luck, a nice Turkish gentleman, dressed in the most outlandish clothes, rescued us. He bought us another round plus potato crisps, and we had a very funny conversation with him. He stood about 5 foot, including his hat, and it was hilarious to see us great big hulks towering over him. I'm a bit over 5'6, Helen is short, but Liz is nearly 6' and very extroverted. The lady owner of the pub spoke to us too, and invited the whole lot of us back again, promising souvenirs. Mahmet the Turk invited us to a club in Muswell Hill, but we couldn't get in and had to hitchhike back to Archway, because the tubes and buses had stopped. When we got in around 2am Sunday morning, we joined the rest of the flatmates in contacting spirits again. We didn't have much luck, as most of the spirits talked in foreign tongues and were very tired. Helen got upset and went to bed, while Liz, Mahmet and I stayed up listening to music and chatting until 7am. Fred, the fireman came over on Sunday, so Liz cut and shampooed his hair for free. I have never witnessed anything quite so funny, as Fred kneeling over the bath having his hair soaped and washed. I was so exhausted by 3pm in the afternoon and crashed and didn't wake up till 8 in the night. I enclosed a great map of London in my letter to Denise, and also an advert about trips to

I don't wear step-ins anymore.

Ireland, which you may be interested in. I have sent away for the brochure, and you can see it when you arrive.

I got a lovely letter from Valmai last week. I wrote her a really long letter yesterday and said Mike will have to build an extension on the house if they persist in increasing the size of their family! Val sounds as mad as ever. She took one whole page to explain she left an aerogramme on the buffet addressed to me, and then found it had disappeared. I suppose she thought the postman had visited one night and took it while she was sleeping. Val also told me she had a letter from Jan saying she had moved into a flat in Bayswater with some other girls and was planning a trip on the Continent during April/May. I think I will write her a note this week, and may visit her, even just to find out what has happened to Miss Chapple. I wouldn't be at all surprised to learn Kris just up and left Jan without so much as a word.

Woolworths is really fantastic over here. Yesterday I bought a pair of stocking tights with a lycra girdle attached, which can be used when the stockings ladder. They only cost about 12 shillings (about 2 Australian dollars). So comfortable, and I must give you some to take home for Denise, or do they sell them at home now?

Betty wrote me a lovely letter yesterday. I seem to have received about 30 letters yesterday in all! She is writing to you very shortly and said if we plan to go to North Wales we should come through Cheshire and visit her. I suppose she will write about this in her letter to you, and I know she would love to have us visit. There is nothing nicer than meeting people you know while in another country, and not just as a tourist. I will always remember those few days I spent with Betty and her husband, and how nice they were to me. Her husband reminds me so much of Mr Seymour. He loves gardening and travelling around.

Liz and Helen are coming with me to a Jazz Concert tonight with Mahmet and a few of his friends. We are all meeting at Charing Cross Station about 6.15, and I think the club is in the Strand right next to Trafalgar Square. Lots of love, Dianne xxxxxxxxxxxx

My next letter clearly showed how nervous I was at the thought of my parents visiting in less than three weeks. I was impatient and lacking in sleep. My description of the Nell Gwynne led to this pub becoming a favourite watering hole for my father and me, especially as it was situated very close to where they would be staying in The Strand.

Friday, 18th April 1969

Dear Mum & Dad,
I received your aerogramme dated 11th April and agree about the car hire business. Last Wednesday evening I went to a recording Jazz Session at the BBC Studios at Charing Cross. It was wonderful, but beforehand we had dinner at the 'Nell Gwynne' Tavern in the Strand close to where you will be staying. We walked up this tiny archway, and the pub was so quaint I must take you there. You have to sit at the counter and look at all this glorious food piled up in front of you. I had ham and veal pie with eggs baked into the meat. The pastry was very unusual, and of course, fattening. It only cost about 5 shillings with a huge salad as well. We met a barrister who talked to us about his job in the Courts. He shouted us a drink too, which was very nice of him! The weather is still fantastic, and I was surprised to hear of your scorching weather at home.
I still haven't heard from Val and David since they went to Ireland 2 weeks ago. They must be still getting over the effects of all that Irish whiskey. It always amazes me how less often one sees people when they live nearby like Val does. Distance definitely makes the heart grow fonder. As you said Dad, during those first 3 days I will be very calm, and not wear the 2 of you out. I will try not to drag you all over the place, but there is so much I want to show and tell you a few weeks just isn't ample time. Maybe we could take the riverboat up the Thames to Kew Gardens and Hampton Court on one of those first days. This would be very relaxing. The

rate I'm going I will wish and pray every day away until you arrive. If only it was tomorrow! Until I see you, All my love, your daughter, Dianne xxxxxxxxxxxxxxx

It was now only two weeks until my parents would arrive in London.

Monday, 21st April 1969

To Our Dianne,

Have been out with Dad since 8.30 this morning. We went down to Wollongong, then back home through Campbelltown, Camden and Fairfield. It has been a glorious day, might add I slept most of the way home, with the sun on my face. We had to buy another suitcase at Roselands, similar to the mustard one you have got, only this was a blue one. On arriving home, we found your letter to us and one to Denise. We got your aerogramme on Saturday. Hope your infection clears up and be very careful using any hand towels. You and Denise used to call me 'Fanatic Fan', but you can't be too careful. Went to St George Leagues Club and met Aunt. I had my usual prawn cutlets and 2 helpings of sweets. Aunt was wearing a nice grey flannel stripe coat and frock. She gets them factory price $8 and saw them at Miranda Fair selling for $15. Dad will tell you what to do at the end of this letter. Russell hasn't been the best and has a postponement of going into the Army for a few weeks. Another letter has arrived for Cliff. Today is another beautiful autumn day. Last Saturday I took Denise to Town, and she bought a nice navy all-weather coat. Naturally, I had the job of hemming it up plus the sleeves, but it looks nice on her. By the way, I have put $30 away for you when I come over. I have taken some of your clothes to wear and have put some money away whenever I use them. You can buy a frock for the wedding. Would like to meet Jan, and if possible, ring and tell her so. I haven't started to think about leaving. Uncle Albert is going to come up and water the garden. Alma and Mr Rogers will water the front. Darling I will close now, hoping you are feeling better, and enjoyed reading 'Anything to Declare'. Love and kisses till I see you on Thursday fortnight, Mother xxxxxxxxxxxxxxxxx Hello love, how are you? We would like you to meet us at the airport. We will be staying at the Strand Palace Hotel, Strand, London, W.C.2. Drivers Licence No. C71922 International 489125. Australian Driving 39 years No Insurance Claim Expiry Date 1971. Air K.L. 127 from Amsterdam arrive London Heathrow 13.55 hours, 1.55 pm London time. Better to leave booking a car until we arrive for when we come back from our trip on Continent. If it is too far for you to come to airport, we could get the bus into town, and you could meet us at the hotel. Love Daddy xxxxxxxxxxxxxxxxx

I had to cancel my weekend trip to Paris just prior to my parents arriving in London. I had been planning it for ages with my cousin Valda, but I felt it unfair to have time off work with my parents, as well as for a weekend to Paris.

Friday, 25th April 1969

Dear Mum and Dad,
    Well, it isn't very far off until you leave, and I suppose, by next week, it will be useless to write any more letters. This aerogramme may just reach you in time, knowing the mail service. I saw Val for lunch yesterday. She has been through a hectic time since Easter, which has left her a bit out of sorts. She mentioned she had written to you not long ago about everything, and how much she is looking forward to seeing you both. David is going to swap his car around for a larger one, so we can all come to the airport to meet you and bring you back to your London Hotel. We had to cancel our Paris trip because of the situation at the office. I am a bit upset, but it is best in the long run. The bosses have been great with the time off I want, and I felt it wasn't right to take 3 days off sick just before you arrive.

I don't wear step-ins anymore.

We put another ad in the paper, for a flatmate to share with Sally. She came last night to see the flat and moves in on the 12th May. Her name is Cathryn Adatte and she is French/Swiss. At the moment she is doing Au Pair work, but next month she will be doing secretarial work at the YWCA. Her boyfriend is very nice. He is a Dental Surgeon at Guys Hospital where they had a heart transplant not long ago. They both stayed and chatted with us for hours last night, and we got to know her quite well. Liz and Helen left for Manchester today, and it is going to be very quiet without them around. Next week we are having a big party, so it gives us a good excuse to clean the flat before you arrive. Sally and I are off to a party tonight. We have no idea how we're getting home, so we may be sleeping on the floor. It's a very miserable morning outside, and combined with the road works, things are very bleak. It's so bad, the sky might open up any moment. We just got our rent bill at the flat totalling 74 pounds. I nearly had a breakdown working it out 6 ways. The things one has to worry about when taking on a flat. Never again! Haven't heard from 'Nece' for ages. Is she all right? Give her my love please. Well, I will see you very soon. Until then, lots of love, Dianne xxxxxxxxxxxxxx

I still hadn't heard from my sister, whom I sometimes called 'Nece'. She had been very busy buying our mother a very weird Mothers' Day card.

Saturday, 26th April 1969

To Our Big Girl,
The weather today has been glorious. I washed Dad's and my bedspreads, blankets and the blankets on top of the mattress, bedroom curtains and the curtains on the front door. Later this afternoon we went to the Cemetery, and took the flowers up for Mother's Day, Sunday week. Nanna's grave looked very nice when it was finished. Have just got off the phone after speaking to Aunt for

over an hour. Aunt called in yesterday with Valmai, Michael, Lisa and Uncle Bill, but I missed them, as we left to go to Balgowlah at 12.30 to play Bowls. I didn't play, but Jack Porter, Dad and Sam Forrest did. Denise sent me a Mother's Day card by post, and I received it this morning. It is not the typical type, but as follows. A Mother is sitting on a chair, and there is the following verse.

'Mum, you've scrubbed for me, and cooked for me, and washed for me, and ironed for me, and cleaned for me, and helped me and taught me, and worked your fingers to the bone for me' On the next page it says.

'So, what's your angle?'

Hope the weather is still holding good. Well Darling, hope you are feeling better, and the tests are OK. Seeing you in 12 days. Love and big hugs and kisses from your loving Mother xxxxxxx at the conclusion of Holy Communion this morning our Rector offered a prayer for Dad and me to have a happy reunion with you, and a safe return home. It was very moving. Well love, today is Sunday. In 5 days, we are on our way to see you. Hope you are well, and everything is O.K. Tell Tina her kiss is getting close. See you soon Darling, love from Daddy xxxxxxxxxxx

Thursday, 1st May 1969

Dear Dianne,

PS: Aunt lent me her folding umbrella. Do you think I will need it?

Received your aerogramme this morning with a letter from Betty. Tell Valda I haven't received a letter from her since last Christmas. Hope she enjoyed her trip to Ireland. Betty asked us to stay with her, if we were touring the Lakes and North Wales. I would like to see her. She said they have had a long winter, but luckily, they didn't lose a single plant or shrub. Russell came over to say goodbye. Denise is going to stay at Russell's place on Friday and Saturday nights. Was speaking to his mother on the phone. Was disappointed you didn't go to Paris, but perhaps you will go another time. Aunt said I have to give her love to you and Valda and David. Tell Valda her mother and father are looking well. Robert came up to see me, and his trousers looked a red colour to me with a white skivvy. He looked very nice. Was on his way to see Lynne. He liked my off-white coat. Reckons I will come back a mini-skirted matron. Well Darling, looking forward to seeing you, and hope you and Valda don't notice too much change in your dear old Mother. Love, kisses and big hugs from your loving Mother. 'May God watch over you, till we meet again'.

The day after my parents arrived home from visiting me, my mum penned an aerogramme. It had been a wonderful reunion, even though she had refused to set foot in the flat at Archway. The first time she entered the flat, the kitchen was piled high with dirty dishes, so it was agreed I would meet her at the hotel in The Strand whenever we went out as tourists. Dad, on the other hand, fitted right in at the Archway flat, and even spent a lot of time in the Archway pub, directly across the road from our flat. We had huge sash windows the full length of the lounge room. When it was open we could sit on the ledge and practically be handed a beer from the bar. Dad loved it as it was frequented by mostly Irish families who had settled in the area.

Another favourite haunt was the Nell Gwynne, the pub close to his hotel. We could leave Mum at the hotel room, and he would spend hours in the Nell Gwynne chatting up the barmaids. We saw many shows and markets, and had fabulous meals out. I joined them on a wonderful bus tour of Ireland, although we were not able to visit Northern Ireland. Mum also returned to numbering her letters to me.

Saturday, 25th June 1969 (Letter 1)

To Our Dianne,
The time is 8.45 pm, sitting in my own chair, watching T.V. and the 'Black and White Minstrels' are on again, in a new series. There is

no place like home, love. The place looked nice, with yellow and red chrysanthemums, sweet peas and two bunches of violets. We arrived at Mascot at 7.20 am Friday and Denise was there. She stayed at Russell's the night before and came in a taxi. The trip from Rome was good. From Beirut to Manila, it was a full plane, but later, Dad and I had three seats between us. He took the armrests out, so I had my legs up, and the swelling had nearly gone by the time we arrived home. In Rome, which is 1 hour ahead of London, we did 2 tours on Wednesday. In the morning we were lucky to go to St. Peters. The Pope had a service for young people from different countries, and also for American sailors. The Basilica is very ornate and huge. We managed to get a position down on the side aisle, and the Pope wasn't very far away. We could see him in comfort. He spoke mainly in Italian. His English is faltering. The parks in Rome are not as well kept as others we have seen on the tour. We had lunch on the tables in the street. I had a pot of tea (2 cups), Dad had a hamburger, a small bottle of Coke, and it came to around 18 shillings. Everywhere on the tours, men are approaching wanting to sell slides. We bought one lot, roughly 50 slides, for one English pound which was very cheap. Yesterday has been lovely. It has been fresh in the morning, but the sun has been nice. Auntie Betty and Uncle Albert are bringing some of my pot plants up in the morning. When you see Valda, tell her I have a pot plant inside the wicker box she gave me. Give my regards to Tina, Liz, Helen, Lou, Jenny and Sally. Love from Mum. Hello Love, hope you are well. We are home in the sunshine. Rome was nice and we had a good trip home. Love to all and look after yourself. Love Daddy xxxxxxxxxxxx

I finally wrote to my parents a week after they left to go home. It had been great catching up with them, especially on our guided bus trip around Ireland.

I don't wear step-ins anymore.

Monday, 30th June 1969

Dearest Mum and Dad,

It is nearly a week since you left, and it seems like ages. We have had perfect weather of course, not one cloud in the sky from 5 in the morning to 10 at night. Had to draw the curtains to keep the glare out at 5.30am last Saturday morning. Sometimes I feel like going into the office very early and finish at lunchtime. Mr O'Dell is away for 2 weeks, and Mr Barton went at midday and won't be back till Wednesday. Did they leave us some work to finish, and all fiddly things too!

I think I told Denise about meeting Noelene Batley last Tuesday night, and about me nearly fainting from the closeness of the Pub. I haven't seen Val since, but will do so, no doubt, before she leaves for Scotland this week. Last night I watched the show about the Royal Family, which did raise a laugh or two from the multitude in the flat, including all the visitors who barged their way in. At one stage during the weekend, I think I counted 10 people in all, sitting in the living room. Liz went to a party at Whopping in your original East End with a chap off the same ship she came over on. It seemed half of London's Underworld was there, plus film stars and models. She drank champagne till it poured out of her ears and had to go to work on the Sunday for stocktaking. It was quite amusing when Liz finally reached home around 8 on Sunday night. She had an 'all dressed up and nowhere to go look' written across her face.

I cleaned like mad over the weekend, especially the bathroom and living room. This morning I woke to find the sink full of dishes belonging to his lord and master.[31] As it is the beginning of the month and rent time, I wrote Lou a nasty note, saying if he didn't have his rent by tonight, he had better leave the country. Getting rent out of him is like getting heat from snow!

---

31   That was my nickname for Louis, the only male in our flat.

Received a letter from Betty last Friday. She now has the phone on, so when I feel like darting up north, she wants me to ring her, which is so much easier than writing. I really wish you had met her while you were here. Never mind, I plan to write and tell her all about you. She would like you to drop her a line once in a while, because she does like hearing about Sydney. Liz has been terribly homesick since she saw you Saturday night. She is waiting patiently for letters from home. I remember quite vividly how homesick I was for months after I arrived. It does wear off when one finds roots to hold on to something, even if what you are holding on to is very unsteady.

Last Saturday night while talking to this American chap, who came down to visit me, I suddenly thought how nice it would be to get on a plane bound for Sydney and pay a visit to 104. I then think about how free and cosmopolitan it is here, which turns me right off Australia. The only thing I desperately miss is you and the rest of the family and the occasional get-togethers. I couldn't live without all the wonder of England, especially London, which is totally non-existent at home. At times when I write home, I am very weary, so I had better finish, and hope to hear from you very soon. Lots of love, Dianne xxxxxxxxxx

Unlike some parents, Liz's especially, my parents wrote at least twice a week, and my Mother kept up with numbering hers. After telling her how homesick Liz was when they went home, Mum took it upon herself to ring Liz's Mum in Wagga Wagga. She was also visiting my cousin Valmai regularly, especially if Aunt had to work.

Thursday, 3rd July 1969 (Letter 2)

To Our Dianne,

Heard on the news tonight, one of the Rolling Stones died. I also saw Prince Charles on TV Tuesday night and stayed up till 1.30am. Thought the Queen looked nice. The Rector announced in Church how pleased he was we were back home, and he read aloud the cards we had sent home. Valmai received a letter from Jan. She is going to write to you and tell you her address. Saturday, I received your welcome letter this morning. Glad it has been fine. We are having cold weather. Tell Liz I am writing to her Mother tonight, and she will have to keep better hours, or she will have bags under the eyes. Hoping you are keeping well (does the brown dress look as nice as the beige?). Glad you have got a purse to match your shoes. Give my regards to the others, and big hugs and kisses from your loving Mother xxxxx Well darling, home again and am back at work. Can't get used to it. Denise was very happy to see us. She was at the aerodrome at 6.30, and she had the house all clean and polished. Hope you are going well, and Tina is well, also your bosses. Tell them it was very nice to meet them, and sorry we didn't have more time to buy a drink. Hope all at the flat are going well, and you have settled down again. Give my love to all. I miss you, so look after yourself and keep well. Lots of love, Daddy xxxxxxxxxxxx

I had some fantastic news to tell my parents. Our flatmate Cathy had asked me to come and stay in her Swiss village St Imier, situated in the predominantly French-speaking Jura Mountains.

Friday, 11th July 1969

Dear Mum and Dad,

I'm pleased you had a pleasant trip home from Rome and happy to be back at 104. As soon as you left, we had some glorious sunny and very warm days. However, I am afraid to say we have seen the last of summer. Haven't heard from Val since she left a couple of weeks ago and have missed our lunch meetings terribly.

Before I get too deep into this letter, I have some very important news. I am off to Switzerland with Cathy on the 1st September to visit her family. I am also going to do some work, which she tells me is in big demand, and more than likely, learn French too. Cathy's family live in a village called St Imier, which isn't too far from Geneva and Lausanne. The village is in a valley between mountains and 10 minutes from ski slopes. I cannot say how long I might be there; it all depends on if I get work to pay my board. If I don't find something I will move on to warmer parts and tour. In other words, I am not going to bother about future plans except have my return fare with me in case something goes wrong. This will be a great chance to get to know the people, and not just skim the surface like an ordinary tourist.

On the way over we are spending about a week in Paris with a friend of Cathy who lives in the suburbs, so there again I will be with an actual inhabitant, even though I won't be able to talk to her. Cathy and I have only known each other since she moved in last May. She thinks it will be beneficial to have someone to speak English with, plus a travelling companion. I don't have to explain how beneficial it will be for me, and I am getting very excited. Told Mr Barton today and he thinks the whole thing is marvellous. He has promised to break the news very gently to Mr O'Dell when he gets back from Spain.

The flat is finishing at the end of August because Liz and Helen are going to Spain. Jenny wants to stay at home and save. Sally is going to Norwich to do her midwifery, and I don't fancy getting new people in again, or spending another winter in the flat. I will send my Sitmar ticket home for you to cash it for me at the office in Sydney. I am sure Val said it could not be done this end. I don't think you should send it back to me (Bank Draft or Traveller's Cheque form) until I get settled, or it will get lost. I will have to send my International Driver's Licence home to be renewed too, and maybe a few things I don't want to take with me. Anyway, Mr Barton has ordered me to finish and post this letter, but I will write a longer letter over the weekend. I am so looking forward to getting out of the flat, but not leaving England. I don't really know if I will get back except to see places I haven't visited. Love to all, will write very soon. Dianne

I don't wear step-ins anymore.

I was really missing my parents since they had left England for home. It didn't help when the mail took over a week to arrive from Sydney. I also loved it when I received letters from other family members, such as Valda's Mum, Aunty Betty, and my Mum's sister, Aunt. Aunty Betty had a wicked and quirky sense of humour.

Wednesday, 23rd July 1969

Dear Di,

Well ducks, must say I nearly fainted dead away when I received your letter, as I haven't heard a peep from you since Xmas, and was beginning to think you might have landed yourself a flash job as Queenies aid at Bucks Palace. So pleased to hear you are well and enjoying yourself like crazy. I saw a photo of you your mother had, and I really am wrapped in your short blonde locks and told your mother so too. I think it looks fab. Valda and David are now in Spain, lolling about in the sun and having a ball, I hope. We are pleased to hear you are going to move on to another country, and I can just see you now hanging five off the Swiss Alps, yodelling up somebody's Khyber. But do be careful and don't climb too high, will you? Robert is well and still taking Lyn out. They have been going around for 12 months now. He still insists it is not serious. What an actor! What sort of a summer are you having at present? Our winter hasn't been too bad at all so far.

Rube and George said they both had a good time abroad, and we thought they both looked well when they came home. How did Rube's pointy toes go over up Carnaby Street?[32] Did you enjoy their stay? Valda rang me up last Wednesday, gee it was great. I am so looking forward to seeing them again. I get sick on the tummy

---

[32] My mother was famous for wearing high heels with extremely pointy toes. When she died in 2009 at the age of 87, my sister and I found three wardrobes filled with boxes of shoes, stacked neatly on top of one another. She frequently accused me of being a hoarder, but her shoe collection covered decades of shoes from the 1970s onwards.

thinking about it. Al has missed Val very much too. It will be 2 years next month since she went away.

We had a smashing night out last week at the 'Top of the Cross'. The food was terrific, and the view was really great. A good band played soft music and we had plenty of wine but had big hangovers the next day. Also went to the Mandarin Club for a smorgasbord lunch the other day. It was great, as much as one could eat for $1.00. Too much! Well ducks, have run out of news so will close now, and remember, if you can't behave, be careful. Lots of love from all of us, xxxxx Betty B. Yates, Sunny Sydney, Australia, 'Down Under.'

I sent an extra-long and ultra-stimulating letter to my parents. I was now getting excited about living in Switzerland.

Friday, 25th July 1969

Dearest Mum and Dad,

As I struggled to the kitchen this morning, low and behold I tripped over stacks of mail, all except 2, for me: a letter from you and Dad, Denise and a bank statement showing 50 pounds on the credit side, and a cheque book with a compliments slip from the Manager!! He must be happy since I got out of the 'red'! And what a super day it is – so sunny and air pure enough to breathe. I took a different bus this morning and walked the length of Harley Street from Regents Park end, and the sights I saw along the way. Arabs dressed in their long robes, and all the cabbies stopped for me at crossings, plus a little lady on a bike who smiled at me as well. Londoners are really very happy when the sun is shining.

Had a great weekend just passed, as our American G.I. friends from Ipswich came for a visit. We had a small party Friday night, and then I was talked into going to the British Grand Prix at Northampton. I spent most of the time in a huge parka sleeping on the side of the track. Visited the 'Wagon and Horses' pub in Hertfordshire, a favourite

I don't wear step-ins anymore.

of Val and David, and then got back in time for another party at the flat, as Sally was leaving. Sunday morning around 4.30 am I had a nap until 10 am and then cleaned up with the help of friends who had stayed. Cathy told us she would make Spaghetti Milanese, so Liz, Cathy and I hiked all over Hampstead, Hendon and other places looking for a shop selling spaghetti. We left around 3 pm and didn't get back 'till 6. The meal was superb. We washed it down with Bitter Ale, and I had 3 helpings, much to everyone's amazement.

After so much gorging, we turned the box on to find the spacemen on the way to the moon. We all sat down, and it was hilarious because David Frost had this big show on, plus a great coverage of what was going on up there. Everyone was in great form, and sarcastic and very funny remarks were being swapped the whole night from Liz, Helen and myself. David Frost was taking 'phone calls from people, and he had a panel of very distinguished guests discussing the Moon. He had Cilla Black, Engelbert Humperdinck, Miriam Hopkins, Eric Sykes, and an Australian entertainer Ken Dodd. They also had direct link ups with TVs at Trafalgar Square and a disco called 'Revolution', which is a great hangout for celebrities and way-out people. The entire cast of 'HAIR' was there, Jackie Stewart (he had just won the Grand Prix), Richard Harris (Camelot) and Jane Asher. Cilla Black has had a nose job and looks so much more attractive. I would have thought it might have affected her style of singing.

Have you heard of Ken Dodd?[33] Remember when we went to Madame Tussauds, and we came to a group of entertainers like Sophia Loren and Jane Mansfield? Well, he was the one with buckteeth and bulging eyes. I have only seen him on TV with his Diddy Men puppets and didn't feel crazy about him either. When I saw him on David Frost, what a change. He is very clever and so funny. At one stage he was imitating the spacemen talking to 'Huston'. In between sentences he blew through his huge buckteeth, and it sounded just

---

33   I now regularly watch Ken Dodd, sometimes when he is hosting the Sydney Mardi Gras Parade on television.

like the pips on the radio they use when talking. Helen and I were the only ones listening at this time, and we just broke up and rolled on the floor in hysterics.

This went on until 2.30 am Monday morning. At about 3 am, the station went via satellite to outer space, and we witnessed Armstrong climbing down the ladder to place his foot on the surface of the Moon. I can't describe the feeling I felt when I saw this happen. It was just as though I was dreaming; yet I didn't feel a bit tired. Helen, Cathy, Sally and one of the American G.I.s Lee, watched it as well, and they felt the same. We saw it so clearly and the whole experience was amazing. I only got a few hours' sleep in the morning, and just before leaving for work, we saw them getting back into their spacecraft on the return to the mother ship. Naturally, I am getting fed up with hearing about the whole thing. All this up-play of news takes the aweness away from it. I am grateful for having been alive to watch this fantastic event, and to be able to tell my children about it. Just think back to when you were young, and the thoughts you may have had about the Moon, if any, and how impossible it all seems, you witnessed a man walking on this same Moon! What a thought.

One hypocrisy is while men are walking on the Moon, 3 major wars are still being fought on Earth, plus numerous smaller ones. It seems such a waste of good money and brains could be working to solve the problems here and now. Man is man, and will always strive to conquer the unattainable, even if it means putting himself into debt for a million years or wasting thousands of lives in the process.

On Wednesday night I met Cathy after work at The Strand, and we had dinner at the 'Nell Gwynne'. Pat was very upset he hadn't received a postcard from you, so if I were you, I'd pick a very nice card to send to him. Before I had time to balance myself on the stool, Pat was making me a Veal and Ham pie salad, which I paid with luncheon vouchers. Cathy had a French roll with ham. He asked me all about your trip home, and still raves about the Tuesday arvo before you left. He also sends his regards and hopes to hear from you very soon.

I don't wear step-ins anymore.

We stayed there for hours, and then walked down to Trafalgar Square before meeting a friend of Cathy, who was taking us to a debate at the House of Commons. The sights I saw while sitting near the fountain were unbelievable. One man had long blonde hair as long as Liz's, but dead straight and very thick. His girlfriend was combing it, and I think she was silently hoping it would transfer to her own head, poor dear. The tourists got an eyeful that evening and was it a hot one too. People were dabbling their toes in the fountain to keep cool, as it was so hot. We then walked down to Westminster and stood watching the river on Westminster Bridge. All the people on boats were enjoying themselves. The Debate was about Crime, and British Rail selling to foreign countries. Some members didn't like it at all because of the present situation in English economics. This chap who took us in is in charge of Education at the W.M.C.A. and gave us some very interesting information while we were with him. He told us one of the suffragettes had tied herself to the spur on the boot of a politician's statue in the hall and broke it completely off. We had to sign a form saying we wouldn't throw bombs or make a lot of noise while the debate was in session. It was so typically English, with the speaker in his wig, and all the members of Parliament falling asleep while one man was talking on the most boring subject. We stayed for a good half hour which was the most we could bare. Helen and Liz went to see a flat last night, but they were very disappointed. They might be staying on until the flat ends at the end of next month. By the way, the address in Switzerland is 34 Pierre-Jollissaint, 2610 St-Imier, Switzerland.

Mr Barton just informed me I am free to use his thatched cottage in Paignton near Torquay, whenever I like. Cathy and I had intended doing a trip before leaving, and we might make our way down to this part of the coast in 2 weeks' time. Isn't he sweet? Valda rang me last Thursday, just before they left for the Continent, and will be going through Switzerland in September, which means I will get a visit. Great, just great.

Dear Dad, thank you for your huge piece of news. When I get home, we will tour the whole way around Australia by car. I would appreciate you lining up some jobs for me with nothing to do with typing, or taking shorthand, or in an office. Everyone sends their love, and Pat at 'Nell Gwynne' would like a postcard off you post haste, so continue your fine effort of writing such informative letters. He asked me why I was drinking beer, and I told him I only drink shots with my Father. Before I get too fat and start growing a beer gut, you had better send me a drinking allowance. The girls in the flat have the hide to ask me when the off-licence opens and closes, as they think I live there - what a cheek!

Lots of love to you and Mum. Good to hear you are losing weight, and I will write soon. Tell the 'little tart' I am writing to her after getting back from Cheshire on Sunday evening. Also, I am getting my hair tinted back to the original colour next Tuesday. I don't intend having foreigners do it when I leave. Dianne xxxxxxxxxxxxxxx

It was the one-year anniversary of my leaving home in August 1968. I was only a couple of months away from travelling to Switzerland via Paris, and disaster happened in the form of Lou Pocock. He decided to run out without paying his rent, leaving me holding the bag.

4th August 1969

Dearest Mum & Dad,

I didn't want to write at this time, as things are very bad with me, and I am afraid this letter may sound depressing. Lou left without paying his rent, and I have been lumbered with all the money problems to sort out. Switzerland is a long way off now, and I am quite upset to say the least, at missing this trip, but I can't go without some money saved. Liz and Helen are undecided about what they want to do but indicate to some extent they would like me to share a flat with them. I think 2's company but 3 is a crowd, so I feel I should start

I don't wear step-ins anymore.

looking again. On the brighter side, Mr Barton wants me to stay on with another rise and my Tax Rebate is due very shortly. I am told it is a sizable sum! No word from Val yet. I do miss her very much even though we only saw each other very infrequently. My hair is back to its original colour and I will be sending some prints very soon. I will write again when I get over this mess. Your loving daughter, Dianne xxxxxxxxxxxxxx

Straight away my Mum and Dad wrote back to console me. My Father even offered to send me money to cover the rent Lou refused to pay me.

9th August 1969

To Our Girl, Saturday,

We received your aerogramme this morning and was disappointed to hear you are not going to Switzerland. You should have made Lou pay in advance, and he certainly hasn't any principles. If you know where he went to school, I would go there and try to see him. It certainly teaches one a lesson. Sometimes love, these things happen for the best, but at the moment you might not be able to see it. God never closes a door, unless he opens a window. By the way, Denise bought some lovely red and white carnations, purple stock and yellow daffodils. Our place looks like a florist shop. Russell came to dinner tonight, and I let them have dinner on their own. Denise set the table, and they dined by candlelight with Mother being the waitress. They had T-bone steak, chips and peas, plus a large dish of strawberries and cream. They have gone to see Valmai in Hospital, then on to Libera's place as she is 21, and is having a party. Her Mother and Father gave her a lamb's wool coat. Denise will tell you all about it. Was Mr Barton pleased you are staying? July was the hottest July in 23 years. The mornings are getting lighter, and the weather has been lovely, although we could do with some rain. Hope you received my last letter with the money to get your coat fixed. Well Darling, hoping to hear from you, and glad you wrote and told us all about it, after all this is what God made 'Mums and Dads' for. Big hugs and kisses from your Loving Mother xxxxxxxxxxxxxxxxxxxxxxxxxx Dear Dianne, how are you now? I didn't think much of that Bloke living with you. Darling let me know how much you are short. You can square things up later. Write to me and let me know as soon as possible so I can help you. Remember, I'm still your Dad and will help you. Hope all the girls are well and Tina. Sorry to hear you are not going to Switzerland, but you know what you are doing. What you want to do is make everybody pay a week in advance, so keep your chin up. Let me know so you won't have to worry. What about your licence and things? Do you want me to fix them for you? Love from Dad xxxxxxxxxxxxxxxxxxx

In only a few short days, I had the money from advance rent, and was able to go to Switzerland after all. I had also been talking about travelling home overland with Liz and Helen, the two Australian girls from Wagga Wagga who rented the last bedroom of the Archway flat. But before that, Helen got married, leaving me and Liz to travel home together in 1970.

Tuesday, 12th August 1969

Dearest Mum and Dad,

Thank you so much for the 15 dollars. I took my coat in and they are shortening it without taking any fur off for a fiver. As every man and his dog are on their holidays of late, I won't have time to get it cleaned before I leave for Switzerland.

Cathy and I will spend a week in Paris with her friend, who has been kind enough to invite us to her flat as she lives by herself. Paris is very empty of people while the holidays are on, so she is pleased we will be keeping her company. The only expenses will be food and the Metro (underground trains). The overall boat and train fare

I don't wear step-ins anymore.

to Neuchâtel in Switzerland is only about 12 pounds, which is very cheap compared to transport in the UK.

I have a job lined up, and the firm is fixing up a work permit, which will save me lots of red tape. Cathy showed me her snaps of St. Imier in winter and it looks divine. Forget my last letter. I wrote it after a rotten weekend spent on my bed, with a blinding migraine so bad I couldn't move an inch. My trouble is I worry too much about little disasters. Judy, one of the nurses who used to live in the flat, invited me for a weekend sail on a Thames Barge in Norfolk on the Broads. I will send some snaps soon of me at the wheel and climbing the masthead. I've got a lovely tan. Went for a swim in my undies because I forgot my costume. I swam in the river near Ipswich when we docked at the village of Pin Mill, and I met some lovely people while I was away. These ships are very rare now. The one we had was 69 years old, and used to carry bricks all along the coast, and up the Thames to the London Docks. I enjoyed myself so much and can't wait to get the slides developed and send to you.

I am all alone at the office since Monday as Mr Barton is in Malta, Tina is in Spain and Mr O'Dell is up North and back tomorrow. Brought the Radio to keep me company, and it is pelting with rain at present. It has been terribly humid in London for weeks. This didn't do me any good, after not bathing from last Thursday evening until Sunday night – no baths on Barges, only cold water and a pump toilet! What next, it is raining but the sun is out!

In all sincerity, the thought of coming home frightens me, simply because I don't think I would settle down to anything. Liz and Helen feel the same, so this isn't stupidity on my part alone. I was just not born to be Australian, as now I feel I belong on this part of the equator, even to the point of liking this weather more. Sorry, I am getting deep again.

Liz and I went down 'The Angel' a few weekends ago to the market and had a great time. The market is called 'Chapple Street', and gives off a ring of Marrickville, if you know what I mean. This street is a lot different with the Jellied Eel sellers and second-hand stalls. Liz and

I both bought a book of poetry. I bought a Wordsworth edition with steel prints showing scenes from some of his best works. Liz got a nice Coleridge edition which I recite from. I get cries of delight from a varied audience at the flat. I recite the 'Ancient Mariner' from start to finish, without even a drink of water or something. (Let me get some air). We stopped at this ice-cream palace and had a lime soda, plus a huge 3 decker ice-cream. Lots of love, Dianne xxxxxxxxxxxxxx

When I think of what I had to go through to renew my licence or cash in a travel ticket, compared to what could be done now via the internet, it astounds me!

15th August 1969

To My Dear Mum and Dad,

I am enclosing my Sitmar ticket for you to cash. If a letter is necessary from me to authorise you to do this, please write back in the very near future. Would you also renew my Driver's Licence please – I think you already have forms signed for this purpose. Jenny just phoned me to say she has 2 girls for the flat until it finishes this month. This means they will pay Lou's rent. Generally everything looks very bright now, except for the noticeable decline in the weather. It's getting more like winter every day, and another reason to look forward to leaving this sun-forsaken country.

As I mentioned in my letter of Tuesday last, I will be back in London next January to meet Liz and Helen and plan our trip overland to Australia. They are as enthusiastic about this as I am, and Helen had me up till 2 am this morning, talking and raving about it. We got so tired I fell asleep on Liz's bed (she was away) with the radio on until about 6am. I woke to turn the radio off, and then we slept until 8.15 when we had to rush around to go to work. Lots of love, Dianne xxxxxxxxxxxxxx

I don't wear step-ins anymore.

My mother refused to get her hopes up about me actually going to live in Switzerland. My dad, on the other hand, loved the photo I had sent home, showing my hair returned to its former colour. He even said I looked beautiful, and ended his note wishing me a great trip to Paris and Switzerland.

Sunday, 17th August 1969

To Our Dianne,

Darling, I won't believe you are going to Switzerland, till I actually receive a letter from you when you arrive there. Auntie Betty called in last Sunday, and I told her you weren't going after all. I hope everything turns out all right for you. Today has been cold, and this morning I felt tempted to stay in bed but decided to get up at 6.40am. After all, if I can't put myself out to thank God for the things I have received, how can I expect Him to grant the requests I make. I'm going to see Valmai tomorrow afternoon, as I meet Aunt at Sydenham Station about 2.15 pm. It saves her a long walk to Bethesda Hospital. Dad said you would have to register your Sitmar Tickets in case they get lost. Will ring Auntie Betty in the morning about how to cash in your tickets and write at the end of this letter. Have been watching the revolt in Belfast on T.V. and can't see the sense in it. Hope it never comes to this for us. Where are Liz and Helen going? Have you sent any of your records home? We haven't bought a new needle for the radiogram since you went away. Dad and I have watched the 'Graham Kennedy Show', and he certainly grows on you. I like the skit where he has his breakfast with the other chap. They certainly get away with more than our TV chaps say. John Laws is leaving 2UE and going to 2UW. With his advertisements he is earning over $1000 per week. Well darling, will close now. Hoping you have been keeping well, and you can tell me if I shall write to your address in Switzerland. Love and hugs from your loving Mother xxxxxxxxxxxxxxxxxxxxxxxx Well here I am again. The weeks go past so quick. How are you love? Received your photo. It is a good one.

I like it. Better this way. It makes you look more beautiful and like yourself. Hope all your troubles are over, but don't forget to let me know what I asked you about in my last letter. Dianne re your letter about Ticket of Sitmar Australia. For credit you will have to send a letter to us with authorisation for Mum or myself to collect refund cheque. We will need another one to the Commonwealth Bank of Australia Marrickville address, so I can pay into your account. When doing these letters have your signature witnessed by someone and company name, like your boss (2 signature witnesses). Also see how much to register these with your tickets. You know what the mail is like. Hope Tina and the girls are all well. Darling, look after yourself and keep your chin up, and have a good trip to Paris and Switzerland. Best of luck and love from Daddy xxxxxxxxxxxxxxxxx

Mum was still not prepared to send any letters to Switzerland until she got a card from me with a Swiss address on it. I had sent some postcards from Paris on the way to St Imier, but this was my first letter to my family since leaving London by train.

1. Tony, Leon, Me and others at bar in Fairstar ship travelling to London August 1968

2. Kris, Jan and Me in Tahiti first port of call August 1968

3. Jan, Kris and Me drinking in our cabin before arriving London September 1968

4. Jan and Me sitting on steps of our first flat in Montagu Square London W1 September 1968

5. Roof of Archway flat near Highgate - Me, Helen, Cathy, her boyfriend and Mahmet November 1968

6. Mum and Me - Petticoat Lane London when she and Dad visited in June 1969

7. Dad and Me on steps of St Pauls London June 1969

8. Me, Mum and Dad Bus tour of Ireland June 1969
9. Me in my kangaroo coat Mt Soleil St Imier Switzerland - Winter 1969/1970
10. Osvaldo posing in snow Mt Soleil St Imier Switzerland - Winter 1969/1970

11. Me and helpful guys I met at Reggio Calabria Italy - April 1970
12. Inside of Sundowners bus at beginning of trip from London to India - July 1970
13. Viewing a broken axle on bus in remote part of Turkey July 1970

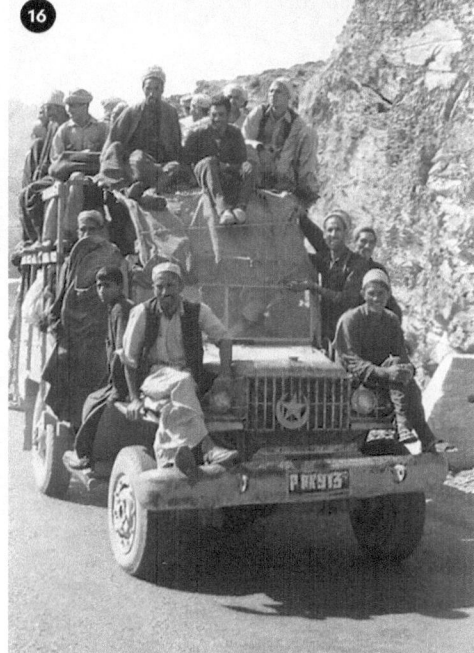

14. Waiting for our repaired bus Turkey township August 1970
15. Liz and me having a rest in ruins Persepolis Iran August 1970
16. A busload of locals travelling through the Khyber Pass between Pakistan and Afghanistan August 1970

17. Kabul Markets - Tribesman giving me a camel ride August 1970

18. Me and a python outside Delhi hotel September 1970

19. Me and Liz in bus with bubble pipes - India September 1970

20. Women shopping in Kabul Afghanistan August 1970

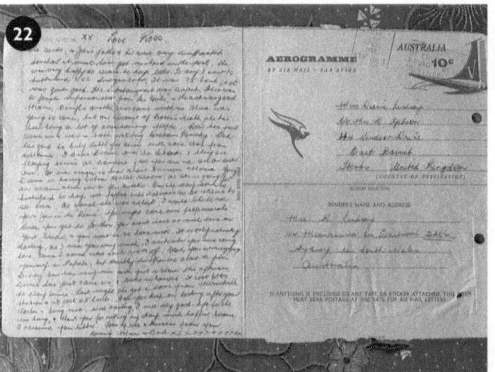
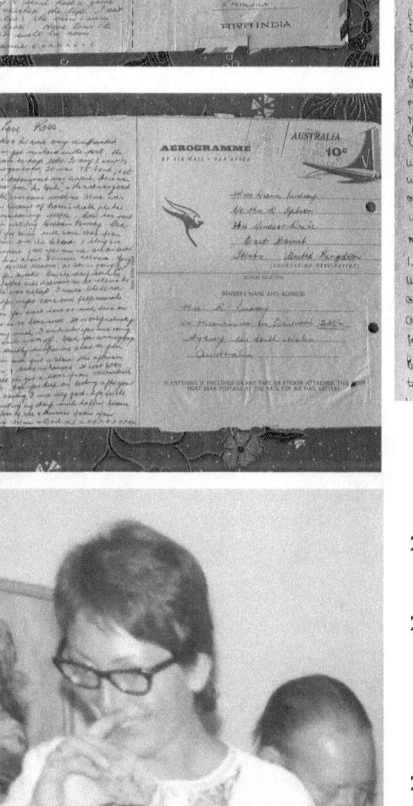
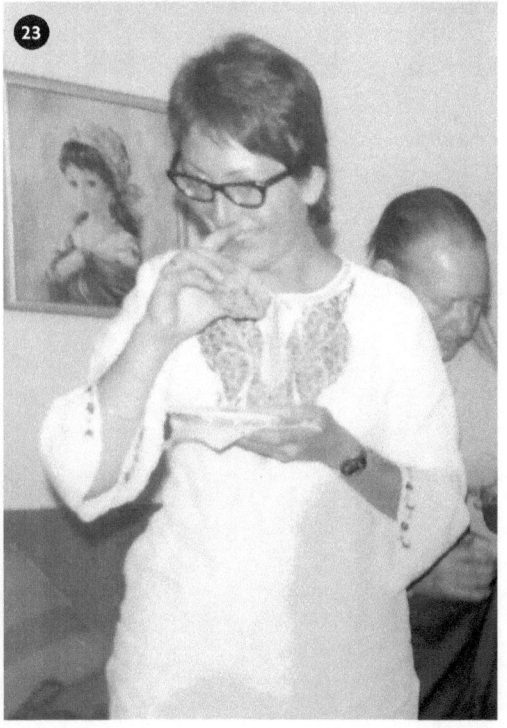

21. My aerogramme written to my family from Kashmir September 1970
22. Mum's aerogramme to me sent to my cousin's house in Barnet Hertfordshire which I received when I arrived in London September 1968
23. An aerogramme written by my sister to me when she worked at the Commonwealth Bank in Sydney August 1968
24. Me at home after arriving at Mascot airport, only a 10 minute drive to where I grew up in Earlwood. I was eating my favourite Aussie food September 1970

25. Me and Mum standing in front of the back trellis around Christmas 1970 a couple of months after arriving home

Part 3
St. Imier
Switzerland

Monday, 8th September 1969

Dearest Family,

    I am now sitting in bed writing to you from Cathy's house in Switzerland. I have a flock-filled eiderdown over me. There is a window beside me, and it feels like I am looking at a postcard of mountains. I can't believe life could be so beautiful as when I arrived here. The village is snuggled between two mountain ranges, so green and filled with masses of forests. Cathy's family is just the same as our family. They fight and argue over the dinner table, and in many ways, it's just as if I was home but with a different language. Cathy's father owns 3 floors, which are like separate flats. One sister and her family live on the 1st, Cathy's parents on the 2nd and there is an empty one on the top, which Cathy and I hope to rent while we are here. I prefer this arrangement as we could maintain our independence and pay our way, as you will no doubt agree with?

    Starting to learn the first stage of the language and can't wait till I can speak fluently. I watched TV last night and was surprised how easy it is to understand by just watching, with Cathy giving me some clues here and there. Am starting a bank account here so I can receive the deposit from the flat at Archway. It may take some time but will amount to about 80 pounds to be split between Liz, Helen, Cathy and myself. Not bad!

I am very worried about Liz and Helen, for they decided to hitch around Scotland and Wales, as they couldn't find a suitable flat to stay in during Winter. I just hope they are not in too much difficulty. When they packed their rucksacks, I had to persuade them to let me re-pack them, as they had too much stuff which was just not necessary. When I was at Outward Bound, I learnt a lot on this, and felt they were very inexperienced[34]. Mahmet went with them which was good. They were planning to stay and work up North, and he was coming back to England to study. All I am waiting for is a letter from them to know how they are getting on.

Cathy's sister has 2 gorgeous children called Cendrine and Pascale, who are just wonderful. The youngest, Pascale, looks very similar to Denise when she was young, except she wears huge glasses. She has a haircut just like Denise had when we went to Suva. I will take a photo and send it to you later after I settle down. Just had lunch, which is a ritual. The whole family comes home at 12 and it is the main meal of the day. At each meal we drink wine and eat bread without butter. Coffee after meals is not usual, but Cathy's mother knew I liked coffee, so we have it. The town is very small and built around a square with a Catholic Church at one end and a Protestant Church at the other end. The churches have always fought against each other. We had a look at the Protestant Church this morning, and it was built in Roman times. Most unusual design, with tunnels underneath leading to a castle in the mountains. These tunnels were used during wars. Each man in Switzerland must spend 3 weeks a

---

34   In 1964, not long after starting my first job with W.D. & H.O. Wills at Todman Avenue Kensington, I was encouraged by a staff member to spend 10 days with Outward Bound at Fisherman's Bend on the Hawkesbury River. I loved it. My mother wanted me to go to June Dally Watkins' deportment classes and learn how to be a lady. I refused, and my younger sister Denise completed them instead of me.

I don't wear step-ins anymore.

year in the Army as part of his service to his Country, and one sees a lot of soldiers while here.

I am enclosing 2 tiny engravings to remind you and Denise of Sacré Coeur Church in Montmartre Paris. It can be put on a bracelet or worn around the neck on a chain. When I go back to Paris, I am getting a couple more, as they are so lovely! Hope you and Denise like them. Awaiting your letters, yours with lots of love, Dianne xxxxxxxxx Dad, have not forgotten you, and will send something very soon from Switzerland.

My mother wrote about Bethesda Hospital in Marrickville, where my cousin Val had her baby Cassandra. Owned and run by the Salvation Army, this was where I was born in 1947. I did not find out until 2012 that I had been adopted immediately after birth, and brought home to live in Earlwood. My cousin Valmai had been affected by witnessing unmarried mothers giving birth to babies that would be taken off them. She was unable to say anything to me until three years after my mother, Ruby, passed away in 2009.

Monday, 8th September 1969

Miss Dianne Lindsay
34 Pierre-Jollissaint
2610 St-Imier Switzerland

To Our Darling Dianne,

Received your card this afternoon and was pleased to get it. Keep sending me one each week, as it makes my mind more at ease. Hope you enjoy yourself in Paris. We noticed the toilets as we had a tour of the city. Let me tell you the news, Valmai had another daughter, Cassandra Lorraine, born on Thursday, 28th August, in the afternoon. She was 6 weeks premature, as Dr. Segal had to bring her on. She weighed a little over 4 lbs, but later in the night, Matron had to transfer her to the Children's Hospital at Camperdown, next to

Wade House, where you had your tonsils removed. She is still in the humidicrib. Denise came with me on the following Saturday morning to see her, and one little foot was pressed on the glass. It was as long as half of my finger near my thumb. They had a tube in her nose to help her breath, but she is holding her own. Matron at the Bethesda Hospital (Salvation Army) gave her a tentative Baptism, as she was so small. At the Hospital there are a few other babies in the Humidicrib, and one is not as big as Cassandra. How do you like the name? I hope God spares her, so remember her in your prayers. We are in bed watching the TV, as today has turned out cold. Yesterday, Fathers' Day, we went to Kogarah R.S.L. Club, and had our dinner there. Auntie Betty, Uncle Albert, Uncle Harold and Auntie Ruby went with us. What do you know, I dug the lemon tree out on my own, and have another Christmas Tree to put in its place? I have cut back those two other trees in the backyard, and although I say it myself, the backyard looks very nice, especially around 6 o'clock in the night. The umbrella tree near the garage is growing beautiful. Remember when I cut it back and Dad said I had killed it? The roses in the front are beginning to sprout and are looking beautiful. I will say goodbye now Darling, as 'Ironside' with my pin-up man Raymond Burr, is coming on next on TV at 8.30 pm. Give my regards to Cathy, and may God watch over you, while you are thousands of miles away from me. Big hugs and kisses from Mother. xxxxxxxxxxxxxxxxxxxxxxx Hello Darling, very pleased to hear you got out of your troubles with the flat. Glad to hear you liked Paris and the tower and sights, and you are enjoying yourself. Give Cathy my best and congratulations. Well, the football finals are on. St George got done, Balmain played, Souths got done by 1 point. Balmain play Manly next week, and the winner plays South for the final. I watch every game. You would not know your Dad. I have lost 2 stone and took my new suit to the tailor this morning to have 4" taken out of the pants. Well you will enjoy Switzerland. It is a lovely place. We enjoyed every minute we were there. Look after yourself and keep your chin up. Let me know everything about Paris. Best of luck and love from Daddy xxxxxxxxxxxx

I don't wear step-ins anymore.

Switzerland had very strict employment laws for other nationalities. I had to go by train back across the border into France and then re-enter, having my passport duly stamped by the Swiss authorities.

15th September 69

Dearest Mum & Dad,

I now find I'm unable to get a job, unless I cross the border and apply for a permit, which may take another week. In the meantime, I must study my French and take a few lessons with a lady who teaches languages and lives next door. I wrote to our landlord at Archway now I have a Bank Account in St. Imier, and it won't be long until I get part of the 90 pounds deposit back. He said before we left most of it would be given back, and I have to split it 4 ways, taking Lou's share for myself as I paid his last month's rent. 'Good things come to those who wait'!

It's very peaceful here and taking a lot to get used to. I have been doing exercises, what with all the good food I consume now. I clean my teeth, even after lunch, as Cathy's mother puts so much garlic in everything, except coffee and breakfast cornflakes (thank goodness!) We went for a hike to the family's winter chalet in the mountains last week, with Cathy's brother-in-law and his 2 children. I found it very beautiful, and we will be spending weekends there when the snow arrives. The cows roam all over the hills, and there is a continual sound of bells clanging when they walk. It is a very beautiful and varied countryside. Cleanliness makes even the soil glow in the brilliant sunshine, under endless, clear blue skies. We went to a village on Sunday very close to the French border, with a sister and her fiancé. We saw some show horses too gorgeous to describe. We found a café where the owner had a baby monkey which I thought was a budgie. It whistled and made exactly the same sound as a budgie. Cathy's job pays over 20 pound a week, but she works from 7am till 6pm with one and a half hours for lunch. People don't have much time for a night life, as they must go to bed about 10pm each night to get up the next morning.

Did you like the pendants from Sacré Coeur (Sacred Heart) – you should have spent more time in Paris, for the Church is a masterpiece and so inspiring, as is most of Paris. Have still not heard a word from Liz and Helen, nor have any idea where they are. I miss these two very much, for we had such good times at the flat. People do mean a lot to other people's lives when parted.

Cathy's fiancé, Richard, who we are meeting next February/March in London when they get married, has posted my painting Cliff gave me to home. It may arrive before the end of the month, so don't throw it out because you think it looks gawdy – You would be surprised to hear it is very rare and part of a dress worn by South American Indians who live near the Amazon. It is very clever and colourful. How is Cliff? If you have his address, please send it over, as I would like to write to him.

Please hurry up and write soon, for I feel more than ever cut off from the news, living amongst these nice, but foreign folk. Lots of love, Dianne xxxxx

Dear Dad, haven't received the Parka yet, but it won't take long to arrive and glad you liked your card. Were the letters okay for my refund of my Sitmar Ticket, and do you need anything else? You will note I'm having great trouble getting a job in St Imier. Lately, I have felt like packing the whole thing in, but I must visit all these places before I come home. The trouble is travelling through Europe and England is impossible in Winter, which is already setting in. I know Liz and Helen are in London, and my job is waiting if I want it. I could work at something else and then travel next Spring. Send me your ideas please, as I'm at a dead end if nothing happens here. It's also good of you to send me a copy of the Australian paper, for I don't hear any news of home here. Don't forget to tell me who wins the Grand Final. I'm backing Balmain, but then Souths always manage

I don't wear step-ins anymore.

to pull something out of the bag at the end. Love and kisses Di
xxxxxxxxxxxxxxxxxx

I became so jealous of my mother's descriptions of food. I would try to outdo her whenever I had the opportunity. My hosts, Mr and Mrs Adatte, went out of their way to make my lunches memorable.

I think it's Friday, 19th September 1969

Dear Mum and Dad,
   I read your letter yesterday after lunch, which consisted of Roast Lamb (N.Z.), beans, potatoes and bacon pieces (like chunks of steak) and red wine. (I insist Father makes a wine cellar when I arrive home so we can have wine with our meals). Cathy bought an English newspaper for me – very rare around here – and after scanning this, I read your very enthralling weekly episode. Thank you very much for the $2 – it was nearly pinched by Cathy's father! It was nice of you to write a note to Cathy, which she read and translated to her parents. She will be writing to you in thanks. It was a great pity you didn't meet her, for she speaks perfect English and is such a nice person.
   Before I write further on anything – things haven't been going too smoothly in regard to a job, simply because of red tape. It seems as a holder of an Australian Passport, most employers don't want the time and expense involved in getting me a working permit. It is a difficult task, as Swiss do not have a lot of contacts direct with Australia. If I had been British, it would have been no trouble. Yesterday I was given a trial day at a factory where Cathy's sister works. It involved cleaning bobbins of fine wire with petrol from 6.45 am to 11.50 (lunch) and then 1.30 to 6pm, including a 10 min. break at 9am. The personnel manageress told me I would have to do this every day for the next 6 months, excluding weekends and 11 days off at Christmas, if they were going to get me a work permit. The wage was 600 Swiss Francs a month = 60 pounds a month or $A30 per

week. The day I spent doing this was torture. All day I sat on a chair with a small machine in front, placing a bobbin on one wheel and letting it spin on another. I took 2 pieces of rag, dipped them in a bottle of petrol and held the wire. One bobbin takes at least an hour to clean, for it must be done 6 times.

I may have a chance, if there is a more interesting job open, or if another firm, Longines, is willing to employ me as an English correspondence typist. If these fail, I still may be able to find work on a farm of a friend, where I would be paid board and lodging plus a small weekly allowance. If all this fails, I have no choice but to leave. Everyone has been so helpful, but if I have no employment, it is useless and wrong to live off other people. Last night I was so mad, I felt like taking the next plane home. Cathy's fiancé had a phone call from Helen this week, and they are in a town close to Ipswich in Sussex. Helen told Richard she would be writing to me very soon.

Last Tuesday I took the Funicular Cable Car to the top of the mountains to a place called Mount Soleil which is a very small village. I was up about 8 or 7.30 and left around 9am by myself. I just walked along a small road past farms and cows wearing their bells. The view was unbelievable with the mist still hanging on the top of the mountain range, and the sun became very warm. Instead of getting the car back, I took the track and walked for over an hour and a half down to St. Imier, just in time for lunch which I badly needed. Lots of love Dianne xxxxxxxxxxxx

Sunday, 21st September 1969

To Our Dianne,

This afternoon at 4pm, I watched 'The Royal Family' on Channel 9. It finished at 6pm and I enjoyed it. It was on Channel 2 at 7pm. In some of the scenes, the Queen looked her age, considering she can have all the best treatment for her skin and wear the most beautiful

I don't wear step-ins anymore.

clothes. Dad and I had a glorious day at Katoomba yesterday. We left at 8 o'clock and went up via Liverpool and the back road to Penrith. The day was beautiful. We went to the Church Missionary House, near the Scenic Railway. It is kept very clean and well looked after. They have the meals cooked for us, and we only have to set up and clear the tables and wash up our own plates. For lunch we had Shepherd's Pie, and peas, with sweets, bread and butter and fruit. For dinner we had braised chops, beans and potatoes, with apple sponge and cream. The blossoms are just starting to come out, and the colours were gorgeous. I have to buy Dad a lottery Ticket as I picked the losing team, but he will tell you all about it. Denise and Russell went into Town this morning to get our plane tickets to Melbourne for Thursday and come back Friday night. The weather down there has been very cold and wet. We are still using our electric blankets. Can you believe Denise is banking, and if she keeps on doing it, she'll get her 18th birthday present? How is your French coming along, Bonjour ma Dianne! When I was at Katoomba yesterday, I bought a book of Peter Marshall's Prayers. They were condensed by his wife and they are lovely. Well Darling, hope everything is going along fine, and hope you have got your working permit. Think of you often, love and big hugs from your loving Mother xxxx xxxxxxxxxxxxxxxxxxxxxxxxxxxxxx Hello Dianne Darling, back again. The weeks go so quick. We received your Cards of where you are staying. It looks lovely. Hope you like it and are enjoying yourself. Well the final of the Football was Saturday between Souths and Balmain. It was a great game, 60000 there but Balmain gave them a hiding and walked all over them, final score 11-2. You asked about Cliff's address. We only know what he gave us a long while ago. Cliff Carrington c/- Mrs McLean 4 Aveley Street Kahibah Newcastle 2290. I have bought some Postcards of Katoomba and Sydney which I will send you to show or use to send to England. I wrote to Pat at the Nell Gwynne a couple of weeks ago and will send him a card also. Russell sprayed his car to sell it. I lent him my spray outfit, so he could sell his car before he went into the Army Wednesday week. Hope Cathy and her family are well. Give them my love. Did you get your parka? It was sent airmail. Well Darling, I hope you are well and looking after yourself, from your Papa with love xxxxxxxxxxxxxxxxxxxxxxxxxxxx

Thursday, 30th September 1969

My Dear Mum and Dad,

My second French lesson wasn't too hot, for I wasn't making much sense out of applying what I was avidly learning, especially trying to build sentences. Anyway, it is slowly progressing, and there is another lesson tomorrow evening. As I don't work anymore on Saturday, Cathy and I are off to the local flicks to see a film on England. We are then going to 'Les Chaux Fords' on Saturday for some shopping bargains. I got paid today, and it is only 8 weeks to Christmas. Work gets more hilarious each day. Wednesday afternoon everyone was in a mad mood, so when the music came on at 5pm, one of the older women started dancing behind the machines. It looked like a ballroom, with me chosen to watch for spys, so we wouldn't be caught. They are all gorgeous people, and I'm finding it easier to like Italian more than French, for I hear Italian all day, which doesn't please my teacher one bit!

Cathy has broken her engagement, as she is currently keeping company with a local lad. She constantly gets to bed at 11 or 12, which means I have to drag her out each morning. Can't keep track of this girl! We had reindeer for lunch today. I wouldn't go out of my way to eat it again. Just keep a nice thick steak waiting for me. One of the main water pipes has cracked, so half the village has no water, nor has the factory, and we can't even flush the toilet. Not good! It is getting chillier each day. I'll have you know; I've never felt so healthy. No colds. When I look at those mountains outside, nothing worries me.

Am enclosing some photos taken just before we left the flat at Archway – the other chap in one of the photos is Cathy's ex-fiancée, Richard. Of course, you'll recognise Mahmet, Liz and Helen. Cathy is there, and Dad will remember her from one of his visits to the flat. Liz and Helen are still apple picking, and we hear from them quite regularly. Dad – I was thrilled to hear about the $391 from Sitmar, and thanks for the newspaper from 'Apia Club' in Leichhardt, as the ladies at work are very interested in Australia. Showed them the photo of you and Mum, and they said Mum was 'La Belle'. They wanted to know your ages, but please tell me the right dates next letter. I said Mum was 45ish and you were 50ish-Close? Anyway, they wouldn't believe it, and even asked how old I was! Will write again soon, but you are always in my thoughts. Lots of love to you, Your daughter Dianne xxxxxxxxxxxxxxxxxxxxxx

I was thrilled and impressed that my mother was attempting to write in French. I later found out she had studied French in high school during the 1930s.

Wednesday, 1st October 1969

Notre Fille, Dianne, Mercredi,
Received your letter this morning, and hope you get the position. You have had a good spell, and too much spare time ends in boredom. Russell came in about 8.30 am, and Denise went with him to Marrickville Barracks, down near Auntie Betty's. I met his mother, and she was upset about him going into the Army. His father Jim, her husband, went with them. Russell's bus didn't leave till 4.30pm and will arrive at Seymour, Victoria, early tomorrow morning. Last Monday went out to see Valmai in the afternoon, and she had just finished bathing Cassandra. She is a pretty baby, and it was the first time Val had given her a bath, as she had been too nervous to do it before now. Must let you know, I found my French book, henceforth the French words. Dad, Denise and I left at 8 am this morning and went to Bowral. We had a nice day, although I think the tulips weren't as nice as usual. Monday, Six Hour Day. I have had so much to eat for my dinner tonight, I feel sick. You know your Mother, just

sitting there, eating warm sausages and a salad, plus chocolate biscuits, apple tart and an orange. Tonight, the temperature is 77 degrees and today has been a beautiful day. Washed and polished the verandah, opened my bedroom windows and the sliding doors in the TV room. Spent the rest of the day out in the garden and it was lovely. Yesterday, after we came home from Church, we mowed the front lawn, and it looks very nice. Uncle Albert rang up on Saturday night to ask us to go to St George Leagues Kogarah on Sunday afternoon. I enjoyed the show, and afterwards had dinner in the dining room. I had the usual, prawn cutlets and salad, with ice-cream cake. We played the poker machines but finished with the $1 we started with. Dad wants to know what Bank to send your birthday money, plus the address. Please keep your shoes on, and don't sit on any damp ground. Well, treasure, I will close now, hoping you are working, and give my regards to Cathy. Love, kisses and big hugs from your loving Mother xxxxxxxxxxxxxxxxxxxxxx Dear Dianne, hope you are well and did get a job. We had a lovely dinner at St George Leagues the other night, Roast Duck, Prawn Cutlets, Lobster Salad, Prawn Cocktails and a couple of bottles of wine. Let me know if you want any more postcards. Love from Daddy xxxxxxxxxxxxxxxxx

Sunday, 5th October 1969

Dearest Mum,

After finishing my first week of work, I went to the local café, 'Patio' with an Italian girl who spoke to me at the factory in English. She wanted to ask me about London. We were sipping our coffee, when a waitress came over to say I was wanted back at the house!! I didn't know what it was all about until I saw a familiar Fiat car parked outside. You can imagine what I must have felt when I saw Val and David sitting upstairs! We then went to find Cathy and have a chat at the Café again, where they told us all about their trip so far. I won't tell you much as it will spoil things when they get home. After supper we went and met some friends where we chatted again

I don't wear step-ins anymore.

for hours. As the upper flat was being used for the sister's wedding during the weekend, Val and David were quite prepared to camp overnight. Instead, two of the chaps we were with had room at their flat, so all was fixed up nicely.

We spent Saturday touring around the countryside, stopping for lunch on a grassy slope overlooking miles and miles of valleys and mountains. I took them up the other side of the valley to 'Chasseral', where I will be skiing during the winter. We sat sipping a beer while gazing out at the Alps in the distance. When we got back to the village the whole family had left for the wedding, so we could use the upstairs flat. Val and David both had a wash and spruce-up in the sink, did some washing, then we all sat on the balcony in the gorgeous sunshine over coffee and cake.

There was a wine festival at 'Neuchatel', so off we went. The whole day was so marvellous and happy, except for the occasional nitwits who had been drinking since Friday evening. Val and I were attacked by guys at nearly every corner. My bottom was pinched, and one chap threw confetti at me. I even got some in my eyes, which was not very pleasant. We drank wine, ate hot grilled sausages and a whole chicken, which we tore apart while walking back to the car. The festival goes the whole weekend, but we had quite enough after about 3 hours. They camped overnight on the slopes near the village and left about 11am today. They met all the family, and will be able to tell you how lovely St Imier is to live in. Val started crying when she left, so we had a sob session in the street. I now feel so empty and alone with them gone. I won't see them again until I get home, after being close to Val especially, for over a year while living in London. Having them here made me realise how much our family means to me. While having lunch today with the family, I had to go upstairs and have another cry. I really wish I was home right now. It's very wrong for me to write like this, but I just can't stop myself clearing away what's bottled up inside.

Anyway, Val and David are off to do a few days grape picking for some extra cash. Touring around gets very expensive, as you probably know. We have a flat now. I spent the afternoon putting the place in order. Cathy went to the wine festival and isn't back as yet (6 pm). Thinking of you and the family all the time, Lots of love, Dianne

13th October 1969

Ma Petite Maman Cherie,

Merci for your letter which I just received before leaving to go to 'Lausanne' for the weekend with Cathy and Meyér. He has asked Cathy to partner him at a dinner party. My part was to be chaperone, for tongues wag in a village like St-Imier. I also enjoyed meeting Cathy's sister and her Turkish husband. He is very nice and speaks English. We had lunch there on Saturday and Sunday, which was delicious. Stayed at a type of Youth Hostel, but it was very comfortable and dirt cheap. If you could only see the colour of the trees now Autumn has come. I wake up and each morning they become more vivid. Living here turns me off big cities. I doubt I could live in a large metropolis again. People are much more obliging in a small place.

I told you earlier Cathy got engaged the weekend before we left London, after a whirlwind romance of 3 weeks. Well, Richard keeps writing, asking her for the papers to go to the U.S.A. next year, and Cathy doesn't feel the same, now she is talking French again. Also, she wants to ski until March, which won't fit in with Richard's marriage plans. I wouldn't be surprised to see Richard on the doorstep, when she writes back and tells him how she feels.

We are in the flat now and don't feel so crowded out, as we were in the other room. The flat is so warm with the central heating. I hang my stockings up over the pipes, and they are warm as toast when I put them on at 6am! The novelty of trying to explain what I mean to the people at work has now worn off, and it has become a test of patience, amongst other things. The ones who are learning English, test their fluency with me, and some say the strangest things.

I don't wear step-ins anymore.

We are decorating the flat slowly, but this weekend is free, and we hope to do more. We have a large bedroom, lounge and kitchen, but use the downstairs bathroom and loo. This can be horrible late at night when having to get out of a gorgeous, warm bed, as you must know. It was good to hear from Denise, and of course I realise how upset she is with Russell gone to the Army. Somewhere I read there is a purpose for everything, so no doubt things will get brighter as each day passes. Val took some photos while here, but please overlook my appearance when you see them, as I'm living a real country bumpkin life at present. I don't care how much you rave on about your gorging sessions, as I'm having some very delicious snacks too. I only gorge once a day, not 10 times a day like you do. One thing I would ask you to send me at Christmas, is a small morsel of your delicious, intoxicating and mouth-watering pudding, or have you discontinued the yearly baking ritual. If this is the case, then I've lost another incentive to miss home, and I hasten you to start cooking right away Maman! The mornings get colder and colder, moreso than London! I enjoy sleeping so much, I go to bed earlier each night, and feel better for it. Lots of love, your Dianne xxxxxxxxxxxxxxxxxxxx

Thursday, 23rd October 1969

Dearest Mum and Dad,
It's a riot at this factory. Now the women want me to do night work at a local chocolate factory, from 7.30 to 10pm each evening! Think of all the temptation, especially as they make chocolate liqueurs too! Better than duty-free booze! The Italian women are just so curious about new people. They devise some startling methods of getting information from me. My descriptions make the whole place roar with laughter. One of the ladies, Ada, who has no bottom teeth, is my favourite. She can't take anything seriously, but they all brighten the place up in their own way.

Thank you for the $2. Am putting the money away towards the future, when it will definitely be of use. You seem to be getting some good documentaries on TV of late, especially English ones. Have been studying my French all this week for my second lesson tonight at 6 instead of 9pm, which is so much more practical straight after work. Now it is lunch time and Mrs Adatte is just finishing cooking fish yum yum!! The weather has suddenly stayed very chilly from the morning, so it seems winter is getting ready to settle. One of the songs from 'HAIR' is being played on the radio called 'Aquarius'. It does bring back memories, but they say the words have not much meaning at all in the production playing at present in Paris. Denise should see it while in season. Anyway, I have both soundtracks to bring home, and one is banned in Australia.

The family is well. Life just goes on as usual in St-Imier, for they are all filling in vacation forms at present. Must finish as I have to go back to work soon but am taking some photos to be finished beforehand. Think of you all very often and look forward to your next letter. Lots of love, Dianne xxxxxxxxxxx

Sunday, 9th November 1969

To Our Dianne,

Today has been a beautiful Spring day, and Gerald has been doing his garden with just his shorts on. Did you have a lovely Birthday? We had booked a call at 9.30pm Sydney time, but it was held up, and when they got through, you had gone back to work, so we had to book for the later call. You won $18.00 on the Melbourne Cup. Will I keep it for you, or do you want me to send it over to you? Russell came home on Thursday night and he looks more mature. He has lost about 9 lbs but holds himself erect. Ten boys were rejected after four weeks in the Army. They have enough to eat but have bacon and eggs each morning for breakfast. He goes back to the base on Monday night, for another five weeks, then has 17 days leave.

I don't wear step-ins anymore.

I made Denise a gold linen frock with matching petticoat, and she wore this with her yellow shoes on Thursday night, when she went over to Russell's place. I finished the blue knitted frock, and she wore this tonight to South Sydney Junior's Club with Russell's parents. Denise also went out to Maroubra today for a swim and has got a little sunburnt. I am enclosing $2 for you to buy some Christmas cards, as they prove expensive by the time you have paid postage. Glad to hear you have your parka and should get your newspapers soon. Liked the photos. Wasn't surprised to read about Cathy's engagement woes. Have you any snow yet? Well darling, I will say goodbye, hoping you got all your cards. By the way, Aunt received her Birthday card from you last Thursday, and was pleased to get it. Give my love to Cedrine and Pascale, and also Cathy. Love and hugs from your loving Mother xxxxxxxxxxxxxxxxxx Dear Dianne, hope you are well and glad to hear you received your parka. You were asking about Mum's age. Don't forget her birthday is on December 13th and she will only be 48, seven years younger than Papa. I am 55 on February 14th 1970. Well I hope you are enjoying yourself and the snow is getting closer. Mr Gorton got back in after a lot of fights in Parliament. All the best to my darling and keep your chin up, Love from Papa xxxxxxxxxxxxxxxxxxxx

10th November 1969
34 Pierre-Jollissaint, St-Imier, Switzerland

Dearest Mum, Dad & Nece

Please forgive this letter taking so long to be written. I cannot thank you enough for surprising me on my birthday. The cake was delicious, and the children helped me blow out the 22 candles. They also helped me eat it, as did the rest of the family. Cathy gave me the new Beatles L.P. which I haven't stopped playing (typical). Received my newspapers and thank you Dad, for it's marvellous to see the old 'Sun' again with such typical Australian scenes. You sounded very energetic on the telephone for 3am in the morning, except Denise who sounded fast asleep. She should be over here working at the factory. I'd laugh myself silly watching 'Her Ladyship' get out of bed at 5.45am each morning.[35]

The weather turned really miserable after last Tuesday. Since then it has rained continually, bringing snow to the higher mountains, but thank goodness, not to the town as yet. We had to put the outer windows in to keep the flat warm, and the heating is on full bore. Mrs Adatte hangs the washing in the hallway each night, and you'd be surprised at how quickly it dries in the central heating. Have made some very nice friends at work, especially one married girl who is 26. She is very much like Valda in her attitude. I went along to an Italian Fete on Saturday night with her friends and had a marvellous time. I just can't seem to make any Swiss friends, for they are a little too 'high and mighty'. The Italians seem to accept a person for what they are, and don't stand for any 'airs and graces'. Can't make much progress with my French. Italian is more my liking, as it just flows along simply and is such a happy language. French has no humour to it at all.

Had some people over last Friday night and they didn't leave until 1am. The trouble with this was I had promised to work in the morning. Anyway, the children had played around with the alarm clock, so I turned up at the factory at 6am instead of 7am. Came back to the flat, getting drenched in a downpour, then back to the factory, where I lasted one hour exactly. After shopping, I couldn't be bothered sleeping, and just took my time getting ready for the Dance. Slept until 2pm on Sunday. Cathy was away at her latest boyfriend's house, where his family had a big 'Do' on.

Those 2 postcards of Sydney were lovely. I can't get over how Sydney seems to be changing so rapidly. How is Mascot's new runway getting on? I've been reading the new Jumbo Jets are

---

[35] 'Her Ladyship' was another pet name my mother called my sister Denise, who expected to be waited on constantly.

completed and ready for delivery. On one wall of the flat, I've decorated it with magazine cuttings, and it looks fantastic. Everyone likes it, for the colours look amazing mixed in together. Haven't heard from Liz and Helen for ages, but no doubt they are keeping well. Did you like the photos I sent? Showed your photos to everyone, and they couldn't get over how young you looked. Lots of love, Dianne xxxxxxxxx

My family, Mother in particular, became very agitated if they didn't receive a letter or aerogramme from me each week. Sometimes, especially in a place like St-Imier, weather would play havoc with mail deliveries. Australia also had problems with delivery of overseas mail, due to reduced deliveries or mail strikes.

Monday, 1st December 1969

My Dearest Family,

If you think it's cold, I want you to pop over here, and gallivant around in temperatures 10 degrees or more below freezing (daytime). Went to the Cinema Friday evening, and it was unbelievably freezing walking back to the house at 11pm. I went to an Italian Dance about 3 or 4 weeks back with a friend I work with. I met a very nice Italian chap called Osvaldo, but because of language difficulties, we got our next meeting mixed up. Last Monday, he gave a message to a girl who speaks a little English, so we have been seeing each other since last Tuesday. He has 5 brothers, one speaks English, and a sister, all in Italy. Yesterday we walked around the village, and I just can't describe how beautiful this place is when covered completely by snow. We went past the skating rink, which is at the bottom of the village, and is hemmed in on 2 sides by mountain ranges, where the skiing is tremendous. They had recorded music playing, which gave it an eerie sound, as it echoed through the valley. I had slacks, boots, a jumper Val gave me last Xmas, and my Kanga coat on. My ears were numb plus my toes. We took the train to the next village, Sonvelier, and there is no platform, you just walk across the tracks and get on, exactly as in the movie 'Dr Zhivago'. I feel like I'm living the whole movie, while in St-Imier. At night, I hear the train whistle, and imagine the train journeying through the frozen steppes of Russia. Fantastic feelings one gets when living in different countries. I learn so much about life now and will pray my children have the opportunities you have given me to become a better person. Even so, I get terribly homesick for you, and my past glorious life at 104.

Monday, 9th December 1969

Dear Dianne,

Russell came home by train yesterday morning. Tonight, Denise has gone to the party at work, and wore her new black dress I made her. Russell is taking her out afterwards. Russell's parents gave him $500 for his 21st. Have received two cards from Canada and one from South Africa. Don't forget to write to Betty as I received a nice Christmas card from her this week. Saturday. Was doing the edges of the lawn in the front, when the postman came. He put quite a few letters in the box, and I asked him, did he have an overseas letter, and he said yes. I told him he made my day complete. I don't think I will open the note for the time being. At lunch time your box of flowers came from David Jones. They were apricot coloured carnations and roses, which I have placed near your photo, with your card. The three water lilies I have put on my dressing table. Dad gave me a sheath of flowers, white Michelmas daisies, Christmas bells and yellow lilies. Denise and Russell gave me a sheath of flowers, 2 dozen red roses, carnations and pink gladioli. Dad gave me the usual ($100), Denise gave me a white kid purse and lots of other presents from family and friends. In the afternoon we went to Kogarah R.S.L. and I had my usual prawn cutlets, side salad and caramel ice cream cake. Denise and Russell have gone to dinner at 'The Summit'. Thank you darling, for helping to make my Birthday happy. I put one of your roses on Denise's dressing

I don't wear step-ins anymore.

table. Looking forward to your next letter, love, kisses and big hugs from your loving Mother xxxxxxxxxxxxxxxxxxx Hello Darling, how are you? Mother had a good birthday. You should have seen her when the chap arrived with your flowers. They were lovely. Well, Xmas is only 10 days away now. We finish work at the factory on Friday for a month. I am trying to get Mum to go on a few trips around the country. I hope Cathy and her family are all well, and you have your machine in order now. All the best and love from Pappa xxxxxxxxxxxx

Monday, 22nd December 1969

To Our Dianne,

Denise is outside wrapping the presents, after a session on the phone with Russell. He took her to work this morning. We received your Christmas card today, and it is a very nice card. I went to Roselands today, and Dad bought me $17.45 make up from Revlon. The night cream is to take the lines away from your dear Mother's face. Time will tell. It has been warm again today, but about 2 o'clock, we had a very heavy storm. We had another about 5.30pm, but I am writing this from my bed with only a sheet over me. Mr Heath, the opposition leader to Mr Wilson, is in Sydney for three weeks. I think he is sailing in the Sydney to Hobart Boat Race, which starts on Boxing Day. Tuesday, we had our Christmas dinner at our place, and the dining room table looked nice. Auntie Betty, Uncle Albert, Aunt, Uncle Bill, Auntie Ruby, Uncle Harold, Dad, Russell, Denise and I sat down to eat. We had roast pork and chicken. Everyone received 20 cents in their pudding, so we added to it, and are getting a $6 Opera House ticket. We showed the film of our holidays. Remember Mr Evans, next door to Cohen's? He passed away early on Christmas Day, so there will be another place up for sale (more New Australians). Your Christmas card was lovely, and your presents arrived on Christmas Eve. We put them under the Christmas Tree and opened them on Christmas morning. I had three chocolates from your present, and they are lovely, but very rich. I am going to use the box as a sewing box, and it is very nice. How did you enjoy Christmas? Needless to say, I was thinking of you, especially at the time when we went to Church. I mowed the back lawn this afternoon, and the grass is looking well, no weeds, then we burned some rubbish and had a barbecue. Dad took 4 chocolates into Alma, as she always asks about you. There was a large crowd attending the beach today, and the cars driving down the Coast were bumper to bumper, as far as Sutherland. I hope love, you don't always wear your slacks, and do you wear your 'Kanga Coat' much? Denise wants a sapphire ring when she is 21. Well love, hoping you are well, love, big kisses and hugs from your loving Mother xxxxxxxxxx Hello darling, hope you had a lovely Xmas? I sent you a piece of cake and pudding, and the girl sent it ordinary mail instead of air mail. Hope you received all your cards and cheques. We had a lovely Xmas, and the best was when your present arrived. Thank you, it was lovely. Keep your chin up, Love Pappa xxxxxxxxxxxxxxxxxx"

Wednesday, 31st December 1969

Dearest Mum, Dad & Denise,

The last day of the year, and tonight I'm seeing the new year in with Mrs Adatte, as we are both babysitting. Cathy has gone to Montana, a very posh skiing resort (Liz and Richard Burton have a chalet there). Her boyfriend and family are presently residing in their chalet. Everytime this boyfriend, John Francois visits his grandmother, she never fails to hand him a 100 Franc note (10-pound sterling)! His father owns a timber mill, and in Switzerland, that means money! The other 2 sisters in St-Imier are off with their husbands for a mystery train trip/Dance/Dinner/the works. They don't return until tomorrow morning.

I received a card from Osvaldo in English. His brother knows the language and must have helped him write the message. I had posted one to him, after spending hours flipping through an Italian/English

I don't wear step-ins anymore.

dictionary, trying to compose something myself. Each New Year is the same. This is the 3rd year I've been lucky to have a male admirer, but he's never with me to see the New Year in! I just bought a bottle of Italian Spumante (Champagne) for 4 Francs (8/- Sterling), and Mrs Adatte and I are going to crack it while watching a cabaret from 'Moulin Rouge' on the TV, plus a variety show direct from 'Maxims' in Paris.

Monday night was a scream, for Ella Fitzgerald was on TV live from the Jazz Festival at Montreux, which is not very far from here. She was too much, but beforehand on the news, was a super film clip of the start of the Sydney/Hobart Race showing the Opera House. It looked bloody gorgeous (excuse the swearing) but it did! It looked like a huge bird with 10 sets of wings, and made the harbour look like a setting for a dream. It looked very beautiful. As usual no-one was in the room, so I had a quiet scream of delight all by myself. While Cathy and I watched Ella, we heard a noise outside. After fighting with the curtain, I spotted a policeman throwing snowballs at the window, trying to catch my attention. He turned out to be a good pal of the family and was after a coffee and cognac as it was 10 degrees below freezing. He could also speak English! I become more amazed at the Swiss each day. We had a great laugh together, and he so reminded me of a real Frenchman out of 'Maigret', with his box type hat and huge trenchcoat.

Mr Adatte had all his bottom teeth extracted last Saturday, and typical of men, has been at death's door ever since. Yesterday he had something else done with 4 injections in his bottom lip. When he ate his soup, he kept losing it, as his bottom lip was numb and kept dropping. The three of us watched him and couldn't stop laughing, but he wasn't very amused. Then he said he couldn't eat the sausages, so Mrs Adatte had to cook an omelette. I got the sausages for supper, and they were delicious!

1st January 1970 1.30am. Just came upstairs am watching the New Year in on T.V. The transmission was from a yacht on the Lake at Geneva, where all the usual T.V. mob get together. They showed a really funny French movie, and then took us direct to the 'Moulin Rouge' in Paris. Cathy and I inspected it thoroughly while we visited 'Pigalle' in Paris. I was surprised to find a very interesting lift-out in the 'Australian' newspaper, on a plan to artificially heat the highways through the Alps joining Italy to Switzerland and France, with a system similar to central heating in normal homes.

Cathy rang after lunch from Montana, saying dresses selling for 2 pound in London, are priced at 20 pounds. Julie Christie is at present somewhere in the village! Cathy's sister and husband returned from their train mystery tour at 8am. They came to lunch in their pyjamas, and father didn't arrive until an hour afterwards, infuriating mother. We had smoked ham, beans covered in melting butter, soup before, and I had 2 helpings of Ice-cream cake and 2 cups of coffee. We watched the Vienna Orchestra play nearly the entire works of Strauss, plus a ballet accompaniment. Cannot tell you how beautiful it was to watch, and from the Opera House in Vienna too. Now, it is after 3.30pm, and everyone except me is sleeping. There isn't much action and it is very bleak outside, making me quite content to fiddle around the flat, listening to a Chopin record of his waltzes. Well, I'll finish off so I can post this on Monday, and hope it finds you all well and happy. All my love, Your Dianne xxxxxxxx

Thursday, 1st January 1970
P.S: $2.00 Pappa

To Our Dianne,

The first day in the New Year. Our weather has not been the best since Tuesday, and this afternoon we had a heavy shower. I helped Dad this afternoon with his books. Denise said her culottes were very comfortable, and she has gone out at lunchtime for a drive with Russell. How did you enjoy your New Year? I received your aerogramme yesterday (Friday). I am happy you enjoyed Christmas. Regarding Cassandra's baptism, I would suggest a bracelet or brooch, and I think it would be nice if you send a present from

I don't wear step-ins anymore.

Switzerland. How about a small cross on a chain, even if Valmai put it away till she was old enough to wear it. We went out to Valmai's yesterday, and Cassandra had been playing up. I think she is spoilt. While I held her up on my shoulder, she doesn't utter a sound, but try and lay her in your arms, and she starts. Dad was pushing the pram, and she was laughing at him, and her little legs were pushing against the pram. She is a child who likes a lot of attention. She gained 12ozs in two weeks, which is rather good. She is going on to solids but is still not very fond of the bottle. If she was your first child, you would think twice about having another, on account of how long you have to take over her meals. Lisa comes to me now and is growing into a little girl. I had a lovely card from Mr and Mrs Adatte. Dad is looking in the French book to see if he can translate the French. I hope they liked the card I sent of our wild Australian flowers. Today we went for a drive to Penrith, had lunch, then to Richmond, then to Windsor, through to Parramatta. We stayed at Lake Parramatta for 1 and a half hours, which is a beautiful park near the turn off to Carlingford. I gave the front lawn a good soaking tonight. The back and front lawns are very green, without *any* weeds. Went into City Tatt's last night (Monday). Denise took her clothes and came in from work. We had a lovely meal, and I thought of the times when you and Denise had your Birthdays, when you were younger. They had a candle, cherries and nuts on the table. We stayed in the lounge and came home about 11 o'clock. Hope the cake and pudding arrived in good condition. We have a small pudding left and Dad said it is his. Well darling, I will sign off, love, big hugs and kisses from your loving Mother xxxxxxxx Hello love, hope you are well and enjoyed your Xmas and New Year. We went out for Denise's birthday to City Tattersalls Club. The waitress was from Switzerland and told us what St-Imier was like. Let me know 7 weeks before you leave, so I can stop the newspapers. Keep your chin up and enjoy yourself. All my love from Pappa xxxxxxxx

While working in Switzerland, I had fallen in love with a handsome Italian, Osvaldo. He lived in the next village, but couldn't speak a word of English. I was so desperate for love and affection I grabbed him at a local dance and wouldn't let him go. I began reliving scenes from *Dr Zhivago*. I became *Julie Christie* and he became my *Omar Sharif*. I would trudge through snow drifts, sustaining myself with sips from my hip flask filled with locally made cherry liqueur. He taught me how to make proper spaghetti bolognaise, which my granddaughter Ellen loves. She even wants me to teach her how to make it.

The family I was living with in the small mountain village of St-Imier, was horrified with my wanton disregard of propriety. I would visit Osvaldo and not return until the next day. The town was shocked, but I didn't care. I was reliving *Dr Zhivago*, one of my favourite movies of all time. I only had a few more months before my work permit would expire, so it was necessary for me to travel back to England and decide how I would return home.

Thursday, 22nd January 1970
34 Pierre-Jollissaint St-Imier Switzerland

Dearest Mum and Dad,

Tonight, I needed you more than ever before, as I'm seriously upset about leaving Osvaldo this March when I return to England on my way home. He doesn't want me to leave, but I would not be content here, away from you and the rest of the family. It is the same with him, moreso, as his mother is very ill. It is easy to say, 'time will heal', but I've said this so many times before, and really feel he is the one person I've been looking for, for so long. If only I could pop home for a while and see whether I have the same feelings for Osvaldo, as I do here. Maybe after I have seen Scotland and been around the Continent, my feelings for him may change. I mustn't build my hopes up too much. What else can I do?

I don't wear step-ins anymore.

What do I do Mother? For once in my life I really want to live for another person, however there are so many barriers stopping this from eventuating. I have no right to drag him from his home, nor he from mine. That's only one barrier, so even if you just say you understand my plight, it will give me the injection I need right now. All my love, Dianne xxxxxxxxxxxxxxxxxx

Wednesday, 28th January 1970

To My Big Girl,

You are still Mum's big girl. I received your aerogramme this morning and was happy to receive it. I know how you must feel, but don't rush things. I would suggest you do your Scotland trip, and stay in London. You could have an understanding with Osvaldo, and on your Continent trip, it would be nice if you could meet his family. In the meantime, his Mother could improve in health. On the migrant scheme you can come out for about $20 but have to stay 2 years. You know love, there are much better conditions in our country, than on the Continent. Dad and I will always be there to help in any way possible. Twelve months is not too long to wait, when you have a lifetime together. How old is Osvaldo? In my prayers, I ask God to guide you, especially as you are so far away. Anytime you are feeling lonely, Mum will always be waiting for a few lines from you. Today I went to the St. George's Leagues for the Smorgasbord with Eve, and two other girls. I saw Valmai, Beverley and Bobby there. In the afternoon, we went to Sylvania Heights where Eve's niece lives. She is hoping to sell her house for $80,000. Di don't forget Dad's birthday 14th February, St Valentine's Day. Today it has been raining on and off. Valda likes her position, but David is still being interviewed. Valmai received your bracelet for Cassandra's Christening. She said it is beautiful and so different from the ones we buy here. Have to drive down to Marrickville station at 9.30pm for Denise, as she is working back, and also worked last night. Hope everything works out all right, but don't be too hasty in anything you do. Thinking of you, love from Mum xxxxxxxxxxxx 'All things work together for good, to them that love God.'

2nd February 1970

Dearest Mum and Dad

It's now 7.30 Monday evening after receiving your letter at lunch. At present I'm eating an Italian orange which is red inside like blood – really strange. Have a rotten cold, but at least it isn't flu, which is raging here. Worked last Saturday morning from 7 to 12 noon for double pay and next Saturday as well, so it will pay my board and give me a chance to bank the rest for when I leave. Snowed very briefly on Friday evening and when I left the factory to have lunch at Osvaldo's place on Saturday. It takes 5 minutes in the train to his village, Sonvilier, where he works. The view from the train compared to London tubes is like a dreamland topped with white whipped cream!

Osvaldo cooked spaghetti with a secret sauce, then chops. After all this we consumed bananas on fresh bread and had wine as well. About 2 hours later he concocted a simple custard cream tasting of vanilla and lemon, which he poured over thick biscuits soaked in Italian Rum! Wow, what a feast. I didn't eat anything more on Sunday except 2 hard boiled eggs, then nothing until today's lunch. The children were selling sprigs of mimosa at St-Imier. The flower resembles our very own wattle, so I bought one for Osvaldo and myself. I put them in a glass of water on the windowsill, as the house at Sonvilier is very warm. When I took the glass in to take mine home, the water was frozen solid! Osvaldo sometimes spends the days in his swimming trunks whilst inside his house. I can't wear my glasses as they steam up! Ridiculous!

When I was walking home from the station it was 5 degrees below freezing. Today, after beautiful snow fell all day long, tonight has

I don't wear step-ins anymore.

brought rain. The streets are now like rivers which we have to wade through! It's horrible if the ice is up tomorrow morning, for then it takes perseverance just to walk one step without falling. Sunday was lovely and sunny, the streets were free of snow, so I was able to wear shoes instead of boots, and my Kanga coat over the brown David Keys dress you gave me. Osvaldo took me for a coffee at one of the little bars in St-Imier. One of the girls behind the counter is from Yugoslavia, and speaks about 7 languages, and of course English. She has Sunday off, so I missed having a rare chat with her.

Last week, when I sent the photos, I also posted an article from 'Life International' by ordinary mail, which is about the massacre by American soldiers in Vietnam. It shocked me very much. When I know Russell and other young men from home could be sent overseas and realise this might be seen by them, it sickens me. There was a very interesting article in 'The Australian' I received today about the same thing on a column about religion. 'The sickest, craziest joke of all is the priests and clergy bless the planes before they take off. They pray for the success of the mission...' Before this was said, tortures were described are being carried out by Vietcong and Americans. He pointed out we are all capable of horrible bestialities and are just as guilty to sit back in silence, as the people actually committing the daily atrocities. They tell us Democracy is the gift sent to us from Heaven, but if it continues as in America, Communism will become as gentle as new-born lambs to the next generation. The article continued – 'Evil is triumphing in Vietnam and most of us have remained silent. But who of us can be called good? The evil is within us. Our insensitivity and indifference are as horrendous as the insensitivity of men brutalised by war, who commit the actual crimes. It wasn't only the war criminals who stood trial at Nuremberg: 'it was the whole German nation, and so it will be with us, we, the good, the silent, the respectable people who have done nothing.'

From your latest letter you sound a bit funny Mum. It's not like you to lose $2 in the one-armed bandits. The family here plays bingo all weekend and bring home enough food for the entire following week – salami, cheese, hams, sugar and cigarettes too. At present, I'm becoming more fluent at work with my French, and even Italian, for Osvaldo doesn't speak much French. He is learning bits of English from me, and when he comes here, says 'Hi' to Cathy, and 'yes', 'goodnight'. I nearly wet myself laughing too! He's so gorgeous, very placid, but won't let me put anything over him. Each day I see him, the more attached I become. To think of leaving in March without a hope of seeing him again, really worries me. I hint about Australia and learn my Italian, so we can exchange correspondence afterwards. I want to visit here again before finally leaving for Australia, but it's not right to think so far ahead. It's because I'm too realistic about the future. Your loving daughter, Dianne xxxxxxxxxxx

4th March 1970

Dearest Mum, Dad, Nece,

I was anxious to hear from you but realised it might have been a mail strike clogging up the works. I've only got 3 weeks left before starting out on my trip through Europe, and it's pretty hectic with work taking up so much time. The weather is slowly getting sunnier, and I can feel spring in the air. At 6.30am all the birds commence singing and the sky is a very dark, rich blue. Can Dad do me a favour and ring the Youth Hostels in Sussex Street? Can he ask them where and how I get my membership renewed for travel on the Continent? Also, where can get a list of hostels in Europe? Valda may know something, for I'm not sure of the address in England of Hostels. Thank you, but write soon about it for me, please. Thank you too for the cartoons and $2. I really enjoy reading those typical Australian cartoons, and only wish everyone here could understand them too. Cathy and I tobogganed on Sunday afternoon at Mt Soleil. We went up in the Funicular, sliding back down on the main road, nearly getting killed on the icy surface, but what fun. Our house is right near the Funicular, we even had time to change our wet clothes before going a second time. We got even wetter, and I got a slight burn from the sun reflecting off the snow, which at present is 9 feet deep at Mt Soleil. Going up we saw 2 deer, one even crossing the rail track in front of us. I took more photos, and only need some of the baby and the rest of the family. I'm coming back here to see Osvaldo before he goes to Italy for his vacation. We mustn't plan too far ahead. You and Denise sound as though you're spending wildly on more hair, rings (my ring?). I don't understand this one, but wait until I get home (for Xmas - cake and pudding etc?) Must write to Betty too and tell her I will see her in August, I hope! What do you reckon would be nice to give her? She has done so much travelling, but I'm adamant about buying a souvenir, maybe something for the home they are re-doing? Any clues Mum? Thinking of you all every minute - lots of love, Your Dianne xxxxxxxxxxx

1st April 1970

Dearest Mum, Dad and Denise,

Left work yesterday 65 pounds richer, plus a very nice reference from the Director. I'm intending to finish all the odds and ends, then leave tomorrow morning. When I got out of bed at 7am (can't sleep longer), and walked out to go downstairs, I saw it was snowing! Right now, there is 3 inches of it, so I'm contemplating visiting the Church to pray for it to stop. The trouble is, St-Imier nestles in a long valley between 2 mountain ranges, so one can see the weather moving off the peaks down through the valleys. It makes me so depressed looking at snow falling, when all my plans are fixed. The Velo Moped bike I'm travelling through Europe on is at present being serviced, and the chap is giving me a chain to ward off thieves. Yesterday he showed me how to clean the spark plug and benzene filter, so this is the least of my worries. He told Osvaldo a tourist left St-Imier a few weeks ago, toured the whole of Turkey and returned in 15 days on a bike like mine! The people at work gave me a lovely card and one of those new long silk scarves in red, green, black and white, which I can wear with anything. Thank you for the $10, plus all the clippings. I have put quite a few paper clippings in my wallet to take with me. Right now, the clouds have parted to blue sky, but it's still snowing slightly. I thought London had rotten weather! I gave Osvaldo your letter and also some postcards of Sydney, which you sent me a while back. He was very thrilled you wrote, and his brother can translate it entirely, although I explained the main parts. We had a good chat over Easter, and he is working here for 2 years, but wants to get a Diploma for Cuisine as a Chef. He will then come to Australia for practise, and eventually wishing to start his own restaurant. At present he works from 7am to 7pm during the week, and Saturday mornings, earning terrific money, but he sends most of it home to pay for the building of his house in Italy. When it is finished, he will rent it out until he decides his plans. It is a form of security very common in Europe. The house is built of mortar, not wood, and will last forever. I think nearly every Italian here has a house back home, which they are paying for, or earning money from. As soon as Osvaldo's house is finished, he wants to come out to Sydney and work in a restaurant. He either wants to study English here, or at night in Australia. If he has a little understanding of English before he arrives, he would have a better chance in job hunting, and it will be less time-consuming. Dad is a good cook too, and he might be tempted to join forces and open a restaurant in Marrickville, or some classy suburb nearby. We could be waitresses and Denise could be the floor show. What do you reckon? My nursing friend Maggie in London, wrote sending me information on London, India, Australia trips costing 110 pounds for 7 days. One is leaving in September, which would get me home by Xmas this year. She even enclosed a deposit form which I might fill out, as it is very cheap. All camping of course, and just have to hop on a boat at Calcutta to Darwin, then go the cheapest way to Sydney. I will definitely be home by Xmas, and now it's really snowing again. Trust you had a good Easter and went to the Show.

I don't wear step-ins anymore.

The weather here has been terrible, but in Italy all the young men took the first swim of the season, as it was sunny every day. When I visit Geneva, I will get the addresses of American Express offices for you to send mail. I will be back here in late June or before, depending on my money. I will write postcards every few days. Love Dianne xxxxxxxxxxxxxxx

I was mad as ever! And I still do crazy things - like trying to get my motorbike licence in my early 60s. I had bought a second-hand Velo moped bike in St-Imier, and was planning to travel through Europe on it. I didn't count on it being the coldest spring on record in Switzerland, as I was preparing to leave. This was very mountainous country, including the Simplon Pass into Italy, which I had to cross. At one stage of the trip, I had to put newspapers inside my jacket just to keep from icing up.

Friday, 3rd April 1970

Dear Mum, Dad & Nece,
Am writing this in a hotel bedroom 20 kilometres before Lausanne, after leaving St-Imier at 1.30pm. It has been snowing in St-Imier continually, but today the sun shone, so I left, only to become intensely cold and sunburnt. I had to soak my feet in hot water to thaw them out. The scooter broke down half way and cost me 1 pound to get it started. Now it makes a terrible noise, and I don't like my chances of ever getting out of Switzerland. Don't intend rushing things, just breeze along while the thing still works. Now it's 7.30 the next morning at the breakfast table, but it is snowing here. The bike is 10 inches under snow, and I'm wondering how to continue. Whether to leave the bike and get trains and buses. Had a nice breakfast and telephoned Cathy. Her mother's sister died, and they are at the funeral, so I'll have to ring this afternoon from the Hotel. The lady who served me was German but told me in French it was the first snowfall in April for many years. I'm not having much luck. Can't do much until I speak

to Cathy, except watch the blizzard rage outside. I forgot to send the last aerogramme but will send it along with this one. Please forgive me for not keeping you informed. I really am wondering whether I'm 'all here' or ready for the Head Shrinkers. No one in their right mind would leave a comfortable house to ride a scooter through mountains of snow, only to find more snow. Can't get temporary work here in Switzerland, so might as well tour around. It is hard when alone, and I miss you all much more than I realised. I miss Osvaldo too, but he can't come to Australia until his house in Italy is finished – another year or more. Maggie, the English nurse, will have time off from the Hospital in summer, and then we hope to go to India in September. This means I have April, May and June free. At least I am lucky to have my things safe and sound at Cathy's place until I get back. Hope I haven't depressed you with all my news, but even I'm starting to think the whole thing is ridiculous. Will write again soon, and with much better news too. All my love, Dianne xxxxxxxxxxxxxxxxx

5th April 1970

Dear Mum, Dad & Nece,

Am back in St-Imier after coming from Lausanne on Saturday evening with the bike. After seeing the chap I bought it from this morning, I find out the valve which keeps oil in the motor has disappeared! Bike or no bike, I leave tomorrow evening by train to Italy, where there isn't any snow, unlike Portugal and Spain are having on the Atlantic coast. During the weekend I wanted very much to get a plane home, as it isn't nice having problems when there isn't a friend to share them with. Was at Osvaldo's place at 8am, getting him out of bed, but I was so happy for he was wonderful and very pleased to see me. Even though we speak different languages, it is easier to talk to him than Cathy. Although she speaks English, she has very little insight into feelings except her own. It only cost me a pound for my room and breakfast at the village 20 kilometres before Lausanne,

I don't wear step-ins anymore.

and 10/- to bring the bike back with me. It is very light and easy to transport. If the guy can't fix it properly by tomorrow, I'll sell it and go by train from town to town, seeing as much of the places I want to see, like Venice, Florence, Rome, Pisa and Sicily. Continental 2nd Class trains are dirt cheap, costing about 5 pounds, maybe less to get to Venice by the Express travelling at night and arriving 8.30am. Somehow, I don't feel very at ease here, for the Swiss are terribly uppish about anything out of the ordinary. Everyone is giving me dagger looks while I walk around, and they work from 7 to 6, saving to go away 3 weeks every year, to somewhere warm where there isn't a trace of snow. I wrote a really terrible letter from the town near Lausanne, but when I feel like this, I hate writing. Next time I'll send postcards saying I'm well and fix up where you can write to me. Anyway, when I've finished touring, I have to come back here to collect my things, so you can send mail here at the time I'm nearly back in St-Imier. The man at the bike shop said it will cost 12 pounds to have the bike repaired. I am going to see him again with Osvaldo tonight, to find out why it has happened, and somehow get him to take it off my hands or fix it without asking for such a high price. It always happens to me. Is Denise home now and back to normal after her annual holiday? She sent me a most unusual card from the 'Gold Coast', saying she'd leave when the money ran out. Another year of borrowing ahead. Give my love to all, and I'll write soon, more than likely, from somewhere in Italy. I'll be thinking of you all, no matter where. It's one day closer to when I reach home. Love Dianne
xxxxxxxxxxxxxxxx

8th April 1970

To Our Dianne,
    Still no letter from you darling, and I patiently go to the mailbox each morning. Watching the TV news tonight I felt a sense of pride, as the school children at the Melbourne Cricket Ground sang the

National Anthem in the presence of the Royal Family. Prince Charles flies back to Sydney today, and leaves later tonight for the Expo Japan, then back to London. The mornings and evenings are drawing in, so have ten extra minutes in bed each morning. My wedding ring was finished last week, and we are very pleased with it. I went to the Show[36] on Tuesday in Easter week. Dad had to go to British Tobacco in the afternoon for a 'cocktail party', so I enjoyed myself on my own, looking at the flowers and cake decorating. I watched the ring events for a couple of hours, then it came over very dull, so I made my way back to the car, and arrived home about 5.30pm. We had a fair amount of rain over Easter, but the other days were nice. I will be counting the weeks till Christmas but will try not to be disappointed if you are staying longer. I hope everything turns out for the best for Osvaldo, for he seems to be a worker and has a vision for the future. That was a nice gesture of your workmates giving you a card and scarf. Was happy to receive your card from Venice. Dad and I stayed there for 2 days. We saw St Mark's, then went on the ferry to the beach. I think it was the Lido. Also had a ride down the canals.

We are having an Indian summer. The days are lovely. The city is starting to look very nice, with the flags and bunting, in blue and yellow. Today the Queen is 44 years old. Last Sunday (19th) the football was a draw, then they had a further 20 minutes, but there were no more goals scored. It was the first time since 1912 this has happened. Tuesday, your aerogramme arrived from Florence, and I can imagine how you must feel. Your card from Rome came yesterday. I was speaking on the phone to Aunt early this morning, and she received hers also. I show everyone Osvaldo's photo, so it is getting around. I think of you each day and wonder what you are doing. You might be on your own sometimes, but someone is always thinking of you. We didn't go out on Wednesday 29th April, as it was a public holiday, and 200 years since Captain Cook landed

---

36 The Royal Agricultural Show, held at Easter at the Sydney Showground, was an event the whole family attended every year.

I don't wear step-ins anymore.

at Kurnell. Watched the Queen and Royal Family at the display at Kurnell. They also showed the sailing ships from South America. Do you remember the 'Esmeralda'? It was all lit up. There were 1,000,000 people in Town during the night, and traffic was a chaos. The weather was beautiful. We put the electric blankets on the beds, including yours, and Gail slept in your bed on Wednesday night. Don't be surprised if Mother gets a job, as everything is increasing each week, and the dollar doesn't go too far. Uncle Billy has sold the butcher shop, but Alick is going to run it for a while.[37] No more cheap meat, but surprisingly, I don't eat the meat like I used to. But I certainly love the sweet things like 'cakes and cream'. I haven't had a card from you this week, but trust God will look after you for me. xxxx Mum.

I had to forget about taking a crazy adventure on a motorised bicycle and just catch trains instead. I also hitchhiked from Rome to Sicily with people I met along the way at youth hostels.

15th April 1970

Dear Mum, Dad and Denise,

Reached Florence today about 1pm and went to the Youth Hostel on the outskirts of the City. This has left me little time to go back in and see anything today. The hostel is palatial with private grounds, but I'm in a dormitory with 11 other girls. I am wondering what they are like, because there are notices all over the place saying, 'We Take No Responsibility for Theft'. At least we get a locker. 2 girls have come in speaking English and saying 'Hi'. I feel so stupid, but just asked about the food, which started the conversation rolling. Had a good Sunday

---

37   Our family friend, Uncle Billy, ran a butcher shop in Wiley Park, a suburb of inner Western Sydney. Every birthday and Christmas from an early age, I received a book from him, such as *Moby Dick*, *Swiss Family Robinson* and my favourite, *Animals and Other People*. The latter was by Louis Bromfield, who also wrote *The Rains Came*, a book about India which was made into a movie with Tyrone Power.

in Venice. Tried the fish in batter from the Adriatic. Even though they looked like tiny octopus, they were very delicious! Went and had a good look over the Lido where the beach is and tried some more fish. On the way back it became dark, but the sky shone purple into the water, making it very lovely indeed. The train today was very slow coming here, but it isn't a trip you can do overnight. The only train this morning was at 9.45am, taking 3 hours. Leather is the big buy in Florence, and I had a brief look at the markets just across from the station. They were huge, and some of the sale items were very cheap. Time is going very slowly here. I wish it was tomorrow when I could start touring around and see Michelangelo's 'David'. Am wondering what you are doing right now. It's horrible sometimes not hearing from you at all, but it won't be long until I get to St-Imier again. Sometimes it's very lonely being with just myself, but travelling alone, one can please oneself, where and what they want to do. It is now Wednesday after 2 whole days seeing as much as I could yesterday with 2 Americans and an Australian boy from Narwee in Sydney. Today they left, so I went around alone. Tomorrow I fancy going onto Pisa before Rome, then Assisi and Perugia, which is Etruscan. Have talked to many interesting people, who have told me stories of interesting places to see. For lunch yesterday, I went with some people to a student mess only costing 450 Lira (8/-) for a 2-course meal, which included fruit and as many bread rolls as you could eat. We were so full, we found it hard to move, even though it took us one hour to get a seat! Trouble is, all the meals are starchy, sometimes there is only spaghetti twice a day. I saw Michelangelo's 'Pieta' today, which is of Jesus taken from the Cross. I was so moved, except 4 loads of tourist buses came in and crowded around, spoiling the view. His works literally breathe as you look at them, but I will cringe if I see another 'Madonna and Child'. It seems every painter since the beginning of time has done one. The weather has been good, but it still gets cold at night. My bunk is right on the window, and it doesn't help to keep warm, when one of the girls leaves the window open all night. They only give us one blanket each, so I will have to sleep with a cardigan on tonight. I am really well, so don't worry, and I will send mail from Rome. Miss you lots and wouldn't mind some good home-cooking. Love to you, Dianne xxxxxxxxxxxxxxxxxxxx

There is no way I could have told my mother I hitchhiked from Rome to Reggio Calabria. She would have had a heart attack. It was pretty scary. One male car driver, who was wearing a type of naval uniform, tried to put the hard word on me and my female companion, whom I had met in the hostel. He tried this when we were getting close to the ferry to Sicily. I grabbed his keys from the ignition and threw them out the window into the sea, and we made our escape on foot to the waiting ferry. I loved Sicily but was amazed at seeing men in public transport carrying handguns in shoulder holsters.

Sunday, 3rd May 1970

Dearest Mum,
    Last Thursday I finally caught a train from Reggio Calabria, the town where the boats from Sicily travel to Italy and vice versa. I had to wait 2 days until the train strike ended, but what a train trip! Left at 4pm and didn't arrive in Milan until 9am the next morning. It was moreso terrible because I hadn't eaten all day. I had some prunes about 7pm, so all night and morning I was wanting desperately to go to the toilet. The train was so crowded, people were sleeping on the floor between the seats, some having to stand up for hours. Got a train at Milan for the Italian/Swiss border at 12.30 and saw some beautiful lake and mountain countryside. Going through the Alps was exciting, but there is still a fantastic amount of snow, even on the mountains around St-Imier.
    Osvaldo has 4 days free this week, and he may come to London with me, before I leave for home. I can't continue travelling alone, because my mind is always filled with thoughts of him, even when I'm with people from the hostel. If it means waiting another couple of years for him to arrive in Australia, or for me to make another trip

to Italy, I would rather spend those years with you in Australia. I think back to the day I left, and how filled I was with so much enthusiasm to see every piece of Europe. Now I have no other inclination, except to spend the rest of my life with Osvaldo. I've had one month away from him, and realise it isn't just a casual romance, but much more serious. Please don't tell everyone I'm coming home, just you; Dad and Denise meet me at the Airport. I will tell you the flight No. when I book it in London. Also, I won't need all the return passage money, as I still have quite a bit in the Bank here. What Bank and Account No. can I charge it to in Sydney? If it is better to send money to the Commonwealth Bank in London, do so, or send a letter there telling me the Account No. of the Bank at home. I'll write again soon, or telegraph about the money in London. Lots of love, Dianne xxxxxxxxxxxxxxxxxxxxxxx

I travelled back to London, where I would work and save for my return journey to Australia by bus. I lived with Liz and Helen in their flat in McKenzie Road, Islington, not far from where we had lived in Archway, near Highgate Hill.

It was an uneventful time, except for Helen getting married and me being invited to the buck's party, where I got chained to a light post by Mahmet, who was the spitting image of Cat Stevens. Three months later, Liz and I boarded a Sundowners bus and headed across Europe, Asia Minor and India, eventually ending our trip in Kathmandu, Nepal.

Part 4
Islington London, and Sundowners Bus Trip Home

9th May 1970

Dearest Mum, Dad and Denise,

Got to London last Thursday afternoon with Osvaldo, and am staying with Helen and Liz, my flatmates from Archway, in their lovely flat at Islington. Osvaldo went home on Sunday, leaving me so lost as to what to do. Liz and Helen are wonderful friends. I'm really dying to leave, for it is hell knowing I won't see Osvaldo for another 6 months or maybe a year. Even though I love London, I would rather be with you and the family. Osvaldo was overcome by London, spending most of the time unable to speak at all. I forgot it was Mothers' Day until last Friday, and hope you received the telegram in time. Also, I trust you had a nice day last Sunday. Well, I'm having lunch with Liz today in the East End. Oh, she works in a pub near Camden Passage. It's a fab place with a nice clientele. She looks great pouring beers for all the men. Am waiting for your reply. If you can send a telegram or a Bank Draft, it may be easier and quicker. Just as long as I get home soon. All my love, Dianne xxxxxxxxx

On arriving in London and meeting up with my former flatmates, I changed my mind about going straight home. My mother was not happy, and now I realise I should have kept my mouth shut tight and not given her false hopes. My dad understood that I wanted to make the most of the time I was away. He also knew I didn't want to come back home and go straight into an office job. I could do better than this. He had always wanted me to run the business with him. My mother had other plans for me. She saw me coming home, meeting a nice doctor or dentist, then settling down in a house with a white picket fence and raising a couple of kids.

11th May 1970

Dearest Mum, Dad & Denise,
    Well, I'm busy at present with 2 jobs, working day and night. Liz desperately wants to come home with me, but overland through Asia. That's if Dad will agree to loan me some money, just in case I am left stuck somewhere. After doing some calculations, I have 300 pounds with my return passage fare and the money I saved in Switzerland. Even though the coach trip from London to Kathmandu is only 115 pounds, I also need money for food, accommodation and the trip from Kathmandu to Bangkok, then home. There is also sightseeing. Sending my trunk home will take a few hundred, and I should have a bit in hand, just in case. I'm hoping! While I was not working, I cooked and cleaned in the flat, and made my first roasted leg of lamb, fillet mignon with mushroom sauce, scones. Liz is absolutely thrilled about us coming home together, and I told her she must come to Sydney and stay when we all settle in. The tour starts on the 13th July and lasts roughly 2 months. We are making our own way home from Bangkok, so it would be early October when I see you for the second time since August 1968. Seems ages ago! I miss Osvaldo too, but he has written and said he would have liked to stay and work in London and learn English. Even during the few days he was here, with all the raving lunatics in the flat, he was learning so fast. I'm

I don't wear step-ins anymore.

earning 12/- hourly working as a temp. I can't get permanent work, as I only have 8 weeks, so I have to save as much as possible. Went to Petticoat Lane last Sunday and thought of our visit there last year. When I walk around, I suddenly find myself remembering the visits we made together, especially when I was at Victoria Station with Osvaldo. I remembered the time I lost you when we were taking the sightseeing bus around London. Had lunch at Nell Gwynne alone on Monday, and Pat didn't recognise me with my glasses on. He couldn't talk much as it was busy, but he was pleased to receive your card at Xmas. Give my love to all, and I'm thinking it's not long 'til I am with you again. All my love, Dianne xxxxxxxxx

I kept writing to my family, but nothing came back until the 30th of June, a few weeks before Liz and I boarded the Sundowners bus to come home.

Tuesday, 30th June 1970

To our Dianne

Today is the last day of the financial year. Tomorrow our new Medical Scheme starts, but as usual everything is up in the air. Today (Wednesday) has been like a Spring Day. I did some gardening and hosing in the front, and it was lovely. Well darling, hope everything is going well, and have you seen Betty? Hope you have a lovely trip and meet some nice people aboard the coach. I will be thinking of you each day, where you will be, and may our loving Father watch over you and Liz, love, hugs, and kisses from Mother xxxxxxxxxxxx Hello Darling, hope you are well and ready for your trip. Make sure you see everything and have a good time. Hope Liz is well and looking forward to the trip. You should have a good time together. Let me know when you will arrive in Australia. Stick together and keep your chin up, all my love, Daddy xxxxxxxxxxx

My mother wrote a week later as I hadn't written to her immediately. My sister had been asking to flat with me when I got home, and my mother was furious, especially as she had renovated the house and made the front sitting room into my bedroom with its own verandah entrance at the front of the house. My mother also wrote about Aunt not being well. She knew how close I was to Aunt, and I really wish she had not told me because I began to worry.

Wednesday, 8th July 1970

Dear Dianne

Denise received your letter today, but we haven't had a letter since Friday week. She said she might be flatting with you and Liz when you come home, so I might sell up and move into a smaller house later on. Aunt rang yesterday, and she is not the best. She had to go to the heart specialist and has an enlarged heart. Her blood pressure was very high, and it could lead to a stroke. She has to take things easy and go back to the doctor in a few days. As Aunt said, she is 58 this November, and we don't go on forever. As I have always told your father and Denise, I want the alarm to ring so much one morning, when you turn it off, you'll find I have found my rest.[38] I showed your Itinerary to the chap at Punchbowl Bank today, and he thinks it is fantastic. Denise said you had heard from Osvaldo. Does he write in English or Italian, and how would you understand it? I received your aerogramme this afternoon and was pleased you went to see Betty. We will be thinking of you each day. Love, I will certainly take the advantage of you waiting on me, as your sister would never dream of ever making your dear old Mother a cup of tea. She'll wonder what struck her if ever she gets

---

38 Ironically, my father passed away peacefully in his sleep in 1984, and my mother continued living on her own until 2009. Two weeks prior to her death she had been struck down with a heart attack and stroke. She did not want to be revived, but continued to survive at Royal Prince Alfred Hospital in Newtown. At the end of two weeks my sister and I were told we had to place her in a nursing home. I spoke to my mother that night, pleading with her to let go. She died on the Sunday night, the day before we were due to take her out of the hospital.

married. Well treasure, we will be thinking of you on Monday night, and how far you have travelled. Enjoy yourself, and every day is one day closer to home, and your loved ones. Give my regards to Liz, love, big hugs, from your ever-loving Mother xxxxxxxxxxxx Well, this letter will find you on your way. Don't forget to see everything on your trip. Hope Liz is well and you both enjoy yourselves. Sam Forrest sends his best, and hope he gets a big hug when you return. Well Dianne, have a good trip, and if you want anything, let me know. Daddy xxxxxxxxxxxxxx

My trip home was getting very close now, and there was so much to do before such a huge journey across Europe, Asia, India and Nepal.

Thursday, 9th July 1970

Dearest Mum and Dad
I was at Betty's place in Macclesfield Cheshire for 6 days. Even though it rained most days, we had a nice time looking at slides, talking and coping with the baby Samantha. Of course, as soon as I left, it became terribly hot and unbearable in humid London. My last needle made me feel terrible. My arm was like a tennis ball, all red, and I was on the toilet all night feeling sick. We went to see 'Gone with the Wind', my 4th time, with Liz and Mahmet. Helen is off work until we go, and yesterday I spent 8 pounds at the chemist, buying anti-malaria and diarrhoea tablets, water-purifying tabs, disinfectant etc, and four 36 film rolls. Our trunks went yesterday, and there is my bag, the small mustard one, with books and odds and ends, which is unlocked. It will take a couple of months, and the authorities should advise Dad when they arrive at Sydney Docks. It is getting hard to contain the excitement of only having 4 days to go. By the way, we leave at 7.30 Monday morning, which is rather early, but we have to be in Brussels Monday night. Must go, see you soon, lots of love, Dianne xxxxxxxxxxxxxxxxx

On the 13th of July 1970, Liz and I boarded the Sundowners bus and began our trip from London to India and Kathmandu. Liz was a couple of years younger than me, but she became a wonderful friend and travelling companion, and we kept in touch after our return to Sydney. I visited her in Wagga Wagga, and she visited me when I eventually moved out of home and flatted in Sydney. We wrote to each other, and she used to call me her 'fellow compatriot'. It took both of us many years to come to terms with restarting our lives in Australia. I lost touch with her soon after marrying in 1972. The last I heard, she had moved to Tasmania; and I even tried to look her up when driving through Wagga in the late 2000s on a visit to Melbourne.

Wednesday, 15th July 1970

To Our Dianne,
When I arrived home from visiting Auntie Dolly on Monday afternoon, I had a lovely surprise finding your aerogramme. Wasn't expecting another one, as I received your previous one last Friday (10th). I made a cup of coffee and opened it. It was four o'clock, and as we are nine hours ahead of London, I was visualising you and Liz at 7 o'clock in London. If telepathy was there, you would have pictured your Mother thinking of you, and imagining where you would be. Each morning I tick off the town you stayed at the previous night. Between you and me love, I will be glad when spring comes, as the weather is like the Blue Mountains weather. Everyone is complaining about the cold. Hoping you are enjoying your trip. I think of you each day. Aunt is much better but has to keep seeing the local doctor each week. Love, big hugs and kisses from Mother xxxxxxxx Hello Darling, hope you are seeing everything possible. The football has finished, Newtown won, Manly got beat and they are leading in the competition. We have a big petrol strike and everything is getting serious. No petrol, no buses, no fuel for hospitals and taxis are off the road. If they don't go back on Tuesday, the Government is going to step in. Love from Daddy xxxxxxxxxxxxxxxx

I don't wear step-ins anymore.

Wednesday, 22nd July 1970
Dianne Lindsay

To Our Big Girl,

Received your card from Salzburg, when I arrived home from St George's Club Smorgasbord with Eve. The card is very picturesque and hope the weather has improved. Ours is still very cold in the morning, but today was rather pleasant. Have already sent 2 letters to Athens. The petrol is supposed to be normal tomorrow but has been rationed along with the milk. Wore your orange and white check wool dress, and one of the ladies passed a remark about it. We later went to Penrith RSL with 2 of the chaps from Coles and had a nice lunch. They are extending this club. We came home through the back way, as Dad had to go to Fairfield. Coming out near the poker machines, Dad gave me two 10 cents and I put them in and won $1.70 clear profit. As usual I am going to buy a $2 Lottery Ticket. Saturday, Denise went down to Earlwood to have her hair done for the Ball she is going to tonight. All they had to do was to style it, as she had set the wig and her own hair. They charged $2 and didn't do what she wanted. Libera and Barry called in at lunchtime to show us their new Japanese car, which is very nice. They took Denise and me for a run in it and it was good. It is a new honey colour with black upholstery. In the short time they have had their blocks of land at Budgewoi near Tuggerah Lakes, they have been offered double the price they paid. They have their heads on the right way and are looking to the future. Was speaking to Aunt on the phone last night, and when we were in at the Doctors on Monday for a check-up, Michael and Valmai called in. All the days I am home, no one comes. Michael goes back to work on Monday. In tonight's news it has been 33 days since we have had rain, and today was the warmest July day since 1968. It was like a Spring day, and I noticed the difference in the clothes drying. On Sunday we watched the British Series 'Oh Brother', about the monks and brothers in a monastery in England. They had to go to Rome and showed some parts of Rome and the fountains. Now I am watching the last part of the Carole Burnett Show. Went to late Church today at 1.00 pm. Our new additions to the Hall and Kitchen are nearly completed in memory of our dear Mr Hood. Went out to see Aunt after lunch, then we went down to Beverley's, who was having a barbecue. All the old crowd was there. Graham Foster has a new Rambler, but I don't think everything is the best with him and Eleanor. Hope you and Liz are enjoying your trip. What is going to happen when you both have to go to work? It will kill the both of you. Well, Treasure, once again Hugs and Kisses from your ever-Loving Mother xxxxxxxxxx this one is for Liz x Mother. Hello Dianne, hope you and Liz are enjoying yourself and the trip is going well. Football has got about five games to go, with St George, Easts, Souths, Canterbury and Manly in the first five. The others haven't got much chance. Went to Melbourne for 3 days last week for a new Kmart store at Belmont. The strikes here are all over the place with petrol, milk, wharf labourers, garbage collection, hostesses and nurses wanting more money and extra holidays. Look after yourselves and have a good trip, Love Daddy xxxxxxxxxxxxxxxxxxxxxxxxx

I loved how Dad kept me informed about the Rugby League. He and I always used to sit in front of the TV and watch the games, as well as the 6-day cricket test matches. My first job was with W.D. & H.O. Wills, and when we moved to Macquarie Street, it was not uncommon for me to share the lift with Bobby Simpson on my way to the office each morning.

This was the first letter written from a fascinating place like Istanbul. I was also looking forward to visiting Gallipoli, where our group was actually going to be sleeping on the beach in tents. In 2012, after being told I was adopted, I found out that my birth grandfather, Benjamin Parrish, went to Gallipoli in his early 20s. It was even more amazing that, when researching his war record, I found my grandfather had enlisted under another name. His records showed he initially enlisted in the Light Horse Brigade.

I don't wear step-ins anymore.

Wednesday, 5th August 1970
Mr & Mrs G Lindsay

Dearest Mum, Dad & Denise,

    We got to Istanbul last night and are camping on the outskirts, as all the cheap hotels have no running water but lots of cockroaches! The camp is divine with hot showers - uh uh, sigh. I couldn't resist buying a bottle green suede full-length coat this morning, and it only cost 13-pound sterling. I bargained it down one pound. It comes to the knee, so I have plenty of length to play around with. The money situation is so difficult Mum, for I'd like to bring lots of presents home, but it is a matter of even being lousy with postcards. We all live on bread, cheese and tomatoes as it is, with diarrhoea imminent, if we drink the water. Watermelon is dirt-cheap so we always split one between 4 of us. Istanbul is so fascinating but very dangerous. While crossing from Greece into Turkey yesterday, we talked to a Minitrek Tour operator. They lost 2 girls here in Istanbul. The girls went out to dinner and never came back. Stories like this reach our ears or the drivers quite frequently. From walking around, it is easy to believe. Liz has been ok, but she does get exhausted with the extreme heat we have been having. I bought a nice swimsuit in Athens and we have been swimming many times and had a whole day on the beach at Kavala. It was our last stop in Greece, so I'm getting nice and brown. On the way to Istanbul we've seen a lot of poverty. I found Yugoslavia poorer generally, the children begging or selling small bags of berries. We are such lucky people to have a country like Australia to live in. You would die to see the filthy streets and toilets I've seen so far, where they ask for money so you can stand across a hole in the ground! We've just got back from walking through the bazaars. I found them too commercial and am waiting for Iran and Afghanistan. I can't remember whether you mentioned you liked Athens or not. I adored it but found Istanbul even more fascinating. Haven't had a pinch on the bottom yet! It was 82 degrees at 4 pm today. It is very sticky too, but I'm okay now in the heat, except for when we got into Yugoslavia and I passed out. One of the girls gave me some iron tablets, as I was quite a bit anaemic. Remember you giving Denise and me that mixture with iron in it, and those tablets made from kelp? I should have brought some away, but these tablets have fixed me up now. I was thrilled with the photo of Earlwood but will have to study it carefully when we have a quiet day. At present things are very hectic, for there is so much to see and do in Turkey. We spend nearly 2 weeks here and see Gallipoli soon, sleeping on the beach. Am sending off a few postcards, but before I get home everyone will have one, I promise. Travelling in the bus is getting worse as the roads and weather goes downhill. We play cards or word games, eat and sleep erratically, and it does pass the time, in between looking at the scenery. It is still very hot and sticky all the same. For all the discomforts, I love this type of life. I'm slowly running out of this lovely green paper, and wish everyone well at the homestead, especially my lovely family. Lots of love and kisses, Dianne xxxxxxxxxxxx

During our bus trip, work was divided between the group for a week at a time, when four of us would shop, cook and serve meals for everyone. I remember the markets throughout Turkey, where rows upon rows of goats' heads stared at us as we scurried around looking for something to cook. I could make a mean spaghetti bolognaise, which I cooked with camel mince, our only source of protein, and it proved to be satisfactory and quite delicious.

Tuesday, 11th August 1970

Dearest Mum, Dad and Denise,
Well I'm really getting bad at the correspondence side of things, but at present Liz and I are doing the cooking with a married couple from Melbourne. It means we are up at 5am to put breakfast on or beginning dinner at late times owing to some long mileage days. Last night we slept in Ancient Ruins of Pamukkale, and an area famous for hot mineral springs. We had a swim about 10 pm before

I don't wear step-ins anymore.

getting into our sleeping bags. Sleep was and has been a problem lately. Not that it is too hot, but because we have had no inclination to leave each other's mad company. We had a nice day on the beach before starting a long 2 days on the bus. The people are simply lovely in Turkey, but we hardly ever see women, only men. We met the Sundowner's Coach on its way to England, so we stopped to say hello and exchange news. We heard the gory details about diarrhoea and extreme humidity, plus some people being spat at by the local villagers! Today has been a beach day at a very nice BP Camp. Liz and I joined some chaps, Steve and Bob, in a swim to an island castle about 2 kms from our beach. We took a camp blow up bed and took turns at resting. The sea was very clean and clear, but Liz, who is a redhead, got a little burnt to say the least. The whole countryside here is strewn with ruins and is so interesting. This country has proved very cheap, for we spend less than 10/- per day. 2/6 for lunch in a restaurant, 1/6 for cigarettes. Not bad, but I don't know if I'll have my plane or ship fare from Bangkok, which is 100 pounds on the cheapest deal. Talking of money, have I been sent any letters from the Inland Revenue Department in London? They owe me at least 50 pound or more, and if I'd been able to receive this before leaving, I may not have had to write asking for more money. I also have a feeling I've mislaid Pat's address in Bangkok. Can you send it to me again Dad, and is there a way of me booking a flight to Sydney through him? I got your letter in Istanbul, and please write soon to the next addresses. Last night when we arrived at Selifke Beach, it was my turn at arranging the meal, so I made a pasta dish with a tomato and meat sauce, like Mrs Adatte and Osvaldo cooked in Switzerland. We had so much fun shopping, and it would amaze you to see butcher shops, and the unhygienic way living is here compared to Australia. To Turks it is normal, and the body does adapt after a few doses of the trots! I get it quite regularly, but not too seriously. I was dripping perspiration like nothing else while chopping onions, apples and everyone made a comment about how tasty it was. I'm going to cook 7 nights a week for you, and you better get used to being lazy from then on. I think I told you about Gallipoli, and how impressed I was, especially as each year at school we remembered the Anzacs. I was walking over the same spot where so many died, and visualising what must have happened. I saw a 'Lindsay' on the lists of soldiers, and Liz saw many 'McPhersons'. We also wrote our name in a book at the shrine, which was covered in wreaths. Must go, as one of the drivers wants me to give him a massage. Liz cuts hair and I massage like we did in London. If I don't hear from you about the money, then I'll telegraph from Bangkok or Singapore, but please, write soon. Liz is in the same predicament, as some places have been very expensive, and not cheap like we were led to believe. All my love to you, Dad and Nece, Dianne xxxxxxxxxxxxxxxxxxxxx"

Tuesday, 18th August 1970

Dearest Mum, Dad and Denise,

   Yesterday at about 11am, after leaving Erzurum Turkey at 7.30am, Liz calmly remarked about one of the back wheels rolling along beside us. Well, we had broken an axle 50 kilometres from Agri, a town not far from the Iranian border. We had to hang out in the desert-like countryside boiling tea, chasing frogs and goats in the river. Liz started riding one of the horses and shepherds began annoying us. Now, we are in a hotel, which smells like a public toilet, and can't walk outside unless in a group or with a man, for fear of being stoned or spat at. This has happened already to 2 girls who were wearing dresses. The men follow us into the showers and are forever trying to touch us. I will be the most patient person by the time I get home, but this may not be until November, because we could be here for 2 days or maybe 2 weeks. I don't know whether you got my last letter, as Turkey recently devalued their currency, consequently increasing the cost on most items. I said in the letter, after working out expenses on 2 pound a day, which includes everything, Liz and I will run out of money by Bangkok and won't have our plane

I don't wear step-ins anymore.

fare to Sydney. We have enquired about ships from Singapore, but it works out just as expensive. This accident has taken a big piece out of our budget, even though we have been living very cheaply. Everyone is in the same situation. The plane fare is 112 pounds sterling from Singapore, and we've been told the safest way to send this money is in Traveller's cheques to American Express at Delhi. I could do a 'fly now pay later' plan with Qantas from Singapore, but if you can send 100 pounds to Delhi through American Express, I will be indebted to you. I don't want anything for my birthday because you have already given me so much. I'm certainly learning some lessons about living while here, but it's an experience, and thank God for you and Dad. All my love, Dianne xxxxxxxxxx

22nd August 1970

Dearest Mum, Dad and Denise,

At last we are in Tehran (Persia) sitting, or cooking in the bus, while waiting for our room numbers at a grotty looking hotel. We left Agri Turkey, yesterday at 3pm, and drove all night and day to make up lost time. The border gave little delay; however, we did experience the most disgusting toilet in existence. It is not easy to describe, although I'll always remember the smell until I die! Before leaving the Persian border, we passed Mt Ararat. I took a photo, especially because it is the mountain from the Bible, upon which rested Noah's Ark after the Flood. The countryside is rapidly becoming more interesting, but I get more depressed by the poverty, and the way these people use animals for tasks we would use trucks. I've already noticed each day to most, is a battle of survival. We sit at home, casually enjoying each moment, because we don't have to fight for such mundane things as bread and water. Over here, water is a commodity to be bargained for! In Turkey we rarely see women, but in Persia we see many, some extremely beautiful, and always covered from head to foot by a flowing robe. Tehran is filthy everywhere, and so bustling, with all kinds of people and animals. The children run around, doing work we wouldn't dream of doing. They are sometimes more aggressive than adults, even the ones likely to speak some English. We had great difficulties with the men in Agri. I had to kick one man and throw a wet towel at another, after being 'handled'. We had an interesting conversation with the Police Chief, who explained it was better for a woman to settle accounts, than have her friend do it for her. After 4 days in a Turkish Village, I could handle any aggressive male. Have read your two letters and one from Betty, so I picked up some aerogrammes while at the Post Office, to answer you straight away. We are here for one whole day, and then Isfahan, which is a much more beautiful city. From there we travel to Persepolis, the ancient town of King Darius 1 (remember him in the Bible?). There is so much to write about. I'm glad you are following my trip on the map and reading my little travel books. They will be a joy to read again when I get home. Some people on the bus are getting attacks of illness from eating bad food, but as yet, I've only had a little dose of diarrhoea. Liz has been sick a few times, but she won't take any medicine, and we end up forcing her to take something. Have just had a shower, made some coffee, and am finishing this off before having a nap. We met some American soldiers in Agri, who gave us Army rations. As Tehran is expensive, I may eat these later instead of wasting precious money. Did you get my previous letter about the 100 pounds? I don't know whether it may be easier to have it transferred to a Bank in Delhi. Anyway, Liz is having her money sent to Delhi and leaving it to her father to decide the safest way of transferring it. Three people are flying from Tehran to India, because the delay has put their plans out of whack. One girl is pregnant, so she and her husband have no other alternative. I count the days till I see you, maybe late October now, because our drivers want to keep the Itinerary as planned, so we won't miss out on anything. As I said before, you must not give me this money, as it is a loan, definitely not a gift. You mustn't fuss over me when I arrive home, for I want to fuss over you from now on. All my love, see you very soon, Dianne xxxxxxxxxxxxxxxxxxxxxxxxx

I don't wear step-ins anymore.

We arrived in Isfahan, the home of breathtakingly beautiful mosques. I was so very lucky to meet a local man, Ahmed, who gave me a copy of a famous book *The Rubaiyat* by Omar Khayyam, and explained the architecture that I had never seen before. He was a teacher at a local school, was married and spoke excellent English. We had a lovely time together, and he asked if he could write to me when I arrived home in Australia. *The Rubaiyat* is still in my bookshelf with Ahmed's photo inside the front cover.

25th August 1970

Dearest Mum, Dad and Denise,

I'm in Isfahan right now, and feel it is the most beautiful and exquisite city I've ever seen. I could write pages about our stay, because as soon as we set out for our dinner the first evening, we were very fortunate to meet a local man speaking very good English. As well as having a guide in him, I was even luckier to start speaking to an old man, whose native country is Armenia. This man has relatives all over the world including Australia. We talked for ages about things generally. He has lived an interesting life in India around 1920 where he met Gandhi and told me what a wonderful man he was. Isfahan is so beautiful, and I have brochures to show you. Every house is decorated with a Persian mosaic motif, some in the way of long strips, and others with entire walls. The main colour is turquoise, and every tile is a work of art. The mosques are a blend of centuries, tiles and mosaics. If there is a Creator, I felt closer in this mosque than in any ordinary church. Before sunrise, lunch and dinner, a man calling from the minaret calls everyone to prayer. It is the most beautiful sound. It is now night. We travelled over rough country, but had our first rain for weeks, the last time way back when we were in Germany. Liz and I are in a room with 5 other girls, 2 sleeping on the floor. We have one cold shower, all for the price of 3 shillings per night. What more could we ask for! Tomorrow we head for Mashhad, the second holiest city for Moslems after Mecca. One of the holy leaders is buried in the city's gold mosque, and Moslems come from all over the world to pay homage. The Sundowner's bus which we passed in Turkey, said a few of their people had been pelted with rocks when they said they were tourists, so we will have to be careful. In Agri, where we stayed to have the bus repaired, we had fruit pelted at us by the locals, so it isn't new to us. We had a terrible fright while driving along a wet and slippery road. All of a sudden, a truck came towards us out of control, and we must have missed being hit by inches. It's not uncommon to see a couple of accidents each day. Not long ago we passed a burnt-out truck on which 20 people had died the night before. Last night in Tehran, I spoke with some children from Kuwait, a kingdom off the Persian Gulf, who speak English as their second language after Arabic. They write from right to left, and it looks very similar to shorthand, but much more flowing and attractive. I wrote to Osvaldo in Agri and gave the address for Pakistan, so he may reach the address in time. I hope he writes as I miss hearing from him. Every time I send a postcard it seems to be full of stock Italian and French phrases. All the same, I'm dying to get home and start learning Italian so I can answer him in proper sentences. It's now the 1st of September, and our bus has another broken axle, this time one day out from Tehran, in amongst the dirt tracks. It's 1 o'clock in Mashhad and I haven't slept since 6 am yesterday morning. We decided to hire a local bus, but at 11.30 last night, the driver decided he had to sleep until 4 am, when we would continue until 9 am. It was like being with a maniac, and even worse when we found out he had been on the opium. We had a few locals on the bus, 2 women and a tiny baby. They spread out on the floor of the bus. Liz and I are so fed up with some of the selfish people on this bus. Last night I felt like going back to Tehran and catching a plane home. I will write again very soon, because there is still lots to tell. Dad, if my greetings don't reach you by Sunday, have a wonderful Father's Day. Lots of love always until I see you. Dianne xxxxxxxxxxxxxxxx

I don't wear step-ins anymore.

My mother's letters were a treasure trove of gossip and important information about weather, especially in areas where I would later live, like the Blue Mountains. When I was researching my adopted parents, I found out they had spent their honeymoon at the Hotel Gearin in Katoomba, and took countless photos of visits there with my sister and me during our childhoods. On researching my birth family, I found that my birth mother, Adelle Olive Parrish, had lived in the Blue Mountains villages of Leura, Wentworth Falls and Bullaburra during the 1980s and 1990s.

Tuesday, 1st September 1970

To Our Darling Dianne,

First day of Spring, and 4 feet of snow at Katoomba, heavy rain in Sydney (I couldn't go to Bowls) and temperatures well below average everywhere. Snow was 4 inches deep in the streets in Katoomba, and up to 4 feet deep in drifts. At Wollongong, hail was as big as 20-cent pieces. There are flood warnings for the Murray and Murrumbidgee Rivers. There were the worst floods last week in Tasmania for years. We received your aerogramme yesterday, Monday, as I was going out to Aunt's place. We are glad you are back on the road. When you write of the poverty, which is why some of Church Missionaries go out to those people, helping them to produce food. Doctors and nurses (who could be earning big money back home) administer to the people in the name of our Father. This is why I have three mission boxes. Valmai and Beverley went for a picnic with Pat and Eleanor. This time Lisa wouldn't speak to me until I was leaving, when I gave her some money. They are going up to Roselands today, as the children don't go back to School till next Tuesday. Cohen's place across the road has only one fireplace standing. Everything has been pulled down. Last night, we could see all the lights towards the airport, and they did look pretty. Aunt saw Auntie Betty, Valda and David passing her place last Sunday, and they stopped to speak to her. Valda was upset, as the sale for the place in Earlwood had fallen through, and they were looking around. You would be astounded at the price they are asking. The semi next to Auntie Dollies' place in Camperdown is $12 per week. Ken had only a week away on his honeymoon, as June had to go back to work this week. Saw Lesley Uggams being interviewed as she landed in Sydney. She is going to do a show at South Sydney Club. She is still very nice, and hopes to eventually settle in Sydney, as her husband is an Australian. Dad and I are both in bed watching TV, with the electric blankets on. Denise is outside watching TV and George has called in. At present love, the rain is pelting against the bedroom windows, and I wouldn't change places with the Queen. I will get Denise to ring Kerrie for you. Well, darling, Dad wants to post this letter tomorrow, so I will have to love and leave you. Another week has passed, and may God keep his loving arms over you till you are home with your loved ones. Love and kisses from Mother xxxxxxxxxxx Well my big girl, I have fixed up your money. You go along to the bank in New Delhi, show your papers and passport, and they will give you money to the amount of 120 pounds sterling. Go to the Chartered Bank 17 Parliament Square (or Street) New Delhi, India. From the Commonwealth Bank of Australia Marrickville Branch. I hope you are enjoying yourselves and Liz and you are well. The time is going and don't forget to let us know when and what time you arrive in Australia. Look after yourself, love Daddy xxxxxxxxxxxxxxxxxxxxxxxxxxxx

During my travels on the bus, I referred to the people of Iran in my correspondence *as Persians.* I felt it more appropriate than calling them *Iranians.* It was such an ancient land, and I had read so much about it in the Bible, and in Sunday School.

I don't wear step-ins anymore.

2nd September 1970 Already!

Dearest Mum, Dad and Denise,
   Today, after a lovely sleep of 5 hours, we're off to Afghanistan. It's 6.15am right now and the Persians are supposed to be bringing us breakfast. They make a gorgeous waffle-sort of bread, jam and butter, as well as a large glass of tea. I've become a fanatical drinker of the local tea, which is terrific without milk, (another luxury unheard of here) except for a concoction of yoghurt and soda water! A glass of tea can cost up to 3c, no more, and usually less, which makes it the cheapest drink going. Liz and I are both fed up with the stupidity of one of the drivers. Yesterday (it's too long a story), he came in later with our own bus, and somehow rearranged the room to his liking, leaving us without a bed. After screaming and standing up to him, we got them to put beds in the basement. The money situation is chronic. They keep telling us it is going to get cheaper, when each time we are roped into paying for something extra. Making matters worse, we have countless holdups and breakdowns. This time we have a new axle, a spare one and the prospects of another being held in Lahore, Pakistan. However, we are thinking of placing bets on what will break next. They are so tight on this bus, when we asked for 2/- for our guide, who has been terrific, the drivers refused. They didn't mind when Joffe, the guide changed money and fixed our accommodation. Thank goodness Liz is here, for we know each other's ways and get on very well together. She is so different from when you met her in London. Her parents are coming to Sydney when we arrive, and we will telegraph the flight number. I would be happier if just you, Dad and Denise came, because it may take ages for the plane to arrive, and we could get on the wrong flight. Liz is having her money transferred from a bank in Australia to another bank in Calcutta. Is it easier for Dad to do this? It will be an asset if you have my passport number to include in the credit note - G400678. Can you send me Pat's address in Bangkok please Dad, for we would like to visit? I just can't wait to get your letters in Lahore, lots of love, Dianne xxxxxxxxxxxxxxxxxxxxx

**17ᵗʰ September 1970
Kashmir, Srinagar**

Dearest Mum, Dad and Denise,

    We arrived in Kashmir last Saturday evening, but had to get a local bus from Jammu, which is 13 hours' drive away. It was a very tiring journey. I slept most of the time sitting up, after not being able to sleep in the terrible humidity of Pakistan and the flat countryside. Firstly, I must tell you lots of things. India is truly fascinating, especially because religion is within everything. Our first stop, Amritsar is the capital of the Punjab, the part of India where people are mostly Sikhs. (They believe in goodwill to all races and religions). We visited their Temple, which is made of pure gold. It is situated in a lake, surrounded by a courtyard and white walls. Many people of the faith visit to bathe in the water or sit in the courtyard on the tiled floors praying. As you enter the temple people give offerings of bread, and there is music playing. It's the most beautiful Indian Temple music I've ever heard. Some of the women were very attractive in their saris, often wearing a red mark on the forehead to indicate high standing. We were given a piece of honey-type bread on leaving, a custom from the religion. Kashmir is a Muslim State, as they don't drink any alcohol. They do smoke these huge hashish bubble pipes, which they pass around. We are living on a houseboat in the middle of Dal Lake surrounded by mountains, some covered in snow. Most of the people on the bus left this morning for Delhi via the 2 previous stops, but I stayed with others for 3 extra days. It is such a beautiful place to recover from half a dozen bouts of diarrhoea. If I don't have the 'runs' it is constipation. We had some bad food coming to the Pakistan border, where there was one toilet, and the flush chain didn't work. About 6 of us had it bad, so we waited in line. I had to go back for an encore visit, as did others. Getting through some borders has been sheer hell, especially in Afghanistan where we had a 'little Hitler' in charge. He made us wait nearly 5 hours while he did his prayers. He then made us stand in front of him for inspection to receive our passports. We brought in Indian rupees illegally from Kabul, buying them on the black market. There is no such thing as an official bank rate, and this is how Afghanistan balances their economy. We fly to Delhi on Thursday 1pm and I can't wait to see the view. I've had a chap called Jimmy, taking me around getting me discounts off all the things I've bought. It costs $1.75 American a day here for 3 meals, hot water included and 1/- for a buggy ride around town. I've been trekking up to the mountains on a gorgeous horse called 'Sunflower' with some of the group, and later had a game of golf when we reached the top. I sat and watched some eagles and the view. It is so much like Switzerland here. Have tons to tell you. lots of love, Dianne xxxxxxxxxx

19th September 1970
WMCA New Delhi

Dearest Mum, Dad and Denise,

I have never been so rushed about in all of my life these past few days in Delhi. To make matters worse I haven't even seen one tourist attraction. After staying in Kashmir 2 extra days we flew to Delhi. We experienced terrible heat last Thursday afternoon, and arrived to find no mail and trouble with Nepalese Visas. The next morning our tour leader came back with mail, but no word from you. So off I went to American Express, and after patiently urging them on, they found 2 from you and one from Betty. I then rushed to the Bank. They found the money transfer after another search, but our passports were still at the Embassy! We rushed back, but no, we had to come at 9am the next morning. Off we went, a New Zealand girl and me, but we struck a nasty little man who mixed them up, and not until 10.30 did we receive our treasured passports. Bursting with anticipation we got our moped taxi (1/- each). He got lost on the way, but on reaching the Bank we found all Banks are having a strike. At present the workers are all in a group at the doors chanting obscenities, getting carried away, and the street is crowded with riot police, ready to act if the groups start fighting. We haven't seen anything of Delhi except the inside of an Embassy and one Bank! It's over at last, so all is well! The Company, because we have suffered 3 breakdowns on the trip, gave us a night out last night at one of the best restaurants in town, so all of us dressed up.

    I wore a trouser suit of white silk with a blue Kashmir motif around the neck. I hope to wear it off the plane, so how is Sydney weather progressing? I think most of the flights from Singapore arrive in Sydney early morning, but I'll write from Singapore or Bangkok if I decide to fly straight home from there. Some are talking about hiring a car in Bangkok to drive to Singapore. I want to come home even now, because Kashmir was the perfect place to end a trip like this. I am fed up with the disorganisation of this tour, as has everyone else. Have got some lovely things for you, which were reasonable. I've been very well lately, and just can't sleep because I'm thinking about getting home. Am posting a parcel from here as my luggage is quite a lot. We have to take our suitcase to Kathmandu, so this will save me lugging extra things around. Last night for dinner I had prawn cocktail (5/-), mushroom soup (3/-), mixed grill (9/-) and ice cream and walnuts, with pineapple, strawberries and cream (5/-) plus coffee and 2 apple juices. Yesterday was a Hindu holy day and therefore no alcohol is served. Even on normal days it is difficult to obtain alcohol. One of our drivers, a stupid aggressive fellow at most times, and a cockney, downed half a bottle of rum before dinner, and poured the rest into his glass from under the table. There is always someone wanting to spoil things. He had to be dragged away from a waiter whom he tried to pick a fight with. He generally dampened the end of a terrific night. I met a lady from Argentina who spoke some Italian and French. We had a chat about things in general, and she and I exchanged addresses, in case either of us visited each other's countries. One meets nice people everywhere. It won't be long. Betty is in the process of writing you. She so likes to read your chatty letters, and so do I Mum. Thank you for getting

I don't wear step-ins anymore.

me out of a spot again. Will write soon. Can I request one lamington or pineapple or mulberry pie when I get home? I'll do some special cooking for you. All of us talk about our favourite food on the bus, and I'm dying to taste a lamington or homemade pie. Lots of love, Di xxxxxxxxxxxx

Tuesday, 22nd September 1970
Laurels Hotel, Agra, India

Dearest Mum, Dad and Denise,

It's a glorious day in Agra, and I've been up since 5am visiting the Taj Mahal, as well as using a whole roll of film of the different views possible. We have seen so many buildings by Shah Jahan, the Persian King. This temple built for his wife, is everything I expected it to be and more. There are no other people around at 5.30am, so we waited for the sun to cast a glow on the enormous dome, adding more to the reflection in the pools. We hired rickshaws and even got to ride them ourselves last night. Yesterday, coming into Agra, was our most interesting day, animal wise, because we saw so much wildlife. Monkeys pestered our hotel in Jaipur. We didn't get a visit in our room, but some girls did. Jaipur was terribly poor, with an odour of excrement and death! You would be appalled by the living conditions. People lived in the streets, begging, some lame or blind. People feel nothing, not even pity, because mothers sometimes maim their children in order to get money from tourists. On the road to Agra we saw camels, peacocks, monkeys, cobras, vultures feeding on a dead cow, and so many different coloured birds. We always see lots of local people going to the toilet, anywhere, but they keep themselves covered! Yesterday we saw one little boy bending down while his brother poured water over his bottom. They don't use paper, but if necessary, the left hand is used, while the right hand is for eating. We fly out of Kathmandu on Wednesday 30/9 for Bangkok, then train to Singapore.

The first day out of Delhi and we got stuck in sand. Thought we would die from sunstroke and dehydration, until a local truck pulled us out. When we reached a drink stop, I downed 3 orange Fantas without stopping. The perspiration loss is unbelievable. In all, 8 people have left the tour so far, for various reasons, but mainly because the bus was in such a bad condition on leaving London after only 3 days service. Now after 3 broken axles, flat batteries, we have only a week to go with the bus. Two and a half months on a bus! Lots of love, Dianne xxxxxxxxxxxxxxxxxxxxxxxx

Sunday, 27th September 1970

To Our Dianne,

Today has been wet and miserable, not like our Spring. Denise went to a Ball at the Trocadero last night with Diane Redgrave. Diane came at lunchtime, and Denise has gone out with her. Diane still works part-time at Bankstown RSL and is working tonight. On Friday night, Dad and I went to Marrickville RSL Club for dinner, and later saw Jane Powell, who looked lovely in a yellow pleated chiffon frock, with the bodice sequined. They had a very good supporting show. I am going out to Aunts tomorrow, Monday. Eve is coming with me. Next Monday week, 5th October is Six Hour day, and beginning of the official Swimming season. Sandra is still dancing at the 'Bunny Club' and Ross is not working at present. They have started on the new house opposite but have been held up on account of the rain. It is going to be a very large house. We were happy to receive your two aerogrammes last week and are waiting to hear from you. We are now watching 'The Andy Williams Show'. Another week closer to you coming home. Sometimes, I think it can't be, when we realise how close it is getting. I was glad you have heard from Osvaldo but realise how hard it must be to translate your words. Denise wants me to go to Town next Saturday to have another look around at sapphire and diamond rings. She wants to go to Diamond Traders.

I don't wear step-ins anymore.

Last week we went to Angus and Cootes, and the gentleman brought two trays out, and she was trying them on. I suppose he must have thought we had money but was very obliging. The petrol war is back on again. Our garage has cut the price to 42 cents, on account of the garage at Bayview Avenue selling the cheap Melbourne petrol. You will notice a difference in Homer Street with the Home Units being built, but the bus trip home from Town through Newtown is still the same (Hell). Well, treasure, I will say goodbye, hoping this is the last letter I have to write, and counting the days. Love, big hugs and kisses from your ever-loving mother xxxxxxxxxxxxxxxxx Well darling, you are getting close now. Hope you are well. You won't know Sydney when you see all the changes. The football has finished. Souths got there again beating Manly in the finals. Your cases have arrived. I will be going into town to the Customs Department to see if I can get them cleared. I have no paperwork on them and hope I have no trouble in getting them. I suppose by the time you receive this letter you won't be far from Australia and home. Hope you got your money without any trouble, and you are still in one piece after all those Countries. Everybody is asking where is your daughter, saying it won't be long now. Well, this will be the last letter you will get, so look after yourself and all the best till we see you, Love Daddy xxxxxxxxxxxx

Many in our group changed their itineraries during the bus trip. Some flew home as early as Athens. They were sick of delays or outrageous costs which were not factored in before we set off from London. Liz and I joined a few friends from the bus to take a side trip to Kathmandu. We drove in a local rickety bus up a scary winding dirt road, and were fortunate to get a view of Mount Everest from an army outpost along the way. Liz and I then caught a Thai Airways plane from Kathmandu into Bangkok. I remember that the plane had an orchid painted on the tail, and we had smoked salmon and champagne during the flight. The most horrible memory was waking up in a hotel room in Bangkok the next morning, with the floor covered in cockroaches. We adored Penang and the amazing train trip to Singapore. Liz wanted to visit Bali and pleaded with me to join her, but I was desperate to get home. To this day I have never had an inclination to go to Bali.

After a morning sightseeing, I caught a Qantas plane from Singapore and came into Mascot Airport the following morning as the sun rose over Sydney Harbour. I shuffled nervously through Customs with my stash of hashish Liz and I had bought from the markets in Herat, Afghanistan, concealed in a packet of *Moddess* sanitary napkins. Memories flooded back of us sitting in the hotel room toilet, smoking hash from bubble pipes and imagining the flushing was a waterfall. I looked and felt gaunt, even anorexic. My scrawny body was exhausted from countless bouts of diarrhoea. I wore my favourite cream silk flowing trousers and blue embroidered top, made especially for me in Delhi. Mum, Dad, Denise, Aunt, Val, Mike, and the babies Lisa and Cassandra were there. So was Ruth and Kevin, who I had been bridesmaid for at their wedding just prior to leaving Australia in 1968. We drove in convoy the short 10 minute drive across the Cook's River at Tempe Railway Station, up the hill past the Tempe Tip to 104 Minnamorra Avenue Earlwood. A spread of Aussie delicacies was laid out for me. My favourite lamingtons took centre stage, surrounded by vegemite sandwiches and Mum's homemade mulberry pie. Mr Cohen's mulberry tree across the road had supplied the fruit, and it was topped with freshly whipped cream.

My bedroom was now at the front of the house, off the front verandah, with a less open view of the airport. Mr Cohen's house sold a few years earlier, and the new owners put up a two-storey mansion which blocked out the previous uninterrupted view. A flimsy plastic fold-back door, with an equally flimsy latch, was the only thing separating my room from the hallway. Directly opposite was my parents' bedroom. The dark rosewood pianola on which I learnt pianoforte from age 7 to 12 was gone. My mum had given it to Aunty Betty, who hardly used it.

I don't wear step-ins anymore.

Weeks went by as I caught up with family, old friends, and new friends from the Sundowners bus. I was drifting into a depressed state, drowning out my sorrows while listening to the LPs I had sent home by sea from Switzerland in a wooden trunk. My mother badgered me constantly to get a job. I submitted, and began working as a secretary to a Partner Director of a company of accountants. My father's accountant worked in the same company, situated close to Wynyard Station in George Street, Sydney. There I met Julie, who also lived in Earlwood at the other end of Homer Street going towards Canterbury. We got cleaning jobs at the Sydney University Library so I could save for my first car, a Morris 1100. These were the 1970s, the days of *Honi Soit* the student newspaper, and of course, *OZ magazine* by Richard Neville. The library looked like a cesspit on Monday mornings. I would go to bed at 8pm and get up at 4am. Julie picked me up in her white and red striped *Fiat 500 gogo machine.* Her father had allowed her to have it *hotted up* so she would drive like a racing car driver to the library, which was only a couple of villages away in Newtown. We would just get home in time to shower, change, and hop on a bus or train to commute to our day job at Wynyard. It became harder and harder to keep in touch with Osvaldo while working two jobs and partying on weekends with old and new friends. My Dad would put on BBQs for when the Sundowners Bus Gang got together for a reunion. It turned out that quite a few lived in the Sydney area, and one of the boys, Bob, became an admirer, even turning up one day with a huge bunch of roses, and asking me to marry him.

Liz and I were miserable, and just wanted to go back overseas. I spent many weekends driving or catching the train to Wagga. We loved going to the local RSL club to cause general mayhem and flirt with the country boys. She would visit me in *The Big Smoke*, especially when I moved in to a flat with Julie and two boys we met at *The Elizabethan Inn,* a fancy pub in Darling Point. In between visits, we wrote to one another often, while trying to settle back in to society. We tried to keep in touch, even when I later married one of those boys I flatted with in 1972.

Forty years flew by. My marriage had ended and both my parents had died, my father in 1984 and my mother in 2009. I had moved to the Blue Mountains in the mid 2000s and shared a house with my two sons, both in their 30s. In January 2012 my cousin Val, who lived a 10 minute walk away, decided to tell me that I had been adopted at birth. I immediately began the tortuous search for my birth mother, and in the following September, I found and briefly met my birth mother, Adelle Olive Parrish in Cootamundra Nursing Home. She had settled in Cootamundra during the 1990s, but was struck down with a form of dementia. Our meeting was brief, but I felt she knew me, even asking me for a cuddle. My cousins came with me, and she even allowed my cousin Mike to take a photo of me and Val holding her hands. Three months later, at the end of December, she passed away. The Nursing Home invited me to a Memorial Service, where the Matron introduced me to the residents and staff. Many told me they felt my mother had died of a broken heart because she was made to give me away, instead of keeping me. I was able to make contact with Tina, who my mother adopted two years after giving me up at birth. Tina had been collecting information about her adopted mum, and gladly spent a week with me in Hervey Bay, Queensland. A few months later Tina spent two weeks with me in the Blue Mountains, sharing photos and learning more about our Mother. Tina commented many times on how much I looked, and even sounded like my birth mother.

Not long after Tina left, I began transcribing the letters I had written to my adopted mother Ruby, while overseas between 1968 and 1970. I typed each letter onto my computer, as well as her letters to me, and all the others I had received from family members and friends. Reading them, especially those from my adopted mother and father, made me realise how fortunate I was to be adopted by Ruby and George Lindsay at birth.

Ruby was strict and found it difficult to show affection to me. I later found out she became very involved with St George's Church of England and was confirmed as an adult, specifically to prepare for

I don't wear step-ins anymore.

my adoption. My mother taught me to sew, to knit, to crochet and as I read in her letters, she adored me. George, on the other hand, was loving and very affectionate, but loved the *grog*. He ran a successful family electroplating company with clients like G.J. Coles, Kmart and a company that made funeral caskets. On the weekends, after doing the lawns, he always found time to take us to Manly beach, the Koala Park in Pennant Hills or the Blue Mountains. We went horse riding, or camping at places like The Entrance and Narrabeen Lakes. He even talked Mum into holidaying in a caravan and taking my beloved fox terrier Trudy, given to me on my first birthday. He showed me how to fish and drive a car. He encouraged me to be free, to take off the 'step-ins' and try everything.

www.ingramcontent.com/pod-product-compliance
Lightning Source LLC
LaVergne TN
LVHW040048080526
838202LV00045B/3538